DISCARD

GLOBAL NEIGHBORS

THE EERDMANS RELIGION, ETHICS, AND PUBLIC LIFE SERIES

Jean Bethke Elshtain and John D. Carlson, Series Editors

This series aims to explore dilemmas and debates at the intersection of religion, ethics, and public life. Its high-caliber books will include both single- and multi-authored volumes by scholars, public officials, and policy experts discussing the religious and moral meanings of pressing social issues. At a time when people puzzle over the connections between religious belief and civic practice, this series will offer valuable perspectives to a wide range of readers.

PUBLISHED VOLUMES

Does Human Rights Need God?
  Elizabeth M. Bucar and Barbra Barnett, Editors

*Global Neighbors: Christian Faith and Moral Obligation
in Today's Economy*
  Douglas A. Hicks and Mark Valeri, Editors

Religion and the Death Penalty: A Call for Reckoning
  Erik C. Owens, John D. Carlson, and Eric P. Elshtain, Editors

GLOBAL NEIGHBORS

*Christian Faith and Moral Obligation
in Today's Economy*

Edited by

Douglas A. Hicks *&* Mark Valeri

WILLIAM B. EERDMANS PUBLISHING COMPANY

GRAND RAPIDS, MICHIGAN / CAMBRIDGE, U.K.

© 2008 William B. Eerdmans Publishing Company

Published 2008 by
Wm. B. Eerdmans Publishing Co.
2140 Oak Industrial Drive N.E., Grand Rapids, Michigan 49505 /
P.O. Box 163, Cambridge CB3 9PU U.K.

Printed in the United States of America

13 12 11 10 09 08   7 6 5 4 3 2 1

Library of Congress Cataloging-in-Publication Data

Global neighbors: Christian faith and moral obligation in today's economy /
    Douglas A. Hicks and Mark Valeri, editors.
        p.   cm.   — (The Eerdmans religion, ethics, and public life series)
    ISBN 978-0-8028-6033-0 (pbk.: alk. paper)
    1. Economics — Religious aspects — Christianity.   2. Economics — Moral and
    ethical aspects.   3. Globalization — Economic aspects.   4. Globalization —
    Religious aspects — Christianity.   5. Globalization — Moral and ethical aspects.
    I. Hicks, Douglas A.   II. Valeri, Mark R.

    BR115.E3G56   2008
    261.8'5 — dc22

                                                          2008011997

www.eerdmans.com

Contents

SERIES FOREWORD   vii

CONTRIBUTORS   ix

PROLOGUE   Producing Endurance:
A Story of Faith and the Global Market   xi
   William Goettler

INTRODUCTION   Christian Faith and the Global Market   xviii
   Douglas A. Hicks and Mark Valeri

I. Near and Far Obligations in the Global Market

1. Who Is My Neighbor? An Invitation
   to See the World with Different Eyes   3
      Thomas W. Walker

2. *Agape* and Special Relations in a Global Economy:
   Theological Sources   16
      Eric Gregory

3. Global Poverty and Bono's Celebrity Activism:
   An Analysis of Moral Imagination and Motivation   43
      Douglas A. Hicks

Contents

II. **Christian Witness and Mainstream Economic Theory: Four Critiques**

4. Human Nature and Human Needs
in Recent Economic Theory   65
Kent Van Til

5. Economic Justice Requires More than
the Kindness of Strangers   89
Rebecca Todd Peters

6. Free Markets and the Reign of God:
Identifying Potential Conflicts   109
Jeff Van Duzer

7. And God Said, Let There Be Many:
An Argument for Economic Diversity   133
Janet Parker

III. **Labor and Vocation in the Global Market**

8. Knowledge Work, Craft Work, and Calling   167
Robert D. Austin and Lee Devin

9. Christian Manufacturers at the Crossroads   196
Shirley J. Roels

10. A Christian Perspective on the Role of Government
in a Market Economy   224
Rebecca M. Blank

11. Critical Economic Engagement:
On the Perennial and Novel Dimensions   248
Douglas A. Hicks and Mark Valeri

INDEX OF NAMES AND SUBJECTS   265

INDEX OF SCRIPTURE REFERENCES   275

Series Foreword

The Eerdmans Religion, Ethics, and Public Life Series brings together insightful and cutting edge books that reflect on the religious and moral dimensions of politics, culture, and society. At a time when religion pervades the public square, this series opens up various forms of scholarly inquiry, moral and religious reflection, and policy studies — all contextualized in light of debates and challenges we face in twenty-first century life. Overall, the series includes a broad array of perspectives from diverse religious faiths, moral traditions, academic disciplines, political persuasions, and professional vocations. Some books in the series bring together scholars, public leaders, political officials, or policy experts within one volume to discuss the religious and moral meanings of timely issues and to provide a venue in which their work can be mutually informative. In addition to these multi-authored volumes, the series will feature monographs that make vital contributions by enriching ongoing conversations or initiating new ones. Books in the series are intended for a wide readership, including academics, clergy and religious leaders, government officials, journalists, students, policy experts, leaders of public institutions, and interested citizens generally.

Global Neighbors: Christian Faith and Moral Obligation in Today's Economy, the third volume in this series, explores a panoply of dilemmas and concerns for those seeking to live faithfully as participants in increasingly complex, differentiated, and mediated global markets. The book takes up daunting questions that Christian communities heretofore — from the early church in ancient Palestine, to medieval villages and Puritan townships, to modern Christian cultures up through the twentieth century — could not have conceived. Hence there is a need to undertake radically new conceptions of how to live out and apply one's religious and moral obligations in an interdependent global economy. One finds in this volume practical guidance for how to sustain commitments to love one's neighbor and care for the poor and the marginalized. More importantly, the editors and contributors urge that readers pay heed to a prior task: the need to expand the conceptual horizons of Christian faith and community. The premise is that Christian life in late- or post-modern times has become shaped by powerful economic and social forces that cramp deep moral and religious obligations to others, especially to those in need. The challenge, then, for contemporary Christians is to recapture and re-appropriate theological resources — beliefs about human needs and human nature, suffering and love, family and community, social relations and transactions, vocation and the meaning of work, and, finally, the moral status of one's neighbor — in ways that resonate with Christian traditions and address the unique challenges of our day. An eminent cast of diverse contributors — scholars, pastors, and policy experts — weigh in to offer illuminating and insightful guidance that aid the reader in this task.

A final word is in order to alert readers that, in spite of the subtitle, this book is not simply for Christians. An expansive array of ideas, actors, and forces from "secular life" — popular culture (Bono), economic theory (Adam Smith and Amartya Sen), moral philosophy (Peter Singer), governmental life (Robert S. McNamara and the World Bank) to name just a few — pack the pages to follow. Those of many different faiths or no faith — all — have a stake in the thorny problems that the various authors uncover as well as their efforts to untangle our market-based presuppositions and to create openings through which we may see and think more clearly about our global neighbors. Ultimately, the collective wisdom of the authors and their essays will enable citizens of this new century to climb out from the nettles and underbrush of intricate global market systems so that they may strive anew to live out their various religious convictions and ethical commitments to the least of those living among us.

JOHN D. CARLSON *and* JEAN BETHKE ELSHTAIN
series editors

Contributors

Editors

Douglas A. Hicks, Ph.D., Associate Professor of Leadership Studies and Religion, University of Richmond. Author of *Inequality and Christian Ethics* (Cambridge University Press, 2000); *Religion and the Workplace: Pluralism, Spirituality, Leadership* (Cambridge University Press, 2003); and co-editor of the three-volume *International Library of Leadership* (Edward Elgar, 2004).

Mark Valeri, Ph.D., E. T. Thompson Professor of Church History, Union Theological Seminary and Presbyterian School of Christian Education, Richmond, VA. Author of *Law and Providence in Joseph Bellamy's New England: The Origins of Divinity in Revolutionary America* (Oxford University Press, 1994); editor of *The Works of Jonathan Edwards,* Vol. 17: *Sermons and Discourses, 1730-1733* (Yale University Press, 1999); and co-editor of *Practicing Protestants: Histories of Christian Life in America, 1630-1965* (Johns Hopkins University Press, 2006).

Additional Contributors

Robert D. Austin, Ph.D., Professor, Managing Creativity and Innovation, Copenhagen Business School, and Associate Professor, Harvard Business School

Rebecca M. Blank, Ph.D., Henry Carter Adams Collegiate Professor of

Public Policy, University of Michigan, and Robert V. Kerr Senior Fellow, Brookings Institution

Lee Devin, Ph.D., Emeritus Professor of Theatre Arts, Swarthmore College

William Goettler, M.Div., Co-Pastor, First Presbyterian Church, New Haven, CT, and Lecturer, Presbyterian Church Polity and History, Yale Divinity School

Eric Gregory, Ph.D., Assistant Professor of Religion, Princeton University

Janet Parker, Ph.D., Associate Pastor, Rock Spring Congregational United Church of Christ, Arlington, VA

Rebecca Todd Peters, Ph.D., Associate Professor of Religious Studies, Elon University

Shirley J. Roels, Ph.D., Professor of Business and Director, Lilly Vocational Project, Calvin College

Jeff Van Duzer, J.D., Dean, School of Business and Economics, Seattle Pacific University

Kent Van Til, Ph.D., Visiting Assistant Professor of Religion, Hope College

Thomas W. Walker, Ph.D., Senior Pastor, Palms Presbyterian Church, Jacksonville, FL

Producing Endurance:
A Story of Faith and the Global Market

William Goettler

Denny McFadden was a smart and creative kid. Growing up in an Irish Catholic family on Long Island meant attending weekly Mass with his family. From his early teenage years, the Mass was far more than an obligation to him: the liturgy touched him, and he felt strengthened and renewed by the Eucharist. Denny's parents, immigrants who had both made their way through the public university system, talked about their faith daily. At the dinner table Denny heard talk about the concepts of Catholic social teaching. At his parochial high school in the 1980s, he learned that Christian faith meant being for racial justice and against militarism. Faith was, after all, about how humans treat their neighbors. Denny joined a small group of students who traveled to New York City with the school's priest, Father Riley, to protest apartheid. Faith made sense to Denny.

But Denny was not to become a seminarian. Instead, he delighted in mathematics, in the technical, and in problem-solving. At eight years old, he had mastered Rubic's Cube; at ten he became a champion at chess. When the time came to go to college, engineering was the obvious choice. And he succeeded in mechanical engineering, first winning academic prizes and then job offers. Denny's early career thrived, and he delighted in his tasks in a series of manufacturing positions. At a start-up firm on the tip of Long Island he created finely engineered measuring devices. He moved to a public utility, and then on to the Cyberton Corporation, where he began to work on industrial uses for laser technology. The work was demanding, but he was good at it.

More and more challenging demands were made on him in industry. Though he was married in 1993 and soon had two small children, Denny did not see much of them. He was needed at the lab from early in the morning until late in the evening. He was dependably home only on Sundays, when the family attended Mass together. Promotions came rapidly, and he knew that the hard work was worth it, that the sacrifices were for the good of his character and for his family's well-being. He started to make good money, and he moved his family from a modest first house into a larger home in a better neighborhood, not far from the water off Long Island's north shore.

Often, in the middle of a day at work, Denny would think of what Father Riley had said about the apostle Paul, about the amazing miracle of Christian hope, that stunning calculation of the life of faith: we boast in our sufferings, knowing that suffering produces endurance, and endurance produces character, and character produces hope, and hope does not disappoint us.

Denny's successful research and work seemed to make use of his gifts in ways that pleased even that sense of holy calling. He was, by every measure that he knew, increasingly successful. This work must be his life's purpose, he knew, because it was work that seemed to be not only fulfilling but holy to him. True, these were just machines; but the company was growing and becoming profitable. The public stock was rising, and people were employed. And part of this thriving economic enterprise was because of his hard work.

In the fall of 1999, Denny was called to a meeting of department heads. The economic news was growing bleak, he learned. But there was a way for the company to continue to survive: it would do this by moving the production of all new electronic components to Mexico. In fact, the engineers gathered that day were the ones who would make this transition possible. The company could be saved by their work: they would build a new plant, an exact duplicate of the plant on Long Island. And they would train the workers. It would happen quickly, in just eighteen months. They would be away from home for much of that time, but it would, in the end, be a good thing for all involved.

A good thing — except for the New Yorkers who would lose their jobs, Denny thought. And except for his family, who would see even less of him. But if this was the only way for the company to survive in the tough economic climate, then he would do what it took. Suffering produces endurance. . . and endurance character.

The announcement of the move to Mexico was delayed while the company kept the New York employees busy. Denny heard the challenges to workers to be more productive, the warnings to the union to back off on demands, even as he traveled south to create the jobs that he knew would replace those workers, regardless of how productive they were or how hard they worked.

Denny spent much of the year 2000 in the border town of McAllen, Texas, and the Mexican town of Reynosa, where the new plant was quickly coming into being. Cyberton was not the only American plant under construction in this boomtown atmosphere. The North American Free Trade Agreement (NAFTA) was about to make doing business across the border easier and cheaper than ever before. And it was a good deal for the Mexicans, too. NAFTA required that a high percentage of the workers be Mexican nationals. In an impoverished country, the jobs that Cyberton would offer were good jobs indeed. Mexican men were already traveling from far in the south of the country to apply for work. Machine operators would earn less than $3,000 a year; skilled workers, those with two-year college degrees, would be given the title of "engineer," and they would be paid about $20,000 annually, with full benefits. The real engineering, of course, would still be done on Long Island. But every Mexican job would be documented, and the company would receive the credit due for encouraging not just cheap labor but skilled professionals.

A mile from the industrial plants, new cement blocks of apartments were also going up quickly. The workers moving to the area realized that they could conveniently share these apartments: each worked a twelve-hour shift, which meant that two workers could live in the space normally needed by one. Half the usual cost for a rental.

And the working conditions were good — identical, really, to those in the States. The plant was well air-conditioned and kept spotlessly clean. After all, Cyberton owned the plant and fitted this Mexican plant according to the standards of its other plants. They would not tolerate unsafe conditions. The investment was high, but everyone believed it was worthwhile. Only the outside air of the region seemed to suffer, because of the growing number of industrial plants that were being quickly built. But the filthy air in this new town was not of much concern to the Mexican workers. They would stay here as long as they could stand being away from their families; but they could always go home again.

Denny found that he liked the Mexican workers. They, too, were faithful Catholics. They were highly motivated, happy for this chance at economic success. Denny even found himself feeling angry at the American workers. If their union were not so strong, if their pay scale was not so high, perhaps the plant could have stayed in New York. But they never seemed to be satisfied, the American workers. They demanded a standard of living that just couldn't be supported by the company, that is, if the business was going to turn a profit. Dividends had to be paid. After all, this was not a nonprofit corporation.

The Mexican workers, by contrast, were eager and enthusiastic. They were grateful for the jobs, and they worked hard — and without complaint — for four dollars an hour. In just fourteen months, the first plant was completed. And by the spring of 2001, Denny and his colleagues were training the new Cyberton workers for the task of building another plant. Denny missed his daughter's first school play and his son's first tooth. But the stock price was maintained . . . almost.

The Mexican plant opened to great fanfare, and it was successful for the entire year, and for the next. Denny made sure that he was in Mexico when the announcement of the jobs moving to Mexico was made at the home plant on Long Island. He went to Mass and prayed for the workers who would be displaced. But his position was not affected, because Cyberton's corporate offices and the research labs would be maintained on Long Island. After all, it was an American company. When Denny returned home, he walked the production floor to share in the sadness of the workers who were no longer needed, many of whom he knew well. They looked at him with a pain and distrust that he hadn't seen before. As bad as he felt, he knew that this was just the way of economic systems. This was business. Suffering produces endurance.

Things continued to go reasonably well in Mexico. From time to time the workers there, when they learned what their American predecessors had earned, agitated for more money. But when they did, they were reminded that there were plenty of Mexicans who would be glad to have their jobs. The unions knew the importance of their "no strike" pledges. And most of them were just happy to be employed.

But then, in the summer of 2002, the market tanked again. Orders seemed to dry up overnight, and the company's stock price fell by nearly 40 percent. Something had to be done. The call into the meeting at corporate headquarters felt all too familiar to Denny. He didn't listen to much of the explanation, and what he did hear confirmed his fears. Costs are too high. Operating our own plant, even in Mexico, is too expensive. We need workers who are willing to accept lower wages. The city of Guangzhou in China — not far from Hong Kong — is the answer. Four dollars a day instead of four dollars an hour. Fewer unnecessary and costly safety regulations. More profit. Save the company.

Even better, Cyberton would not have to build or even own the plant in Guangzhou. Industrial capability was already there. American companies would simply sign on with contract manufacturers, provide them with the equipment needed to make the electronic equipment, and send their own people as teachers to do the training. Cyberton would not be in the awkward position of promising to stay forever. These would essentially be temporary workers. The contract company would provide housing in dorms, as well as food for the workers. The American company's hands would be clean: they would have no responsibility at all to the employee.

And the finished product would be exactly the same as the product that was once produced on Long Island, exactly the same as what was now being produced in Mexico. And with even fewer rejected components. That was hard to believe. The micro-electronics required in production had become smaller and smaller each year, ever more difficult to actually manufacture. The old American plant, and the new Mexican plant, had increasingly found it necessary to rely on robotics. But the Chinese women who would be hired by the contractor, teenagers really, had tiny hands, and the contractor promised that the work would be nearly free of error.

These female workers would leave their rural villages when they finished high school. Their wages, woefully inadequate even by Mexican standards, were higher than anyone in their family had ever dreamed of. They would work constantly for four or five years, sending almost all of their earnings home; then they would go back to their village to marry. How interesting, Denny thought, that even the workers in a country that wasn't even Christian knew that their goal — the point of it all — was to get home again, to build a family, to embrace the values they held most dear.

Working conditions would not be as nice as in Mexico. A part of the work of the American trainers and inspectors would be to keep an eye on the conditions. Nobody wanted another Bhopal. Who could handle that kind of publicity? But neither employee relations nor workers' wages would really be Cyberton's problem. And even more attractive, the contractors already had in place the kind of quality safeguards that had been observed across Asia since W. Edwards Deming had moved to Japan after

World War II, when the products were junk. His processes to inspect, test, and correct for quality assurance were now the Asian standard.

There was no fighting progress, Denny realized. Corporations were learning to be more nimble, to move around in search of quality and cost control. Americans didn't want manufacturing jobs, the Long Island unions had made clear. And as a country, he knew, the United States was moving beyond that. The American economy of the future would be about funding, innovation, and ideas. But concerns lingered in his mind when he thought about India, where the focus of every level of schooling was increasingly on software development and technical skill. Every software support line now seemed to be answered in Calcutta. Soon Indians would not only be supporting American products; they would be offering better and cheaper products of their own.

The United States was known for innovation. But if the corporate bosses continued to insist on teaching others to do the work that was once done on Long Island, then not just a lot of jobs would be lost in the long run, but eventually the American place in the world economy would erode. Would he bear part of the blame for that kind of failure? Would these painful trips away from his family lead to such an end, not only harming his family by his absence in the short term, but in the long term as well, endangering the jobs that his kids might someday hope for? Denny had had just such a dream recently: on this trip to China, after he would show his production plans to his Chinese counterparts and spend five days uploading data and developing working relationships, he would be, he suddenly realized, redundant. Cyberton wouldn't need Denny McFadden anymore. And he'd be just as jobless as those whining union workers on their picket line, those whose demands were too great for a profitable business to take seriously.

Denny couldn't think about that today. He was handed travel documents; a private limo would pick him up at his house, and he would take a first-class flight to China. He needed his rest. Denny would be part of the first team to fly to Hong Kong, then travel up to Guangzhou. On this first visit they would inspect the factory. They would bring along the design specs, the same documents that Denny had created for the plant in Mexico. The goal would be to create an identical facility to the long-closed plant on Long Island and to the soundly operating one in Mexico. He would be in China a week from today.

Leaving meant that he would miss his wife's birthday. He would go, he knew, and would do what was asked of him. Suffering produces endurance. But he didn't feel like going to Mass today.

Cyberton is a fictitious company. However, all other aspects of the above story are drawn from the stories of engineers working for Long Island corporations that must remain nameless, because those engineers still hold those jobs. Like many American companies, these companies have followed just the patterns described in this story during the last decade. And the American workers that they still employ struggle with the same questions that are of concern to Denny McFadden.

Christian Faith and the Global Market

Douglas A. Hicks and Mark Valeri

Denny McFaddden's story serves as an apt prologue for this book. As William Goettler describes him, Denny is a person of faith, commitment, and thoughtful reflection. An engineer in a manufacturing company, he tries to act morally within a global economy that seems to have a mind of its own. He can't seem to win for losing. He wants to do the right thing, but he becomes increasingly frustrated that jobs are moving overseas and that he is somehow complicit in the process. All the while, Denny feels powerless to know how to think or what to do.

Denny McFadden's questions are our questions. How should Christians live in a global economy in which the stakes are so high and the system so complicated? How can we act faithfully and effectively when it is clear that most economic forces are beyond our control? Even when we want to help our coworkers, or assist the poor, how do we know what we should do? How do we balance our working lives with time for family and community? Are potential employees in Mexico or China as much our neighbors as persons from our own country?

Economic globalization is quickly transforming the way we live. Money, messages, and media communication travel instantaneously around the world. The "Made in America" label in our clothes or on our cars means very little anymore, because it may only signify that a variety of pieces manufactured around the world were merely assembled within the U.S.A. In an age of international outsourcing, we are more likely to reach someone in India than in Indiana when we dial up customer service for some product. The larger and more complex the economy gets, the harder it is for us to think carefully about justice and goodness in economic life.

Our traditional Christian moral norms about economic life presuppose face-to-face economic interaction. *Commutative* justice involves fairness in the person-to-person exchange of goods; *distributive* justice involves very tangible laws about aiding impoverished persons within one's own community. Even when the apostle Paul speaks about aiding other Christian communities, he is able to speak in detail on a first-person basis about visiting or corresponding with those persons. Traditional Christian morality in economic life is based on *interpersonal* relations among neighbors, but our contemporary global economy is based on *impersonal* exchanges around the world.

If Christian faith is to help us in tangible ways to live moral lives, we must reconceive our notion of what it means to live as neighbors at a global level. The thirteen contributors to this book — scholars of business and economics, biblical studies and ethics, theology and history — provide a variety of perspectives on how we can rethink and apply Christian morality to the changing global economy, so that we may understand it and live faithfully within it (and despite it). The authors do not agree on every point, but they do generally find common ground in identifying the key issues for assessing the global economy and living in it. Most are writing from a Protestant standpoint, and several explore Reformed perspectives in particular. Yet many of our contributors are conversant with parallel resources within Catholic social teaching (including the papal encyclicals from Leo XIII's *Rerum Novarum* in 1891 to John Paul II's numerous letters on the economy).

These authors emphasize in different ways the need to exercise moral imagination in economic life. They reflect significant creativity in seeing new ways in which we as individuals, as churches, and as a political community can proactively respond to — and even critique — economic forces that sometimes seem beyond our control. As the distinguished economist and political scientist Charles Lindblom has argued, the time is ripe for an "intellectual interchange on the market system between economists, most of whom admire it, and those scholars of history, literature, and philosophy who . . . judge its consequences for values like freedom, rationality, and morality."[1] Our goal is to present just such an exchange: to help others reflect on moral participation in the market and to envision strategies that might transform market relationships.

1. Charles E. Lindblom, *The Market System: What It Is, How It Works, and What to Make of It* (New Haven: Yale University Press, 2001), p. 3.

These essays came out of a yearlong series of meetings of the authors, convened under the auspices of the Institute for Reformed Theology at Union Theological Seminary and the Presbyterian School of Christian Education in Richmond, Virginia. They stand as individual works of scholarship and Christian reflection. As we describe in the following paragraphs, the essays also connect on a variety of points. It is our hope that the following chapters will engage readers in serious conversation, and that these reflections will, in turn, provide at least some guidance and motivation for faithful action.

Near and Far Obligations in the Global Market

The essays in the first section address ways in which the Christian faith calls us to understand our moral obligations to our neighbors, both near and far. Thomas Walker's engaging essay examines the ideas of neighbors and strangers in biblical texts, with a particular focus on the parable, in Luke's Gospel, of the Samaritan who helps an injured man on the Jericho road. This parable is often referred to as "the Good Samaritan," though it is arguably better described as a story about a *neighborly* Samaritan. The parable's remarkable point is that, unlike the religious leaders of the victim's "own kind," who cross the road in order to increase their distance from the man, the Samaritan draws near to the needy person, disregarding social mores that would keep Jews and Samaritans apart from each other. Thus Jesus' parable speaks volumes about overcoming social (if not geographic) distances among would-be strangers. In opening this first section, Walker, a biblical scholar and a pastor, emphasizes that it takes our own theological and moral imagination to see past the distances and the barriers that separate us from persons in need. Jesus calls us to exercise our imagination, and then to respond with compassion and justice.

Christian ethicist Eric Gregory offers an important analysis of some key theological resources in the Christian tradition for thinking about *agape* love for all persons and preferential attention to one's family and fellow citizens. Like Walker, Gregory frames his essay in reference to the Good (or neighborly) Samaritan and the ways Jesus' parable calls its hearers to overcome human-to-human boundaries. He begins his reflections on these issues not with Augustine or Aquinas (though he offers us careful analyses of each) but with the contemporary secular philosopher Peter

Singer. Singer's strong moral call to address severe social and economic deprivation, Gregory suggests, seems to take the message of the parable far more seriously than do many Christian thinkers. Gregory's essay complements Walker's biblical reflection, presenting insights from theological and moral resources concerning the obligation to show regard for all persons and the duties owed to those persons who are our special relations.

Beginning with the parable of the Good Samaritan, Walker and Gregory suggest the power of biblical and theological imagination to enlarge the boundaries of neighborly love in economic exchange. Douglas Hicks, a Christian ethicist and scholar in leadership studies, looks at a contemporary effort that does the same. He focuses on the recent (and ongoing) movement to address severe poverty in Africa: the ONE Campaign, a coalition largely comprised of church-based and other Christian nonprofit institutions. Bono, the charismatic lead singer of the band U2, serves as the campaign's lead spokesperson. Hicks explores the ways in which Bono, named 2005 Person of the Year by *Time* magazine for being a "global Good Samaritan," and the ONE Campaign have sought to motivate Christians and others to respond to their global neighbors in severe poverty. Hicks identifies the successes of the recent antipoverty movement while he also delineates the limitations and future challenges of a celebrity-driven, NGO-coordinated effort. Following the other two essays in this first section, this chapter provides a useful discussion of the Christian call, despite all the challenges, to expand our idea of neighbor-obligation to a global scale.

Christian Witness and Mainstream Economic Theory: Four Critiques

All four of the chapters in the second section use the Christian moral imagination of neighbor to offer a critique of mainstream, neoclassical economics. Ethicist Kent Van Til examines the work of three economic theorists — Gary Becker, Hernando de Soto, and Amartya Sen — for their assumptions about human nature and human need. Van Til evaluates, according to his own account of biblical anthropology, their respective understandings of poverty; in essence, he poses the question of how Christians should think about mainstream economic theory and its alternatives. He expresses appreciation for some aspects of Becker's work, de Soto's recognition of the need for poor persons to have access to capital, and, most significantly, Sen's central focus on basic human capability. Van Til's conclusions for understanding and addressing poverty are constructive and provide the groundwork for adapting existing economic theories and developing corresponding practices consistent with Christian faith.

Sustained reflection on a host of different economic thinkers, from Adam Smith through Gary Becker to Amartya Sen, may muddy the waters of an oversimplified criticism of any one grand economic theory, but one thing is clear: fundamental moral assumptions underlie all economic theories. This is one important point of the chapter by Rebecca Todd Peters, a feminist Christian ethicist and scholar of globalization. She argues that any economic theory implicitly involves assumptions about human values, and that contemporary mainstream economists' denial that their social-scientific work is infused with values is a mistaken notion that has real costs in practice. Peters offers a concise analysis of Adam Smith's two major works in order to establish that the founder of classical economics understood well the role of values in maintaining a just social order. She goes on to suggest that the failure of contemporary economists to name their approach as value-laden has enabled practitioners such as Robert McNamara, former World Bank president, to overlook the actual effects of economic policies on people's lives, particularly poor people's lives. Peters's central claim that values necessarily form any economic theory creates space for Christians and other persons of faith to engage in a careful analysis of their own values vis-à-vis the operational values of the economy.

The next chapter, written by a business school dean, Jeff Van Duzer, provocatively takes up Peters's point by suggesting that there are fundamental conflicts between some market values and what he calls the "kingdom values" that derive from Christian faith. Specifically, Van Duzer suggests that the assumption of self-interest (and the lack of intrinsic attention to the needs of others — for example, customers, coworkers, or the poor) is contrary to the biblical call to love one's neighbor as oneself. He considers various reasons why these market-versus-kingdom conflicts do not get our attention or inspire our concern more frequently. One reason is that "ethical" behavior or behavior that is not exclusively self-interested can hide in market imperfections. Van Duzer suggests that as markets (presumably) become more competitive over time, it will become more and more difficult for firms and individuals that show concern for others to stay in business. Van Duzer's constructive contribution comes from his exploration of how individual and collective actions (at local, national, and transnational levels) can create new space for kingdom values to operate in a modified market structure.

Biblical imagination can illuminate the implicit moral values and deficiencies of the global market in several ways. Janet Parker, a feminist ethicist and pastor, examines reflections and declarations by the World Council of Churches and the World Alliance of Reformed Churches on the global economy. Parker considers the theoretical and practical dangers of an economic system that has taken on a predominant — or hegemonic — status at the global level. She mounts a case for the instrumental value of economic diversity in the world. Parker concurs with Van Til about the effects of the global market on human poverty and with Van Duzer on the conflict between free-market ideology and Christian conceptions of justice. However, Parker goes beyond Van Duzer's analysis in the depth of her critique of the market system as a form of idolatry. Christian actors can play a lead role in assuring that no economic system becomes a totalizing force in the lives of anyone, especially the vulnerable. Like the authors of the earlier essays on the theological and moral imagination, Parker sees a liberating, alternative vision for economic life in the Christian narrative for countering a powerful market system.

Labor and Vocation in the Global Market

The essays offered in this third section focus on how the Christian moral imagination of neighbor works its way into the local and quite mundane context: the nature of the work that Christians can (and should) do within the global market. The notion of vocation, or calling, has long been a part of Christian thinking about economic life. A person's calling extends to all aspects of his or her life; but the sense of a call, particularly in recent times, has often been reduced to what a person does in the work-for-pay relationship, that is, in one's everyday job. The first chapter in this third section, written by business school professor Robert D. Austin and theater arts professor Lee Devin, outlines the ways in which the nature of work is highly dependent on the economic systems of a given time and place. The way we think about vocation similarly varies according to the society in which we live. Austin and Devin offer a fascinating narrative of how work has shifted, from being a craft in medieval times, to becoming stuck in industrial routine, to offering in recent times the opportunity to return to creative, personalized activity. While they are quick to point out that not everyone can find fulfilling work in the current economy, Austin and Devin's distinctive perspective provides a rather hopeful view of human labor in the globalizing world.

Business scholar Shirley Roels comes at the issue of work from a very different place: from that sector of the economy that is closest to the industrial routine critiqued by Austin and Devin as being less humanizing — that is, the manufacturing sector. Roels focuses particularly on the calling of leaders in manufacturing: she asks how they can organize their firms to provide productive and meaningful employment experiences for their workers and how they can contribute to social justice. Roels makes the point that Christian discussions of economic life, for all of their focus on distributive justice, have failed to address what she calls "productive justice." The manufacturing leader can make a real contribution, she argues, to economic life by shaping firms that efficiently produce goods that are of service to human beings. The creation of useful products is a high calling, Roels observes. In the process, leaders and their firms must covenant with their workers not only to pay them justly but to prepare them for future employment (in their firm or in other firms and sectors) in an economy of constant change. Roels suggests that, even if a leader might need to terminate an employee because of dire economic conditions, we can consider it just if the firm has undertaken training and professional development to prepare that employee to face the economic world.

The economist Rebecca Blank, a former member of the President's Council of Economic Advisors and former dean of a public-policy school, widens the idea of vocation for our complex, institution-laden economy. She suggests that, in the end, the Christian conception of neighbor-love, which has traditionally been thought of in interpersonal terms, can partly (but not wholly) be met by establishing and supporting just economic structures. This concept resonates with the robust account of both markets and society that Adam Smith developed, as Peters notes in her essay. And it stands as a critique of the present mainstream economic view that the government's role in the economy should only step into the market to stop market failure. Blank's nuanced analysis of the role of government in Christian thinking about the market brings us back, in a sense, to the widening of our moral imagination about how best to help a vulnerable neighbor on the side of the global road. Martin Luther King, Jr., put it this way: "One day we must come to see that the whole Jericho road must be transformed so that men and women will not be constantly beaten and robbed as they make their journey on life's highway."[2] Blank drives home a point of view that various authors here have suggested: in the global economy, Christian faith requires individual, church-based, and political action. Vocation entails all of these dimensions of life, and the various chapters of this book develop different aspects of that calling.

Perennial and Novel Challenges

The last essay of the volume draws together insights at the intersections of economic theory, Christian faith, and everyday social life. Douglas Hicks and American religious historian Mark Valeri outline an approach based on this premise: The challenge in economic life for Christians in any time and place has been (and remains) to live together in ways that humanize their neighbors and that do not make idols of any ideology. At individual and corporate levels, Christians are called to recognize the dignity of all human beings in any economic system, even as they name the shortcomings of those systems and seek to transform them toward more just economies. Christian morality for economic life may have initially developed in the contexts of interpersonal exchanges and a more tangible sense of the neighbor, but the essays in this volume demonstrate that Christian faith offers creative and profound resources for living justly in the complex and bustling global economy — with all of its potential and its perils.

2. Quoted in Eric Gregory, "*Agape* and Special Relations in a Global Economy: Theological Sources," ch. 2 of this volume, n. 30.

PART I

Near and Far Obligations in the Global Market

CHAPTER 1

Who Is My Neighbor? An Invitation to See the World with Different Eyes

Thomas W. Walker

In his provocative book *The Prophetic Imagination,* biblical theologian Walter Brueggemann argues that the American church is so beholden to the current cultural milieu that it lacks the ability to imagine other possibilities for life and action.[1] Like a fish unable to detect the water in which it swims, modern American Christians find themselves immersed into a cultural milieu whose assumptions have shaped their understandings of reality along with their responses to that reality. With the loss of an imaginative gap between the "American dream" and biblical faithfulness, the typical modern Christian (and for the sake of argument, Christians in any age) often cannot even imagine a dissonance between a modern consumerist ethic and the witness of Jesus Christ in Scripture.

In the realm of economic life and Christian faith, this "beholdenness" is particularly evident as market theories and activities govern not only the realm of economic thought but have moved into the realm of deeper assumptions about human life and ethical conduct.[2] From religion becoming just another commodity to be purchased, to a "Walmartization" of Christian faith and practice (low prices and easy availability), to an ethic of utility, a modern consumerist ethic has captured the imagination of the typical modern American Christian.[3] People have become commodities

1. Walter Bruggemann, *The Prophetic Imagination,* 2nd ed. (Minneapolis: Fortress, 2001).
2. See Vincent J. Miller, *Consuming Religion: Christian Faith and Practice in a Consumer Culture* (New York: Continuum, 2004).
3. For an interesting pastoral reflection and challenge to the commodification of the Christian gospel, see Eugene Peterson, *Living the Resurrection* (Colorado Springs: NavPress, 2006).

3

used to maximize personal profit with whatever makes sense for the market and to protect their own share of defining priorities. As other writers in this volume will show, the global market system depersonalizes individuals so that they become valued solely for their productivity (ability to produce) and their "consumability" (ability to consume), and they become faceless cogs in a global megamachine. While few would publicly claim it for themselves, the old bumper sticker that reads "Whoever has the most toys wins" may be seen as an underlying ethic for much of the daily activity of the "average" person in a culture that highlights "bling bling," pays millions to superstars (whether those stars are athletes or actors), and finds supermarket stands filled with tabloids about lifestyles of the rich and famous. Truly, one wonders at times whether the fish can see the water they are swimming in.

While this may be an overstatement of the current modern American Christian reality, it does paint in broad brushstrokes some of the common assumptions that exist for those seeking to engage our culture with the claims of the Scripture of the Old and New Testaments. It would seem that, even at first blush, Scripture pushes against some of these assumptions about human life and the character of living that seem to dominate the mainstream consumerist economic ethic. The opening narratives in Genesis 1 declare that human beings are created in God's image and carry intrinsic worth through their creation, which is in contrast to the value placed by the global market on productivity and "consumability." Mandates in the Torah and the Hebrew prophets abound concerning the care of the economically disadvantaged (the poor, orphans, and widows). Jesus issues challenging words about focusing on heavenly storehouses rather than earthly ones. It is easy to see that the biblical witness gives rise to imaginative possibilities that challenge commonly held assumptions about modern life. As has been pointed out in numerous books and articles, the Bible speaks more about our money and our possessions — that is, our economic life — than about any other particular subject.

Yet, as Brueggemann suggests, we all have become so beholden to our "way of life" that we have often ignored the disjunctive nature of the biblical testimonies, perhaps not intentionally, but because we have domesticated the stories to the point that they serve a different narrative. Brian McLaren, a leading figure in the "Emergent Church" movement, has adeptly noted the disjunction between a scriptural ethic and the current consumer-market ethic:

"[S]acred" words such as *private* (meaning personal and individual), *ownership* (meaning autonomous personal and individual control), and *enterprise* (meaning autonomous, personal individual control over projects to use God's world for our purposes) seem to fly in the face of kingdom values like *communal* (meaning seeing beyond the individual to the community), *fellowship* (which means sharing, holding in common with community, not grasping as "mine!"), and *mission* (meaning our participation in God's projects in God's world for God's purposes).[4]

Whether or not one agrees with this analysis, the basic question remains about the witness of Scripture providing insight for ethical deliberation that leads to the practice of faithful Christian living.

It is important to note here that the question I am wrestling with in this chapter is not what "the faithful responses of Christian practice" to a consumer culture are, but what the imaginative insights drawn from engagement with Christian Scripture are that might help to shape faithful ethical responses. Given that we are "swimming" in this particular culture, are there biblical images that may provoke our imaginations to ask questions in fresh and different ways that can open possibilities of new forms of faithfulness? Later chapters in this book will investigate in greater depth the intersection between a biblical imagination and specific ethical concerns raised by a market economy. But before we move to that intersection, we will explore at least one biblical image that will enable us to imagine a world different from the given or perceived world around us.

One can find many biblical examples where changes of perception brought about by imaginative renderings lead to new and faithful responses. Brueggemann puts it this way in his 1997 Stone Lectures at Princeton:

> Dip in almost anywhere. . . . They are utterances that assault our closely held worlds. They are surprise raids, surprise assaults on imagination, surprise every time uttered and every time heard, raids that expose the limited ammunition of the rulers of this age, attacks that cut off the supply lines and oxygen lines of easier ways in the world. They cut the communication lines to other resources by suggesting that the

---

4. Brian McLaren, *A Generous Orthodoxy* (Grand Rapids: Zondervan Youth Specialties, 2004), pp. 239-40.

other modes of communication have missed the news. They expose the supply lines we counted on by making clear the genuine sources of life are other than we thought.[5]

From prophets that draw on the powerful images of the tradition to call Israel back to faithfulness, to Paul's use of the image of the body to help the bickering Corinthians see their unity (1 Cor. 12), to Revelation's fantastic images that call forth discipleship in a hostile Roman world, the Bible is replete with imaginative "utterances" that challenge current assumptions and call for faithful response.

A classic example of the entire movement from perception to imaginative confrontation to new perception is evident in the encounter between King David and the prophet Nathan following the Bathsheba affair in 2 Samuel 11–12. Given the prerogatives and power of kingship, David cannot imagine, or see, that he has done anything wrong, even though he has committed adultery with Bathsheba and ordered the killing of Bathsheba's husband, Uriah. As king, David has certain political and cultural prerogatives, and the narration of his activity with Bathsheba and Uriah is reported in the 2 Samuel narrative without comment or judgment. It is simply the most powerful man in Israel wielding his power in ways that are both personally beneficial and that treat others as commodities to be acquired and disposed of in the way powerful people in cultures throughout the world have often used their power. Although the narrative makes no commentary on David's action as it reports the movement of the story, the close of the narrative declares abruptly and unequivocally that what David did was evil in God's sight and imagination: "But the thing that David had done displeased the Lord" (2 Sam. 11:27). What is lost in this English translation of the verse is that the Hebrew words here translated as "displeased" literally mean "was evil in the sight of." What David saw as legitimate and possibly a good use of power, God saw as evil. But how will these contrasting perceptions be engaged in such a way that David can see with new eyes?

In 2 Samuel 12, the prophet Nathan has the difficult task of confronting the powers that be and the assumptions of that power with a different perception of reality. How can Nathan help David see the differences in per-

---

5. Brueggemann, *Ichabod Towards Home: The Journey of God's Glory* (Grand Rapids: Eerdmans, 2002), p. 104.

ception? Even though the prophet was the Lord's spokesman, a direct frontal accusation and assault on David could, at worst, have disastrous consequences for Nathan, and would serve, at the least, to do nothing more than raise David's defensive justifications for his actions. In this precarious situation Nathan disarms David by using a parable in which he paints the picture of a world where a callous king steals the most beloved possession of one of his poor subjects. Enraged at the injustice of the brazen leader's actions, David demands to know who could act in such a way, so that David, the king with the power to act and ensure justice, can see that the perpetrator is justly punished. With this parable as his bait, Nathan evokes within David a different perception of reality, which he then uses to convict David of the "evil" of his action when he says, "You are the man" (2 Sam. 12:7). Seeing with new eyes, David is repentant and moves forward operating within a revised moral framework and seeing the world in new ways.

In our world of consumer ethics, the question can be raised concerning biblical images that can elicit repentance and new, perhaps more faithful, practices of Christian living. Given the move toward depersonalization and commodification of other people in a global economy, biblical texts such as this David story that speak to the treatment of the other are particularly useful, poignant, and provocative for a biblically informed ethical imagination. Since economic activity by definition involves our interaction with others, and since part of the move toward faithful practice involves the ability to provoke an imagination beyond commonly held cultural assumptions, let's turn to an encounter between Jesus and a lawyer in Luke 10:25-37 to engage our imaginations concerning the lawyer's question, "Who is my neighbor?"

Luke 10:25-37

In Luke 9:51, Jesus sets his face to go to Jerusalem and begins a journey that will take him and the narrative to his entrance into Jerusalem in Luke 19:44. As Luke has arranged his Gospel, it is along this way that Jesus is teaching his disciples — through both his actions and the telling of parables — particularly about discipleship in the kingdom of God.[6] Near the

---

6. See David P. Moessner, *Lord of the Banquet* (Minneapolis: Fortress, 1989), for a discussion of the issues related to the travel narrative.

beginning of this journey to Jerusalem, Jesus is confronted by a certain lawyer who seeks to test him. This is no ordinary confrontation, but one that sets the context for our exploration. The interactive movement of this encounter between the lawyer and Jesus reflects the same movement that we saw in the David-Nathan story: Jesus, like Nathan, confronts the lawyer's assumptions about the world, about the identity of the neighbor, and about God's call to a certain way of life with neighbors. He then provides an imaginative reconstrual that calls for fresh ethical practices.

The confrontation begins with a question concerning eternal life: it is a deeply religious issue, and we can presume that this lawyer would know the finer points of the common religious understanding of his day. Yet the lawyer immediately finds that Jesus has turned the tables: instead of the lawyer being able to put Jesus on the witness stand, he finds Jesus turning the question back on him. Jesus asks him to declare the common understanding of the day as found in the Torah, and the lawyer responds with what are commonly known as the two greatest commandments: "You shall love the Lord your God with all your heart, and with all your soul, and with all your strength, and with all your mind; and your neighbor as yourself" (Luke 10:27, quoting Deut. 6:5 and Lev. 19:18). Jesus notes that the lawyer's answer is correct, and he notes the possibilities of life inherent in faithfulness to those commands. Jesus and the lawyer agree in essence on the common assumptions of ethical life that formed the faithful practice of Jews in the first century (and Jews and Christians throughout the ages). There is a shared framework for ethical decision-making that is agreed on at this point by the lawyer and Jesus, an ethic based on love of God and love of neighbor. However, it soon becomes evident that the shared ethical framework has been assimilated differently by these two. While the lawyer and Jesus may agree on the nature of the broad framework, they have drawn out their ethical imperatives arising from that framework differently.

But back in the text, we need to remember that this particular lawyer is not there simply to agree with Jesus; he wants to test him. So the lawyer, desiring to justify himself, asks, "Who is my neighbor?" The question brings forth from Jesus what has become one of the best-known of Jesus' parables, commonly known as "the Good Samaritan." Like the Nathan narrative quoted above, the parable arises in a situation where there have been shared assumptions about life but where the parable teller wants to challenge those assumptions.

This parable has been variously interpreted over the centuries, but a very common interpretation looks at the parable as a morality play that sets forth an ethic of compassion toward the other, a living out of the twin rules of love of God and love of neighbor. In fact, many scholars note that Jesus deflects the lawyer's question to the point of altering it: by the end, the question is not "who is my neighbor?" but "what does it mean to be a neighbor?" — that is, to act neighborly. Jesus' follow-up question at the end of the story and his subsequent command of "go and do likewise" seem to support this interpretive move. By the end of this narrative, Jesus focuses the question back onto the lawyer (as he did earlier in the text and as Nathan did with David), leaving the demands of the neighborly life at the lawyer's feet.

While this is often the typical interpretation of this text, closer attention to some of the details of the Good Samaritan story suggests other interpretative and imaginative moves that can flow out of the text. In particular, paying close attention to language about "near" and "other side" (of the road) suggests that Jesus does not leave the lawyer's question hanging; rather, he answers it and then pushes beyond the question to a call for a specific way of neighborly life. Beginning with the Greek word for "neighbor" *(plēsion),* which literally means "near one," we can read the lawyer's question as "Who is my near one?" In other words, the question raised by the lawyer is: Who is located "near," or contiguous to, me that claims my attention? (See John 4:5, where *plēsion* refers to a field nearby.) Jesus then exploits this spatial characteristic of the word for neighbor in the parable: his play on the spatial implications of near and far drives the action of the story. It is important to note that we are assuming that, for everyone who is near, there must be someone who is "far" and who does not require our direct attention as does the "near" one, the neighbor. It is a common scholarly assumption that the Jewish culture of Jesus' day was defined by definitive social boundaries. There were clearly demarcated near ones and clearly understood far ones.[7] Thus the lawyer is in some sense asking the question about who sits near enough to me to be a "near one" (neighbor) and is hence deserving of the love commanded in Leviticus 19.

Reading the parable anew, with an eye on spatial relationships and

7. See, among others, I. Howard Marshall, *Commentary on Luke,* New International Greek Testament Commentary (Grand Rapids: Eerdmans, 1978), p. 444; see also R. Alan Culpepper, *The Gospel of Luke,* NIB Commentary Series, Vol. IX (Nashville: Abingdon, 1995), p. 229.

given the known spatial boundaries of Jesus' contemporaries, we can quickly perceive an interesting play on these ideas clearly emerging. We see that a certain man on the way from Jerusalem to Jericho has a group of bandits "fall about him" *(peripiptō)*, literally meaning "fall in with."[8] In one sense of the word, they become neighbors (that is "near ones") to this man, but their actions can be clearly understood as the opposite of the commandment in Leviticus 19: their treatment of the neighbor is destructive and harmful.

Following the bandits, a priest comes down the road, sees the injured man and passes by on the other side (*antiparerchomai*, two prepositions meaning "not" and "beside," followed by a common Greek word for motion). Next a Levite comes down the road, and he actually moves forward to see the injured man, but then he also "passes by on the other side" (*antiparerchomai*).[9] While many reasons have been advanced to explain the actions of the priest and Levite, the text does not allow such speculation. In many modern readings of the Gospels, the common assumption is that Luke would have highlighted a story in which Jesus negatively portrays the priest and Levite — because they were his opponents. But since Luke elsewhere shows respect for the office of priest, this is not the place for some kind of Christian triumphalism (Luke 1:5; 5:14; 17:14). In other words, this story is not intended to cast aspersions on the priest and Levite as much as it is to answer the question of who is the "near one."[10] However, in answering the question of who the near one is, the parable clearly shows that the man lying on the side of the road is certainly a "far one" for the priest and Levite, considering that they pass by on the other side and do not come near.

The final character in the parable approaches the beaten body lying on the side of the road, and instead of passing by on the other side, he has compassion for the wounded man. It is intriguing that the word Luke uses for "compassion" here is the one he uses only for the activity of God or Jesus elsewhere in his Gospel (Luke 7:13; 15:20). Of particular interest to my argument is the similar use of the word in another well-known parable,

8. *A Lexicon Abridged from Liddel and Scott's Greek-English Lexicon* (Oxford: Clarendon Press, 1987), p. 551.

9. There are textual problems concerning Luke 10:32 with respect to this fuller reading. See Marshall, *Luke*, pp. 448-49, for a discussion of the issues and argument for the fuller reading.

10. Fred Craddock, *Luke* (Louisville: John Knox Press, 1990), p. 151.

the one typically known as the parable of the "prodigal son," where the text clearly notes that, from *afar*, the father sees the prodigal and has *compassion* on him. Because this third character has compassion, he does not pass on the *far* side of the injured man but comes toward the man *(proserchomai)*. This word has the same base Greek verbal stem as the verbs used earlier to show the action of the priest and the Levite; but now it is combined with a preposition that carries a meaning of drawing "toward," which is the opposite action of the "not by" used earlier of the priest and Levite.

Therefore, in terms of sheer space, this third character becomes a "near one" to the injured man, and his nearness Luke later describes as "mercy" (another word that Luke uses for the actions of God: Luke 1:50, 54, 58, 72, 78). This third person's actions are almost the exact opposite of those who had "fallen in with" the man earlier. Kenneth E. Bailey notes that the bandits take money from the man, whereas the Samaritan spends money on the man; the bandits beat the man, whereas the Samaritan binds his wounds; finally, the bandits leave him for dead and depart with no promise of return, whereas the Samaritan leaves him in the care of others, and he promises that he will himself return.[11] As the lawyer notes at the end of this text, we have learned what the action of a "near one" looks like, one who follows the commandment of love for the neighbor.

It is here that the identity of this third man leaps out at the hearer/reader: he is a Samaritan. Given the enmity between Jews and Samaritans through the centuries, and at the time of Jesus, the latter's identification of a Samaritan man as the "near one" functions to challenge the assumptions of Jesus' hearers about the definitions of near and far that were common in their day. Jesus' contemporaries would have thought the Samaritan to be, by definition, a far one, and the priest and Levite to be, by definition, the near ones. And in the imaginative world created by the parable, the ones expected to be and act like near ones become far ones both metaphorically and literally: they go to the other side of the road. The one expected to be and act like a far one becomes a near one by going to the injured man and acting with God-like compassion.

Thus, while the text does provide a clear ethic of love for the neighbor, it is far from being simply a morality play. Through the interplay of the locative terms concerning the concepts of "near" and "far," the text re-

11. Kenneth E. Bailey, *Poet and Peasant* (Grand Rapids: Eerdmans, 1976), p. 73.

defines the concept of the near one (a neighbor included in the care of God) to being the far one (a Samaritan traditionally considered outside that care). Hence a fuller reading of this text not only suggests an ethic of love but an imaginative redefinition of the neighbor (the near one) to include the far one, who is also deserving of the love we are commanded to show the near one.

As I have noted above, the text establishes that the lawyer and Jesus have the same ethical framework for action: the two great love commandments found in the Torah (e.g., in Deut. 6 and Lev. 19). However, the parable highlights a major difference between Jesus and the lawyer in how they have assimilated that common framework into imperatives for ethical action. The cultural context of the lawyer has limited the concept of neighbor to a very specific subset of individuals. Like the fish not seeing the sea, the lawyer's question ("who is my neighbor?") reflects this subset of boundaries that limit the realm of neighbor. The particular power of the parable is not so much that it defines what neighborly action looks like (although it does that clearly by noting the actions of the bandits and the Samaritans); rather, it is in creating new imaginative possibilities that challenge the restricted view of neighbor and in pushing for more expansive, if not nonexistent, neighbor boundaries. Like Nathan before him, Jesus could have directly answered the lawyer's question by accusing him of the disease of shortsightedness, that is, limited neighbor-view. Instead, by telling a parable, Jesus evokes new imaginative possibilities about neighbors for this lawyer and, perhaps more importantly, for Luke's audience, both ancient and modern.

Later chapters of this book will move on to suggest how our ethical imaginations about this redefinition of the "near one" can be suggestive for ethical decision-making in a global market economy. But before we go to that level of discussion, it is important to note that the interplay of "near" and "far," as well as the imaginative redescription of those categories, runs through Luke's Gospel. At the beginning of the Gospel, the ultimate insider, Zechariah, a priest who ministers in the holy of holies and thus is as physically close to God as one can get, is portrayed as lacking in faith, while the ultimate outsider, an unmarried woman (who could come no closer to God physically than the outer courts of the temple) soon to be an expectant mother, is portrayed as a model of discipleship (Luke 1:5-39).[12] Mary's re-

12. For a further discussion, see Raymond Brown, *The Birth of the Messiah* (New York: Doubleday, 1993).

sponse to God's drawing near to her notes her own reversal of place from far to near, and it indicates that God is about bringing the same reversal of fortune to the world (Luke 1:46-55). Later in the Gospel, another one of Jesus' parables, this one about the prayers of the Pharisee and publican, also plays on the redescription of near and far (Luke 18:10-14). The Pharisee (the insider and "near one") seemingly draws near to God by praying openly about his own righteousness and the distance of the publican (the "far one") from God. On the other hand, the text notes that the publican stands "far off" and refuses to even lift his eyes. By the end of the parable, however, their places have been reversed: the publican is the one who goes home justified and thus in the position of a near one with respect to God. Likewise, immediately following the parable, children, who in the ancient world would have been powerless far ones, are prevented from coming into the presence of (or near) Jesus by his inner circle of near ones, the disciples (Luke 18:15-17). Jesus sternly rebukes the disciples: he teaches them that to become a near one in the kingdom, they must become far ones like the powerless children.

Finally, at the end of Luke's Gospel, when the narrative gathers the reader around the cross, it turns the boundaries of near and far upside down once more. As Luke paints the portrait of Golgotha, those nearest to Jesus during his earthly life (the text literally refers to them as those who "knew" him) are farthest from him; they watch from afar (Luke 23:49: the same Greek word for "afar" as found in Luke 15 and 18). Near ones have become far ones, while those who sought his death and mocked him are the closest to him. We should also note the irony that it is those who are in the closest proximity, but who are far ones in the worldview of Luke's audience, who come up with the final "correct" identifications of Jesus. The sign that is placed over Jesus' head by the Romans identifies him as the "king of the Jews"; the condemned criminal knows that Jesus is innocent and coming into a kingdom; finally, the Roman centurion announces Jesus' innocence after his death. Yet it is these far ones, in terms of their enmity toward him, who are standing near the cross, and it is they to whom Jesus utters the words, "Father, forgive them for they know not what they are doing," thus making them near ones to him (Luke 23:34). It is intriguing that it is Jesus' beaten roadside body that offers compassion to those who are near and yet far. It is almost as though he forms a bracket with the "far" Samaritan, who opened eyes about what it meant to act like a near one. As the Samaritan did in the parable that bears his name, Jesus offers compassion to yet another far one on Golgotha, the criminal on the cross: he promises paradise to a criminal convicted of a capital crime, one who would be an ultimate outsider in all cultures (Luke 23:43).

These few examples, along with the deeper exploration of Luke 10:25-37, point to a theme that runs through the Gospel of Luke: God is at work intentionally in reversing the world, turning it upside down. The first become last, rich become poor, poor become rich, and those near become far while the far become near. This inversion of assumptions regarding reality and its reimagining of the world lead to ethical action, which is suggested by Jesus' last words in the parable: go and treat others like neighbors, like near ones (Luke 10:37). Not only do these texts imaginatively reshape the boundaries of the world, but they highlight examples of particular responses of action. From the father who sees the prodigal son from afar, has compassion on him, and welcomes him home, to the portrayal of the crucified Jesus having compassion on the far ones who are crucifying him, Luke's Gospel highlights clear examples of particular responses of compassion to far ones as though they were near ones. But the presentation of the Gospel with its reversal of categories also suggests that the boundaries of those who are near need to be expanded. As part of this inversion, the Gospel redefines and gives new imaginative possibilities to the category of "neighbor." As Luke's Gospel imaginatively challenges common assumptions about the boundaries of near and far, the result is that *all* people are captured in the term "neighbor," and the challenge to treat all people as neighbors becomes inherent in Jesus' final words to the lawyer, "Go and do likewise": that is, go and act like the Samaritan, full of compassion and mercy — go "love your neighbor as yourself."

Earlier we assumed that we live in a culture defined by consumerism and an economic system that is becoming more global by the day. The boundaries of our economic participation have moved from the local to the extralocal to the national to the international to the global scale. At least one of the dangers inherent in this progression is that the products we buy are no longer made by our "near" ones (defined geographically) but are more often than not made by "far" ones. Yet our economic practices and decisions are, more often than not, defined by "near" boundaries instead of "far" concerns. Like the lawyer in Luke's narrative, our assumptions and our cultural context have placed boundaries on those we consider to be our neighbors. But the distance that exists between the coffee grower in Latin America and the computer consultant who stops at Starbucks each day has collapsed over the past decades. But for the average person, the fish swimming in the water, this distance is not being bridged: the far ones remain far off and are not party to the near economic decisions. Not only is that true, but as Walter Brueggemann might suggest, we are such a part of our economic reality that we cannot imagine the world any other way, and thus we cannot imagine (or perhaps refuse to imagine) how our economic activity has an impact on far ones. Jesus' imaginative reconstrual of the world in his parable of the Good Samaritan, and also Luke's overall telling of the story of Jesus, where far ones are just as much neighbors as near ones, invites us to new visions of the world and to new modes of action that center on compassion and mercy.

We don't know how the lawyer responded to Jesus' challenge. Unlike the story of Nathan and David, in which the text reports David's contrite reaction to Nathan's story, the lawyer walks offstage at the end of Luke 10:37 and is never heard from again. Given the narrative context of the parable within the journey section of Luke's Gospel, whose primary purpose is the formation of disciples, we can wonder whether Luke intentionally leaves us hanging at the end of the story. That is, the parable extends the challenge to reframe the nature of who the neighbor is, not only to the lawyer but also to all who encounter the parable and want to become disciples of Jesus. It is an imaginative challenge that pushes us to specific actions of "neighborliness" as we seek to "go and do likewise."

CHAPTER 2

Agape and Special Relations in a Global Economy: Theological Sources

Eric Gregory

> *But a Samaritan, as he journeyed, came to where he was; and when he saw him, he had compassion, and he went to him and bound up his wounds, pouring on oil and wine, and took care of him.*
>
> LUKE 10:33

The parable of the Good Samaritan continues to fascinate us. It has become one of the most enduring stories about the nature and scope of morality. Few writers, religious or secular, concerned with questions about moral obligation resist its invocation; and no one directly criticizes the actions of this Good Samaritan. He is praised for his deed, a definitive example of compassion at work. The teaching of Jesus also is usually praised for its universal implications about who counts as "neighbor": his willingness to recognize the humanity of any neighbor contrasts with narrow tribal boundaries of moral concern limited to one's own kind. But not everyone shares the same conclusions about what we human beings owe to one another. Christians themselves disagree about what it means to follow Jesus' injunction to "go and do likewise." In fact, much of recent Christian ethics has challenged the supposedly abstract and individualistic altruism associated with moral universalism. In this chapter I would like to examine these disagreements in the context of today's global economy.

The primary question I address is this: How should a Christian, in a country like the United States, understand his or her obligation to strangers in need given the expanding networks of economic interaction and global communications? Here we face perplexing theoretical questions about the nature of morality as well as immediate practical decisions about ordinary life. I pursue these questions by putting traditional Christian beliefs in conversation with an influential argument made by the secular philosopher Peter Singer. Originally provoked by a famine in East Bengal, Singer claimed that affluent citizens of developed countries woefully neglect a moral duty to respond to the grave needs of distant strangers. In his view, humanitarian aid is not simply a kind thing to do; it is morally required. The scope of our duty to rescue those in need does not stop at national borders. To admit this more radical claim would imply drastic lifestyle changes for most people in countries such as the United States. Christians sometimes also talk this way when they read passages from the Bible that enjoin us to feed the hungry, clothe the naked, and welcome the stranger. I argue that Christians have theological reasons to reject Singer's account of the moral life and its demands; but these reasons do not justify rejecting his specific moral arguments. They can swing free from his utilitarian assumptions. Given global economic realities, Christians should adopt his call for a more rigorous interpretation of duties to aid "distant" strangers.

Recent natural disasters such as Hurricane Katrina and the Asian tsunami dramatize these moral questions. They force us not only to reconsider our moral obligation in the face of extreme poverty, but also to renew our commitment to the least well-off in societies vulnerable to natural contingencies and misfortune.[1] Christian communities, often at the forefront of humanitarian response, need to integrate their theological commitments with a moral framework that makes sense of human relationships within a global economy. I do not aim to provide a universal principle that can crank out the "right thing to do" in any given case or for any given person. I also do not wish to defend a rootless concern for "humanity-at-large." To that extent, I will affirm the importance of Christian appeals to creation, vocation, and divine providence. But I do hope to push those within the Christian tradition to reexamine dominant perspectives on charity that have emerged from such appeals.

This chapter is divided into three sections: first, I place my argu-

---

1. For relevant statistics, see Thomas W. Pogge, *World Poverty and Human Rights* (Oxford: Blackwell, 2002). According to Pogge, "Some 2,800 million or 46 percent of humankind live below the World Bank's $2/day poverty line" (p. 2). He calculates that, "if the developed Western countries had their proportional share of [deaths associated with poverty], severe poverty would kill some 3,500 Britons and 16,500 Americans per week" (p. 98).

ment in the context of the reemergence of economic discussions in mainstream Christian ethics; second, I put forth Singer's moral claims about poverty, proximity, and distance; third, I consider various readings of the Good Samaritan parable, including both classical and modern discussions. I use these discussions to show where Christian beliefs recast some of Singer's theoretical assumptions, and why they also support Singer's practical conclusions.

I. The Return of Christian Ethics and Economics

Sustained discussions about Christian ethics and economics have reemerged in academic circles and public life. Christian churches have long wrestled with the implications of their beliefs and practices for issues related to wealth and poverty, and this postmodern period is no exception. In fact, until the end of the Cold War, questions of political economy dominated the agenda of twentieth-century Christian social ethics. Among Protestants there was the flowering of the Social Gospel movement and its critical reception by prominent public intellectuals such as Reinhold Niebuhr. Among Roman Catholics there were the influential treatments of distributive justice in several papal encyclicals and by moral theologians such as John A. Ryan.

More recently, liberation theologies and the civil rights movement have fueled widespread debates about economics and the demands of a Christian faith that emphasizes care for the poor. While professional economists frequently lament the underdeveloped or even misguided "economics" of these discussions, they remain standing examples of efforts to bring religious and moral commitments to bear on material practices. Scores of charitable organizations and actions, both large and small, have emerged from within these earlier contexts. These organizations continue to play an oft-neglected institutional and interpersonal role in meeting basic human needs throughout a world marked by stubborn and extreme inequalities of socioeconomic privilege.

What do I mean, then, by the "reemergence" of Christian ethics and economics? Christian communities have continued to draft statements of principles that should guide pressing matters of economic policy; scholars have continued to assess the relative merits of Max Weber's thesis about the relationship between Protestantism and capitalism; and individual

Christians have continued to offer prophetic challenges to prevailing economic conditions in their scholarship, preaching, and personal witness. And at the level of institutional effectiveness, religious aid and relief agencies have matured into some of the most important nongovernmental organizations (NGOs) in the world.[2] But a central theological focus on economic activity and material possessions has not been a hallmark of contemporary Christian social ethics or political advocacy.

At least three developments in the past thirty years have led to the relative demise of Christian reflection on economic issues. The first is connected to the rise of professional specialization: just as economics has become an increasingly specialized field of inquiry with its own particular culture, so too have theology, biblical studies, moral philosophy, and public policy. These developments have exacerbated already emerging divides between economics and humanistic disciplines as well as divides between churches and academic institutions. In particular, the sophistication of economic modeling and quantitative analysis has intimidated or marginalized nonspecialists, except for occasional broad judgments regarding free-market economics or popular Christian books on poverty.

A second development has been the proliferation of other important areas for theological reflection. Emerging issues in bioethics, the ethics of war and peace, and race and gender, while bound up with economic issues, have placed serious demands on Christian social ethics and church witness. Perhaps more importantly, however, has been the need to address the facts of pluralism in a liberal society. Consider, for example, the intellectual energy that has been spent on the discussions of John Rawls's political theory and the popular debates about the role of religious arguments and symbols in public life. A third development, connected with the second, was the erosion of Christian moral concepts as presumptive parts of ethical analysis. This erosion has coincided with a suspicion of religious communities among some of those most committed to combating global poverty.

It is not my goal to defend these impressions or to judge their relative merits. I note them here merely as a route into the main topic of this essay. Today I think the situation is changing. It is too soon to judge how responses to Hurricane Katrina might invigorate discussions of poverty

---

2. For links to several of these agencies, see http://www.bread.org/learn/links.html. To my knowledge, no major Christian relief and aid organization restricts its activities to fellow Christians. Most groups explicitly adopt universal policies in their mission statements.

within American religious life, but it is clear that religion and ethics have become hot topics both inside and outside the academy. Interest in "business ethics" has flourished alongside an interest in "spirituality" among major corporations and social entrepreneurs. Progressive theologians have undertaken an aggressive unmasking of religious presuppositions implicit in neoclassical economics and challenged the alliance of democracy and free-market capitalism. However, popular support for more radical proposals has proved elusive.

The resurgence of religion and economics in both academic and ecclesial settings owes much to four concrete developments: debates about welfare reform in the 1990s;[3] moral and religious concerns about globalization and consumerism;[4] religious appeals to "compassionate conservatism";[5] and the public influence of philosophers such as Martha Nussbaum, Amartya Sen, Peter Singer, and Peter Unger.[6]

My choice to focus on Peter Singer is motivated by the relative neglect of this central feature of his work among Christian audiences. Most Christian assessments of his work focus on abortion, euthanasia, infanticide, genetic technologies, and the moral status of animals and the environment. Christian responses to Singer rarely discuss his views on poverty and affluence, and usually only in passing.[7] It is not surprising that these

---

3. Mary Jo Bane and Lawrence M. Mead, *Lifting Up the Poor: A Dialogue on Religion, Poverty and Welfare Reform* (Washington, DC: The Brookings Institution, 2003).

4. See Rebecca Todd Peters, *In Search of the Good Life: The Ethics of Globalization* (New York: Continuum, 2004), and Vincent Miller, *Consuming Religion: Christian Faith and Practice in a Consumer Culture* (New York: Continuum, 2004).

5. Marvin Olasky, *Compassionate Conservatism: What it Is, What it Does, and How it Can Transform America* (with foreword by George W. Bush) (New York: The Free Press, 2000).

6. These authors are helpfully discussed in Daniel M. Hausman and Michael S. McPherson, *Economic Analysis and Moral Philosophy* (Cambridge, UK: Cambridge University Press, 1996). For the best appropriation of Sen and Nussbaum in Christian ethics, see Douglas Hicks, *Inequality and Christian Ethics* (Cambridge, UK: Cambridge University Press, 2000).

7. For a notable exception, see Gordon Preece, ed., *Rethinking Peter Singer: A Christian Critique* (Downers Grove, IL: InterVarsity Press, 2002). In Christian media, see Heidi Hadsell, review of *One World: The Ethics of Globalization,* in *Christian Century* 120, no. 4 (Feb. 22, 2003): 59-65; Richard John Neuhaus, "A Curious Encounter with a Philosopher from Nowhere," *First Things* (Feb. 2002); Mark Oppenheimer, "The Utility of Peter Singer: Who Lives? Who Dies?" *Christian Century* 119, no. 14 (July 3-10, 2002): 24-29; and the interview with Nelson Gonzalez in the British magazine *Third Way* (Aug. 2002), available at

other areas receive attention considering Singer's ethical challenge to traditional Christian beliefs about the sanctity of human life.[8] These discussions, both implicitly and explicitly, engage the lawyer's famous question in the parable of the Good Samaritan: *Who is my neighbor?* Modern interpreters point out that the parable itself does not answer the lawyer's question: "Jesus' counter-question redirects attention from the status of others to that of the lawyer himself."[9] Some presume that an answer to the status of others readily dictates a host of resolutions to divisive moral and legal questions. I am skeptical of this belief.[10] The human beings being discussed here qualify by any standard as persons in the relevant moral sense. I also bracket a number of other controversial questions about the nation-state and the market in order to crystallize an underdeveloped issue for Christian ethics and economics, one that is a preoccupation of Singer's ethical writings. Some of these topics loom in the background, especially the relationship of civic identity to Christian identity. My task is more restricted, and it is ambitious enough.

Christians should pay attention to the best social-scientific and economic literature to find ways to reduce poverty and make empirical judgments about how best to provide aid. They should also engage the best philosophical work in ethics. But some perennial issues in theological ethics are also relevant for contemporary Christian responses to world poverty and humanitarian aid. These issues include, but also move beyond, the familiar problem of motivation. Many people think that the most basic problem of morality is motivating people *to be* moral, usually in the sense

---

http://www.utilitarian.net/singer/. In academic religious ethics, see John P. Reeder, Jr., *Killing and Saving: Abortion, Hunger, and War* (University Park, PA: The Pennsylvania State University Press, 1996), pp. 39-43, and Andrew Flescher, *Heroes, Saints, and Ordinary Morality* (Washington, DC: Georgetown University Press, 2003).

8. Peter Singer, *Rethinking Life and Death* (Oxford: Oxford University Press, 1995).

9. Ian A. McFarland, "Who Is My Neighbor? The Good Samaritan as a Source for Theological Anthropology," *Modern Theology* 17, no. 1 (Jan. 2001): 57-66.

10. For example, one classic article on the ethics of abortion argues for a "pro-choice" position based on an explicit concession to the full personhood of the fetus. An appeal to the Good Samaritan parable is central to its case. See Judith J. Thomson, "A Defense of Abortion," *Philosophy & Public Affairs* 1, no. 1 (Fall 1971): 47-66. Current divisions among conservative Roman Catholics regarding the ethics of embryo adoption also reveal the remaining moral difficulties even when the fully human status of embryos is granted. See John Berkman, "Adopting Embryos in America: A Case Study and Ethical Analysis," *Scottish Journal of Theology* 55, no. 4 (2002): 438-60.

of overcoming self-interest in order to help others. Christian theology knows about this problem of a selfish will; but it does not reduce ethical reflection to what motivates people to be moral. It also need not reduce morality to maximizing consequences. But even within the Christian tradition the demands of morality are themselves contested. Classical debates in moral theology about the universality and the preferential nature of Christian neighbor-love are instructive.

Most Christian traditions, regardless of their accounts of universality and preferentiality, reject the view that Christians (either individually or collectively) are responsible for either the *ultimate* or the *entire* moral good of the world. Beliefs about divine grace and providence, as well as an affirmation of diverse human vocations, resist theories of value that consider morality from this kind of perspective. From a Christian perspective, these moral views are liable to impatient temptations to be "like God." Christians are called to imitate Jesus, but that does not mean they are called to love in the same way that God can love.[11] The life of Jesus suggests that even he did not perform every possible act of benevolence, especially if benevolence is reduced to meeting material needs. It is the pride of humanitarianism gone awry — not virtue but vice — that entertains moral obligations beyond human limits and fuels the erosion of appropriate (if penultimate) boundaries of loving. Morality must be morality appropriate to creatures like us, not angels. Christians also think that there are other goods in life besides "moral" ones. Of course, these arguments have been made to justify oppressive political and social arrangements and to pacify possible Christian resistance to them. They can do that. But I want to point to another important problem for their appeals in light of the ways in which human beings *choose* to distance themselves from neighbors.

Mounting evidence confirms that geographic concentrations of poverty and wealth are contingent products of bias and residential segregation that have far-reaching effects on the distribution of goods.[12] These facts invite moral and religious reflection because affluence too often shields the

11. See Gene Outka, "Following at a Distance: Ethics and the Identity of Jesus," in Garrett Green, ed., *Scriptural Authority and Narrative Interpretation* (Philadelphia: Fortress, 1987), pp. 144-60.

12. See, for example, Kevin Kruse, *White Flight: Atlanta and the Making of Modern Conservatism* (Princeton, NJ: Princeton University Press, 2005), and Douglas Massey, *American Apartheid: Segregation and the Making of the Underclass* (Cambridge, MA: Harvard University Press, 1998).

wealthy from the poor. Long-standing Christian claims about the providential or created structure of social obligations need to respond to this evidence. These realities add further support to my claim that familiar theological resistance to utilitarian morality does not immediately dissolve Singer's challenge.

One common approach to moral obligation for mortal creatures like us imagines a series of expanding concentric circles of relationships that should govern one's sense of duty. The Christian tradition, dating back to Augustine, has proposed something called an *ordo amoris,* an "order of love." This view holds that legitimate moral preference can be given to one's family, friends, fellow citizens, and coreligionists. Obligations to the distant needy can be trumped by the qualitatively unique demands of these "closer" special relations. Families, for example, embody a special relationship that justifies the particular care parents rightly show for their own children rather than more needy children elsewhere. Local communities, it is further argued, rightly show particular solidarity with their fellow residents rather than more needy residents elsewhere. Empirical realities should transform conventional discussions of a Christian *ordo amoris.*

Christians today face new ethical challenges in a global economy where economic life draws each of us into ever closer and more compact connection with "near and distant neighbors."[13] Our economic choices, which are involved in a series of impersonal transactions, radically influence those we do not know and rarely consider as we make them. The quest for efficiency has transformed the kinds of interactions that once characterized economic exchange. In a sense, economic globalization has meant both a more intimate and a less familiar world. Available media sources and dynamic migration patterns have expanded our consciousness of others, even though these others remain faceless, either through our own greedy complacency or the distortions of media forms and economic exchanges themselves. Globalization is characterized by a "rapidly developing and ever-densening network of interconnections and interdependence."[14] Once-distant neighbors are fast becoming near neighbors, an

13. I borrow this formulation from a section heading of Karl Barth, *Church Dogmatics* III/4, ed. G. W. Bromiley and T. F. Torrance, trans. A. T. MacKay et al. (Edinburgh: T&T Clark, 1961), pp. 285ff.

14. John Tomlinson, *Globalization and Culture* (Chicago: University of Chicago Press, 1999), p. 18, as cited by William Schweiker, *Theological Ethics and Global Dynamics: In the Time of Many Worlds* (Oxford: Blackwell, 2004), p. 6.

economic analogue of the Christian proclamation that "the far off have been brought near in the blood of Christ" (Eph. 2:13). Perhaps more morally significant than awareness per se are the developed channels of transportation and effective means of aid that make beneficent action at a vast distance feasible. The practical opportunity to provide immediate aid, as the parable of the Good Samaritan demonstrates, constitutes an important aspect of a traditional Christian understanding of moral obligation. The "neighborhood" and the "road" have changed in ways that could not have been imagined by classical Christian theologies. Every day we pass by on the other side of this road — literally and figuratively.

But, given the conditions of finitude and sin, can or should Christians entertain all of these possible moral obligations at the same time? Can a Christian commitment to universal and preferential loves really coexist? Do Christians have *special* obligations, including to themselves? If so, which ones, in what circumstances, and in what ways? Do fellow Christians warrant receiving aid more than family or fellow citizens do in cases of equal or even greater necessity? Is the natural bond of family life part of the created order while bonds of citizenship are merely provisional features of fallen life? Does a "common good" require boundaries in order to meaningfully pursue actual community in real relationships? Are their criteria by which such determinations can be made? Or are Christians simply left to "charity and its nebulous dictates"?[15] I argue that convergences among frequently opposed moralities offer promising avenues for practical coalitions.

Divergent conceptions of cosmopolitanism remain salient, but global economic realities warrant joint advocacy and action consistent with a more rigorous interpretation of duties of beneficence to aid "distant" strangers. Appeals to the Good Samaritan, taking up a Lucan emphasis on

---

15. Garth L. Hallett, *Priorities and Christian Ethics* (Cambridge, UK: Cambridge University Press, 1998), p. 30. Hallett's book forcefully presses the ambiguous deliverances of Christian ethics on questions related to everyday conflicts between the "near" and the "needy." He frames his discussion via A. C. Ewing's example of a father's choice to spend money on his son's university education rather than aid to those starving from famine. After tracing the transformation of an earlier Christian emphasis on the "needy" to a modern focus on the "near," Hallett sides with the former and concludes: "It would be good for him to save the starving, if he can. It would be good for him to become the kind of person who can save them, if he can" (p. 109). Interestingly, like Peter Singer, he also demonstrates that the earliest Christians urged moral parity in considering cases of killing and letting die (p. 64, n. 60).

universalism and concern for the outsider, often ground a strong egalitarian ethic (known as *"agapism"*). In many ways, agapism parallels the morally demanding views of a consistent utilitarian like Singer. The Samaritan "proved neighbor" to the wounded man, foreclosing any effort to unilaterally restrict the scope of persons worthy of one's engaged moral attention. In fact, the most influential treatment of love in modern theological ethics has defined Christian love as an "equal regard" for others that has deep "material overlap" with impartialist notions of justice.[16] Principles such as equal respect and impartiality serve as analogues of divine love.

Christian critics of this understanding of *agape,* drawing from traditional arguments against the impersonality and formalism of both Kantianism and utilitarianism, issue strong theological challenges to this view. Mirroring charges that are often brought against Christian ethics, these critics also claim that Singer's brand of morality is hyperbolic (allowing harm is to be distinguished from doing harm), excessively tragic (aid to some does not entail neglect of others), narrow (reducing suffering and avoiding death are not the goals of a good human life), legalistic (preferring context-specific virtues over imperatives that can be universalized as the basic normative category), and even immoral (special relationships and proximity are woven into the very fabric of a moral life). Responding to these critics by denying the relevance of their theoretical claims will have the additional advantage of creating ad hoc agreements between Christians and secularists in responding to global poverty. It is to Singer himself that I now turn.

II. Singer, Poverty, and Special Relations

Peter Singer's claims about affluence and poverty can be put simply. The clarity of his arguments and his own short parables make them powerful. His reliance on common moral intuitions and disturbing facts about global poverty has combined to accomplish a rare feat for moral philosophy: it has changed the way people actually live. Like the persuasive rhetoric of a good preacher, his reasoning often convicts people without leaving them paralyzed by guilt. In this case, as Singer hoped, it has changed how

16. Gene Outka, *Agape: An Ethical Analysis* (New Haven: Yale University Press, 1972), p. 309.

they spend their money. For many, the immediate appeal of Singer's moral argument emerges from a pair of descriptive sentences:

> Going out to nice restaurants, buying new clothes because the old ones are no longer stylish, vacationing at beach resorts — so much of our income is spent on things not essential to the preservation of our lives and health. Donated to one of a number of charitable agencies, that money could mean the difference between life and death for children in need.[17]

Framing the issue in this way elicits a response. If, as it is estimated, a donation of $200 to UNICEF or OXFAM will save a child's life, then it is unjust to spend that $200 on a trivial luxury.[18] Forsaking new gadgets or expensive dinners in order to save lives is not simply a good thing to do; it is a moral duty. It is true that the movement from a mundane discomfort about going to the movies toward making large transfers of wealth to developing countries may not be apparent to most readers. But Singer provides a rich argument about why it is wrong not to do so.

In his classic 1972 article entitled "Famine, Affluence, and Morality," Singer calls for a radical change in received views about the moral implications of extreme poverty and our capacity to reduce suffering.[19] According to Singer, avoidable suffering and death is a moral failure that is parasitic on unrecognized (though widespread) fallacies about the moral significance of contingent facts such as "proximity or distance" (p. 231) and "cases in which I am the only person who could do anything and cases in which I am just one among millions in the same position" (p. 232). Singer argues that these two distinguishing aspects of responses to global poverty cannot bear the weight they must implicitly carry in the ordinary way we think about supposed limits to moral obligation. They do not mitigate these obligations. *These cases,* at least, do not warrant traditional distinctions between duty and charity that play a large role in both moral philosophy and Christian moral theology.

---

17. Peter Singer, "The Singer Solution to World Poverty," *The New York Times Sunday Magazine,* Sept. 5, 1999, pp. 60-63.

18. Peter Unger, *Living High and Letting Die* (Oxford: Oxford University Press, 1996), pp. 136-39.

19. Peter Singer, "Famine, Affluence, and Morality," *Philosophy and Public Affairs* 1, no. 3 (Spring 1972): 229-43. References in the text are to this essay.

Giving from one's surplus income to reduce extreme suffering or death is not supererogatory: it is not merely a welcome virtuous act above and beyond the strict imperatives of real duties like "do not kill" or "do not steal." Singer entertains a number of practical objections, but I will focus on his two principled arguments. He argues:

(1) If it is in our power to prevent something *very bad* from happening, without thereby sacrificing *anything* morally significant, we ought, morally to do it. An application of this principle would be as follows: if I am walking past a shallow pond and see a child drowning in it, I ought to wade in and pull the child out. This will mean getting my clothes muddy, but this is insignificant, while the death of the child would presumably be a very bad thing (p. 231; italics added).[20]

(2) It makes no moral difference whether the person I can help is a neighbor's child ten yards from me or a Bengali whose name I shall never know, ten thousand miles away. . . . Admittedly, it is possible that we are in a better position to judge what needs to be done to help a person near to us than one far away, and perhaps also to provide the assistance we judge to be necessary. . . . This may once have been a justification for being more concerned with the poor in one's own town than with famine victims in India. Unfortunately for those who like to keep their moral responsibilities limited, instant communication and swift transportation have changed the situation. From the moral point of view, the development of the world into a "global village" has made an important, though still unrecognized, difference to our moral situation. . . . There would seem, therefore, to be no possible justification for discriminating on geographical grounds (pp. 231-32).

Singer wrote these words over thirty-five years ago. Since that time, "instant communication" and "swift transportation" have exponentially increased. And so has the concentration of wealth among the affluent. Debates continue as to whether or not a global economic order exacerbates inequality in relative terms but also helps the poor in absolute terms. Most

---

20. Singer, in fact, supports a more demanding principle: "If it is in our power to prevent something bad from happening, without thereby sacrificing anything of comparable moral importance, we ought, morally to do it" (p. 231).

Christian ethicists, and Singer himself, admit that "free-market economies enable many good things to happen."[21] But continuing realities of abject poverty remain. Malnutrition, unsafe water, famine, preventable disease, and extreme poverty continue to afflict the lives of vast numbers of people in the world.

Singer's essay concentrates on defending the first of his two claims. He considers two objections: 1) that it makes morality too demanding (risking obedience to "real" moral obligations or ones that more immediately involve us), and 2) that giving money is not the best way to help (e.g., it encourages corruption and other factors that exacerbate poverty, such as overpopulation). His "drowning child" analogy aims to dissolve the first objection. And in response to the second objection, Singer allows that other kinds of aid and economic development are consistent with the general thrust of a rigorous duty to aid.[22] Both of these responses, to my mind, are compelling.

In terms of a Christian ethic that affirms some version of love that does justice to all who bear "the image of God," further objections to Singer's modest principle do not appear forthcoming. Presumably, Christians do not need justifications for why they should act morally or take the interests of others (especially the poor) as moral claims. Christians are not skeptics about other-regarding morality as such; they also affirm some version of moral freedom that transcends racial, class, or national boundaries. They affirm the aspiration of moral action that heeds the equal dignity of all humanity. Counter-arguments that the very poor merit their fate by squandering resources are empirically false and, for that matter, morally irrelevant for those called to imitate Christ's love and to give thanks for their own gifts that come from a radical dependence on the gracious charity of God and others. *Reductio ad absurdum* objections also fail in the

---

21. Thomas Ogletree, "Corporate Capitalism and the Common Good: A Framework for Addressing the Challenges of a Global Economy," *Journal of Religious Ethics* 30, no. 1 (2002): 79-106, esp. p. 80.

22. For a helpful, though discouraging, "practical" analysis of different kinds of aid in light of political contexts and histories, see Dale Jamieson, "Duties to the Distant: Aid, Assistance, and Intervention in the Developing World," *Journal of Ethics* 9 (2005): 151-70, and Tony Waters, *Bureaucratizing the Good Samaritan: The Limitations of Humanitarian Relief Operations* (Boulder, CO: Westview, 2001). Jamieson agrees with Singer's demanding duty to aid the distant poor, but he emphasizes the need to "be modest and self-critical about our ability to discharge this duty successfully" (p. 170).

light of the consumer behavior of affluent Christians in the face of global poverty.[23] If affluent Christians were sacrificing anywhere close to the point of their own or their dependents' extreme poverty (what used to be called "evangelical poverty"), then this theoretical objection would warrant more attention. Few Christians reach even the parity considerations of 2 Corinthians 8:14: "As a matter of equality your abundance at the present time should supply their want, so that their abundance may supply your want, that there may be equality." But questions remain. How should we distinguish between vicious luxury and necessity? One imagines all kinds of practical pleas: "This vacation is necessary for my psychic integrity or to save my failing marriage." "This new car or new suit is necessary for my work." "A university education for my child, in the long run, will help her give more aid to the poor." "I can help the poor in my country more effectively than the poor in distant countries." Here we enter the attractive world of utilitarian commensuration of goods.

Few (if any) Christian ethicists endorse Singer's brand of utilitarianism. A Christian ethic need not propose that morality is a matter of maximizing states of affairs or the satisfaction of welfare interests. The diverse examples of Christian saints resist any singular (let alone welfare-maximizing) conception of the imitation of Christ as a model for Christian living or a univocal conception of goodness. Christian ethicists have developed sophisticated arguments that chasten the hold of this understanding of morality. It has devalued Christian affirmations of human excellence across a spectrum of possible creaturely activity, including participation in aesthetics, athletics, intellectual pursuits, and the worship of God.[24]

Others, notably feminist ethicists, have raised concerns about the rhetoric of compassion and service given the historical abuse implicit in calls for individual self-sacrifice directed at women and minorities. It is wise for Christians to remain alert to who, among the relatively affluent, are being called to meet this moral obligation. But Singer's arguments do not rely on a rejection of personal autonomy or the endorsement of any particular ethical theory, utilitarian or otherwise. In fact, he cites Thomas Aqui-

---

23. On luxury consumption, see Robert H. Frank, *Luxury Fever: Money and Happiness in an Era of Excess* (Princeton, NJ: Princeton University Press, 1999).

24. Robert M. Adams, *Finite and Infinite Goods* (Oxford: Oxford University Press, 1999).

nas in support of his conclusions.[25] One would be hard-pressed to dismiss Aquinas as a utilitarian. Theory often helps us with our practical decisions, but moral agreement with Singer's claims does not rely on achieving consensus about ethical theories (something highly unlikely even among Christians). Some will be motivated by his utilitarianism, others not. Undermining his version of utilitarianism or his views on human dignity will not defeat his claims about the moral implications of extreme poverty.

In the next section, however, I argue that objections to Singer's second principle are not easily dismissed from a Christian perspective. Unlike in utilitarianism, proximity and distance have been central topics in Christian ethics.[26] Part of the ethical challenge for Christian theology is the fact that spatial and temporal proximity are never considered merely *in themselves*. Distance has never been "just" geographic distance, but constitutive of the kinds of affinity that make space and time theologically relevant. But I argue against those Christians who emphasize proximity in a way that defeats Singer's practical conclusions, the relevance of which demands revision in light of new economic realities.

---

25. "Now, according to the natural order instituted by divine providence, material goods are provided for the satisfaction of human needs. Therefore the division and appropriation of property, which proceeds from human law, must not hinder the satisfaction of man's necessity from such goods. Equally, whatever a man has in superabundance is owed, of natural right, to the poor for their sustenance" (*Summa Theologica*, II.II.66.7), as cited in Singer, "Famine, Affluence, and Morality," p. 239. Singer repeats this citation elsewhere and glosses it this way: "This particular aspect of his teaching is not one that the Church has chosen to emphasize" (Singer, *One World: The Ethics of Globalization* [New Haven: Yale University Press, 2002], pp. 185-86). For a discussion of Aquinas's views on necessity and property right, see John Finnis, *Aquinas* (Oxford: Oxford University Press, 1998), pp. 188-96. Ironically, some theologians argue that Aquinas's naturalization of property right broke with an older patristic tradition of nonproprietary community. See Joan Lockwood O'Donovan, "The Theological Economics of Medieval Usury Theory," in Oliver O'Donovan and Joan Lockwood O'Donovan, *Bonds of Imperfection: Christian Politics, Past and Present* (Grand Rapids: Eerdmans, 2004), pp. 97-120.

26. Singer claims: "I do not think I need to say much in defense of the refusal to take proximity and distance into account. The fact that a person is physically near to us, so that we have personal contact with him, may make it more likely that we *shall* assist him, but this does not show us that we *ought* to help him rather than another who happens to be further away. If we accept any principle of impartiality, universalizability, equality, or whatever, we cannot discriminate against someone merely because he is far away from us (or we are far away from him)" (p. 232). Hallett affirms this claim: "Mere spatial proximity, in itself, lacks moral relevance" (*Priorities and Christian Ethics*, p. 14).

III. The Good Samaritan, Proximity, and the Ethics of Distance

Like any biblical passage, the parable of the Good Samaritan has been pressed into the service of many different political agendas. One of the more famous conservative appeals came from Margaret Thatcher, then the prime minister of Great Britain. In the heat of welfare debates in that country, Thatcher remarked in a television interview: "No one would have remembered the Good Samaritan if he'd only had good intentions. . . . He had money as well."[27] Others, emphasizing the spontaneity and charitable dimensions of the act, have appealed to the Good Samaritan to reject state-sponsored welfare.[28] Still others find the parable an effective and valid resource for supporting the democratic values of "fairness and concern for the vulnerable" that generate "support of broad or universal health care."[29] While the application to public policy requires an additional step in the argument about the role of the state, the most prominent appeal in American history supports this *kind* of argument. Here are the words of Martin Luther King, Jr:

> On the one hand we are called to play the good Samaritan on life's roadside; but that will be only an initial act. One day we must come to see that the whole Jericho road must be transformed so that men and women will not be constantly beaten and robbed as they make their journey on life's highway. True compassion is more than flinging a coin to a beggar; it is not haphazard and superficial. It comes to see that an edifice which produces beggars needs restructuring. A true revolution of values will soon look uneasily on the glaring contrast of poverty and wealth.[30]

In his last sermon, King returned to the parable in his call for "a kind of dangerous unselfishness" that would "make America what it ought to

27. Cited by Richard Owen Griffiths, "The Politics of the Good Samaritan," *Political Theology* (1999): 85-114 (quote from p. 96).

28. John W. Robbins, "The Ethics and Economics of Health Care," *Journal of Biblical Ethics in Medicine* 8, no. 2 (1994): 1-17.

29. Ronald Thiemann, *Religion in Public Life* (Washington, DC: Georgetown University Press, 1996), 155-56.

30. Martin Luther King, Jr., "A Time to Break the Silence," in *I Have a Dream: The Essential Writings and Speeches of Martin Luther King, Jr.*, ed. James M. Washington (San Francisco: HarperCollins, 1992), p. 148.

be."[31] King's emphases on collective action, structural analysis, and institution-building now holds sway in Christian social ethics, especially in the social teachings of the Roman Catholic Church and mainline Protestant denominations. In fact, one of the great revolutions in Christian ethics has been an emergent conception of "social sin."[32] Social sin points to the collective behavior of groups and institutions that create and perpetuate structural conditions of oppression. Combating social sin requires more than individual effort. In fact, assuming that the individual is the basic unit of moral analysis inevitably fails to address social sin. Many interpreters point out that the Good Samaritan is not a "model of heroic, individual extraordinary self-giving at all, but rather a model of love based on interdependence."[33] The Samaritan acted within — and relied on — a network of communal resources. My focus on *individual* obligation may appear to cut against the grain of Christian social ethics as well as trends in legal and moral analysis that highlight the significance of institutions. It may seem to imply an atomistic understanding of human action and church life. This is not my aim.

As King's quotation suggests, the two approaches are not mutually exclusive. Motivating individual aid need not compete with more systemic or collective responses, either public or private. Given that public responses remain insufficient, individual efforts are needed (and, I believe, vice versa). Moral reflection on institutions and structures is often derivative of claims about individual duties and virtues. Citizens, for example, need to lobby for, or at least be willing to accept, public expansion of foreign aid or the sacrifice of domestic agricultural subsidies for the sake of global farmers. Given the relative neglect of economic ethics in recent moral theology, it is helpful to follow traditional Christian casuistry and begin at an individual level in order to clarify some basic principles and virtues. Talking about individual duties need not deny the importance of communities.

---

31. Martin Luther King, Jr., "I See the Promised Land," in *I Have a Dream*, p. 200. King preached: "The question is not, 'If I stop to help this man in need, what will happen to me?' 'If I do not stop to help the sanitation workers, what will happen to them?' That's the question" (p. 201).

32. See Margaret Pfeil, "Doctrinal Implications of Magisterial Use of the Language of Social Sin," *Louvain Studies* 27 (2002): 132-52, and Stephen Ray, *Do No Harm: Social Sin and Christian Responsibility* (Minneapolis: Augsburg, 2002).

33. Gerald Schlabach, *For the Joy Set Before Us: Augustine and Self-Denying Love* (Notre Dame, IN: University of Notre Dame Press, 2001), p. 150.

A. Classical Resources: Augustine and Aquinas

A brief account of the two most significant classical Christian authors suggests that the moral principles involved in these current debates are not new. Like most patristic authors, Augustine interpreted the parable of the Good Samaritan within the gospel framework of salvation history. He imagined Adam as the wounded man, Jerusalem as the heavenly city, the robbers as the devil and his angels, the priest and the Levite as the Old Testament law, the Samaritan as Jesus, the inn as the church, the innkeeper as the apostles, the promise to return as the Second Coming, and the two denarii as the two love commandments. Augustine's figurative interpretation of the parable has found its share of modern critics. For many, it stands as a paradigmatic example of his hyperspiritual Christian Platonism.[34] But Augustine is not deaf to the concrete welfare concerns that have preoccupied modern readers. In *On Christian Teaching,* he says:

> That the commandment to love our neighbour excludes no human being is made clear by our Lord himself in the gospel. . . . When our Lord was asked, "And who is my neighbour?" by the man to whom he had pronounced these same two commandments and said that the whole law and the prophets depended on them, he told the story of a man going down from Jerusalem to Jericho . . . so it is clear that we should understand by our neighbour the person to whom an act of compassion is due if he needs it or would be due if he needed it. . . . Who can fail to see that there is no exception to this, nobody to whom compassion is not due?[35]

Augustine claims that the worship of God cannot be separated from the "works of mercy" or "acts of compassion" because "God especially commands the performance of such works, and declares that He is pleased

34. For a qualified defense of Augustine's exegesis, see Mike Higton, "Boldness and Reserve: A Lesson from St. Augustine," *Anglican Theological Review* 85, no. 3 (Summer 2003): 447-56. Higton argues that "a Christian cannot interpret this parable without realizing that, even if she is talking about the revelation of an existential possibility, or about a moral lesson, she is at the very same time talking about things which are grounded in the deepest ways of God with the world, talking about things which are established, revealed, and confirmed, in the Incarnation, on the cross, in the resurrection" (p. 450).

35. Augustine, *On Christian Teaching,* 1.31, trans. R. P. H. Green (Oxford: Oxford University Press, 1997).

with them instead of, or in preference to, sacrifices."[36] Breaking from an earlier conception of Stoic reserve as necessary for a life of virtue, Augustine held that investment in the suffering of others is an essential part of a Christian life. His emphasis on loving others makes him "anxious lest they be afflicted by famine, war, pestilence, or captivity, fearing that in slavery they may suffer evils beyond what we can conceive" (*City of God*, 19.8). He does caution against allowing excessive compassion to interfere with prudence and judgment. Identification with another's suffering has limits. He offers the following example that reminds us of Singer's "shallow pool":

> In order to stretch one's hand to another lying on the ground one has to bend down. But it makes no sense to let oneself fall down next to the other on the ground; for then there would be two in need of help. No, one bends down to a person lying on the ground in order to help him up again.[37]

Augustine shares the empirical concern about what today is called compassion fatigue. He also worries that compassion can provoke a self-righteous attitude that demeans the dignity of persons and reduces them to objects, which is a frequent temptation in providing goods and services to the poor. Augustine knows that compassion plays tricks:

> Once you have bestowed gifts on the unfortunate, you may easily yield to the temptation to exalt yourself over him, to assume superiority over the object of your benefaction. He fell into need, and you supplied him: you feel yourself as the giver to be a bigger man than the receiver of the gift. You should want him to be your equal, that both may be subject to the one on whom no favour can be bestowed.[38]

---

36. Augustine, *City of God*, 10.1, trans. Robert Dyson (Cambridge, UK: Cambridge University Press, 1998).

37. Augustine, *Eighty-Three Different Questions*, q.71,2, trans. David L. Mosher (Washington, DC: Catholic University Press of America, 1982).

38. Augustine, *Homilies on the First Epistle of John*, 8.5 in *Augustine: The Later Works*, trans. Juhn Burnaby (Philadelphia: Westminster Press, 1955). Nietzsche would echo Augustine's suspicions, but in the service of exposing Christian morality: "You crowd around your neighbor and have fine words for it. But I say unto you: your love of the neighbor is your bad love of yourselves. You flee to the neighbor from yourselves and would like to make a virtue out of that: but I see through your 'selflessness'" (*Thus Spoke Zarathustra*, trans. Walter Kaufmann [New York: Penguin Books, 1966], pp. 60-61).

However, Augustine does not allow this suspicion to get in the way of his recognition that circumstances arise in human life that can overwhelm individuals. To reject the possibility of responsiveness to suffering as simply disguised self-interest would carry Augustine's doctrine of sin too far. Compassion does not require stripping the neighbor of his dignity in order to rescue a helpless victim. As Martha Nussbaum argues, "People are dignified agents, but they are also, frequently, victims."[39] Augustine tries to find a way to ensure that autonomy, human dignity, and charity are correlated rather than antithetical notions. But how might a Christian discriminate among the many victims who remain agents?

Augustine claims that, while Christian love is unconditional and universal, it begins "at home" and extends "outward." It is necessary that "love, like a fire, should cover the nearest terrain before it spreads farther afield."[40] But what is the "nearest terrain"? Augustine offers this influential picture:

> All people should be loved equally. But you cannot do good to all people equally, so you should take particular thought for those who, as if by lot [*quasi quadam sorte*], happen to be particularly close to you in terms of place, time, or any other circumstances. Suppose that you had plenty of something which had to be given to someone in need of it but could not be given to two people, and you met two people, neither of whom had a greater need or a closer relationship to you than the other: you could do nothing more just than to choose by lot the person to whom you should give what could not be given to both. Analogously, since you cannot take thought for all men, you must settle (rather than by lot) in favour of the one who happens to be more closely associated with you in temporal matters.[41]

"As if by lot." "One who happens to be more closely associated." These are strikingly egalitarian and universal formulations. Augustine suggests that a Christian could not love *every* neighbor but should love *any* neighbor who happens across her way. Our embodied nature places con-

---

39. Martha Nussbaum, *Upheavals of Thought* (Cambridge, UK: Cambridge University Press, 2001), p. 406.

40. Augustine, *Commentary on First John*, 8.4.

41. Augustine, *On Christian Teaching*, trans. R. P. H. Green (Oxford: Oxford University Press, 1997), I.28.29.

straints on our capacity to love others in need (and, as Augustine also points out, our capacity to harm others). Augustine affirms both avoiding harm and promoting good: "There are two ways in which a man may sin against another, one by doing him harm, and the second by refusing to help him when one is able."[42] There is, for Augustine, no strict moral calculus that might determine what it means to love others well. He finds it difficult to reconcile this affirmation of special relationships (including friendship with fellow Christians) on the basis of his commitment to neighbor-love and his conviction that partiality was something to be overcome. Augustine's metaphor of a "divine lottery" may strike us as disturbing, as another Augustinian shock to assumptions of freedom as the power to choose. But to see these gifts in the light of divine providence means that a Christian should neither begrudge particular bonds of affection nor remain so focused upon them that he is unwilling to be interrupted by a strange "neighbor." In fact, the metaphor provides a healthy antidote to more static accounts of preferential love rooted only in an order of creation.

Nevertheless, Augustine stands within a long tradition of Christian discussions of moral priorities rooted in doctrines of creation. His account of the order of charity is not very detailed. His focus tends to be psychological: he is concerned about *how* one loves; he does not engage in abstract speculation on *what* or *who* one is to safely consider as an appropriate object of love. Book 19 of the *City of God* repeats the idea that human relationships are like sets of expanding concentric circles. He expands and intensifies Greek philosophy with the radical claim that "a man's fellow citizens are also his friends" (*City of God*, 19.3). As Emerson would point out, Augustine's circles do not have a circumference.[43] Much like the cosmopolitan Stoic, Augustine wants to be friends with the angels of the "universe itself" (*City of God*, 19.3). Those who follow the way of love must first "care for his own household; for the order of nature and of human society itself give him readier access to them, and greater opportunity of caring for them" (*City of God*, 19.14). Time and opportunity place limits on the realization of universal love that Augustine thinks must await the consumma-

42. Augustine, *The Catholic and Manichean Ways of Life,* trans. Donald A. Gallagher and Idella J. Gallagher (Washington, DC: The Catholic University Press of America, 1966), 1.26, 50.

43. Ralph Waldo Emerson, "Circles" (1841), in *Essays and Lectures* (New York: Library of America, 1983), pp. 401-14.

tion of love, "when God is all in all." Here we see the powerful moral significance of proximity within the Christian tradition. It was left to Thomas Aquinas to develop it with exacting clarity.

Thomas Aquinas, as Singer notes, affirms the rightness of the distribution of "superabundance" given Christian convictions about the common good. Indeed, for Aquinas, this distribution is a "duty of strict justice (not merely 'charity')."[44] Aquinas claims that "there is a time when we sin mortally if we fail to give alms."[45] Singer, however, does not comment on Aquinas's seminal discussion of the "order of charity" that shaped Christian morality and continues to inform practical decisions about aid.

In contrast to Augustine, Aquinas pursues the order of love with his characteristic rigor.[46] Like Augustine, Aquinas focuses on the quality of our loves; but he also develops a hierarchical ordering of the loves themselves. In a passage about the duties of advocating for the poor, Aquinas invokes Augustine's discussion of "place, time, or any other circumstance."

44. John Finnis, *Aquinas,* p. 192. Finnis notes that "misleadingly (in some respects) Aquinas's main treatment of the duty to make one's goods available to the poor (II-II, q.31 a.3, q.32 aa.5-10) is under the heading of 'charity' (love of God and neighbour) rather than 'justice,' though it is outlined again under justice (II-II q.66 a.7)" p. 192, n. 26).

45. *Summa Theologica,* trans. Fathers of the Dominican Province (New York: Benziger Brothers, 1948), II.II q.32 a.5. For Aquinas, "such a situation exists when there is evident and urgent need on the part of the recipient, yet no one else appears at hand to help him, and when the giver possess the superfluous goods, which he does not need for the time being, so far as he can judge with probability."

46. Edmund Hill notes that Augustine's "rather casual way of leaving the order of charity to chance will not satisfy the scholastic mind, certainly not that of Saint Thomas. He devotes thirteen articles to the subject in his *Summa Theologiae* Iia Iiae, q.26 . . . going into great detail. He decides, for instance, that love of parents takes precedence over love of one's children and love of one's father over love of one's mother — other things, of course, such as their goodness and holiness, being equal. . . . Augustine, I suggest, is to be congratulated on not being so meticulous in the matter" (*Teaching Christianity,* in *The Works of Saint Augustine,* trans. Edmund Hill [Brooklyn: New York City Press, 1990-1995], p. 127, n. 28). John Wesley shares Aquinas's lexical clarity: "If you desire to be a faithful and a wise steward, out of that portion of your Lord's goods which he has for the present lodged in your hands, but with the right of resuming whenever it pleases him, first, provide things needful for yourself — food to eat, raiment to put on, whatever nature moderately requires for preserving your body in health and strength. Secondly, provide these for your wife, your children, your servants, or any others who pertain to your household. If when this is done there be an overplus left, then 'do good to them that are of the household of faith.' If there be an overplus still, 'as you have opportunity, do good unto all men'" (John Wesley, "The Use of Money," cited by Garth Hallett, *Priorities and Christian Ethics,* pp. 20-21).

Aquinas's commentary jeopardizes Singer's conclusion by affirming and extending Augustine.

> [Augustine] says *by reason of place*, because one is not bound to search throughout the world for the needy that one may succor them; and it suffices to do works of mercy to those one meets with. . . . He says by *reason of time*, because one is not bound to provide for the future needs of others, and it suffices to succor present needs. . . . Lastly he says, or *any other circumstance*, because one ought to show kindness to those especially who are by any tie whatever united to us. . . . It may happen however that these circumstances concur, and then we have to consider whether this particular man stands in such a need that is not easy to see how he can be succored otherwise, and then one is bound to bestow the work of mercy on him. If, however, it is easy to see how he can be otherwise succored, either by himself, or by some other person more closely united to him, or in a better position to help him, one is not bound so strictly to help the one in need that it would be a sin not to do so: although it would be praiseworthy to do so where one is not bound to.[47]

Aquinas's appeal to prudence in such matters takes the moral sting out of the clarity of Singer-like duties: "But if of two persons, one is more closely connected with us and the other in greater want, it is not possible to decide by any general rule which of them we ought to help rather than the other, since there are varying degrees of want as well as of nearness: here the judgment of a prudent person is called for."[48] Singer might reject this appeal as pregnant with the possibility of moral evasion. Given the role of human sin in constructing relationships of nearness and distance, Christians should also question the role these arguments play in debates about moral obligation. Should the concept of neighbor change with the globalization of the neighborhood? To respond to this question, I return to our modern discussions.

B. Modern Discussions

Modern agapists are not blind to the concerns about the moral claims of special relations. Outka claims Christians can "distinguish near and dis-

47. *Summa Theologica*, II.II q.71 a.1.
48. *Summa Theologica*, II.II q.31 a.3.

tant neighbors and concentrate on those nearest, i.e., those with whom I have to do directly and distinctively."[49] Karl Barth, a vigorous critic of the idolatries of nationalism, also affirms this kind of distinction. According to Barth, the command to love others "does not float in empty space."[50] Love "presupposes that the one or many who are loved stand in a certain proximity to the one who loves — a proximity in which others do not find themselves."[51] Recently, many theologians have once again emphasized the moral significance of proximity as part of the created goodness of embodied finitude. They signal an emerging rejection of twentieth-century universalism that once was celebrated against the narrow particularism of nineteenth-century Christian theologies bound up with nationalism and racism.

Christian social ethics is trying to find a way to affirm virtuous kinds of particularity even as it rejects vicious ones. For example, John Milbank, in *Being Reconciled,* argues that the "specificity of proximity, which is yet also the endlessly surprising gift of renewed contingent arrival, is *our only* creaturely way to participate in God's equal love for all."[52] Appealing to Aquinas, Milbank interprets the neighbor-love of the Good Samaritan to mean "precisely a preferential love for those nearest to us, those with the most inherited, realized and developed affinity with us." But Milbank is quick to welcome "those strangers with whom suddenly we are bonded whether we like it or not, by instances of distress, shared experience or preferred comfort" (p. 39). Agapic universalism, for Milbank, sinfully aspires to a kind of premature angelic status of equal and immediate temporal relationships to all. Human beings are "rooted in our animality, embodiment, and finitude" (p. 39).[53]

Milbank's politics and economics are decidedly socialist, though of a

---

49. Gene Outka, "Universalism and Impartiality," p. 78.

50. Karl Barth, *Church Dogmatics,* ed. G. W. Bromiley and T. F. Torrance (Edniburgh: T. & T. Clark, 1957-70), III/4, p. 288.

51. Karl Barth, *Church Dogmatics,* IV/2, p. 803. Barth affirms a "special solidarity" of the Christian community as "practical and provisional" (*CD,* IV/1, p. 105; *CD,* IV/2, pp. 807-08).

52. John Milbank, *Being Reconciled* (New York: Routledge, 2003), p. 39.

53. The goodness of finitude, for Milbank, includes "our limited range of intense capacity for affection and attention" (p. 39). Milbank here notes a theological analogue to Bernard Williams's argument that ethics should not be so "counter-intuitive or counter-naturalistic as to challenge our natural impulse always to save our own nearest and dearest first in the event of a common catastrophe" (p. 39); see Bernard Williams, *Shame and Necessity* (Berkeley: University of California Press, 1993).

religious rather than a secular origin. His primary aim is not to limit the market as much as it is to revive a culture that is not governed by profit and loss. He laments the passing of public spaces of ritual gift exchange and festival sharing, as well as the loss of a sense of guild vocation and craft within business life. I suspect that he would worry that Singer's proposals traffic too much in the ethical abstraction and austerity of cosmopolitan universalism that makes charity an anxious duty. But my question remains: Does globalization change the way we experience the "sudden bonds" of strangers?

Milbank's concern for a Christian sense of time parallels another British theologian's concerns with a Christian sense of place. Oliver O'Donovan defends the Augustinian claim that "divine providence has instituted distinct peoples with distinct identities (conventionally, though by no means exclusively, defined by territorial border), to set limits to the pursuit of justice, focusing it upon conceivable and practicable undertakings."[54] According to O'Donovan, "God allows only *neighborly* identities, not universal ones, as we are taught by the story of the Tower of Babel" (p. 130).[55] O'Donovan, of course, is also aware of the traditional reading of the Good Samaritan parable as a rejection of narrow exclusivism. He agrees that this lesson abides: "There are many societies where the rebuke of the parable strikes like a meteor against the complacency of racial or class self-love."[56] But O'Donovan suggests that there are "complacent forms of universalism, too" (p. 316). He argues that Christians must today encounter the message of the parable from "the opposite side, drawing out attention to an urgent form of contingent proximity" (p. 317). It was by chance, O'Donovan reminds us, that the Samaritan was going down that particular road. In fact, the parable emphasizes rather than denies proximate relations: "The parable discovers them where they are not looked for, nearer to us and under our very noses" (p. 317).[57] But again, do new economic conditions present distant strangers to us as nearer than we imagine?

---

54. Oliver O'Donovan, "Deliberation, History, and Reading: A Response to Schweiker and Wolterstorff," *Scottish Journal of Theology* 54, no. 1 (2001): 127-44 (quote from p. 130).

55. O'Donovan argues that "the precondition for a world-identity and world-government would be that Martians had arrived" (p. 133).

56. Oliver O'Donovan, "The Loss of a Sense of Place," in *The Bonds of Imperfection*, ed. Oliver O'Donovan and Joan Lockwood O'Donovan, p. 316.

57. In fact, "the mercy of the Samaritan restored that point on the road to the dignity of a real place, a place of meeting" (p. 317). He notes wryly that "among the paradoxes of

Legal philosopher Jeremy Waldron offers a nuanced reading of the parable that might finally help us with this question. Waldron also admits the importance of the traditional readings of the parable that focus "concern across communal and religious boundaries like those that separated Jew and Samaritan."[58] Waldron also shares O'Donovan's concern with "complacent" forms of abstract universalism. Yet he points out that the Samaritan did not "stop and figure out *his relation* to the man who had fallen among thieves" (pp. 341-42). In fact, says Waldron, it is "the person who makes the delicate calculations of moral distance, who would strike us in these cases as the one substituting abstraction for morality" (p. 342). Like Milbank and O'Donovan, Waldron emphasizes "the sheer particularity of the accidental conjunction in time and space of two concrete individuals" (p. 342). The moral meaning of the parable turns on the emphasis on *"actual proximity"* (p. 347). But Waldron adds an important caveat:

> [T]hose who fail to help the man who fell among thieves are portrayed in the parable as *going out of their way* not to help, or *going out of their way* to avoid a decision about whether to help. . . . Their not helping is an intentional doing: a decision to cross the road, a choice not to go out of their way to avoid the predicament. (p. 343)

To focus only on proximity and its special duties neglects this feature of the parable that Waldron rightly elevates. It suggests a helpful practical question for Christians and Christian communities to regularly ask themselves in making judgments about their material resources: Are you crossing to the other side? To ask that question requires more than just being prepared to be interrupted by the "sudden appearance" of a fallen neighbor. That is, it is not an abstract or rhetorical question.

There is a need for more public information about poverty that does not simply overwhelm the public with numbers. Economists and ethicists should work with Christian churches to disseminate clear and accessible data showing the direct impact of economic behavior on our so-called dis-

---

late-modern culture it must rank high that huge reservoirs of compassion can be released by television pictures of suffering in other parts of the world, while anyone who actually stops at a roadside to attend upon the plight of an accident victim, may expect to be treated as an eccentric" (pp. 317-18).

58. Jeremy Waldron, "Who Is My Neighbor? Humanity and Proximity," *The Monist* 86, no. 3 (July 2003): 333-54.

tant neighbors. Singer's modest principle counsels affluent Christians to sacrifice more of their resources in the face of extreme global poverty. In fact, Singer extends his argument beyond humanitarian responses to natural catastrophes to include an entire way of life that aims to reduce absolute poverty.

However, Singer does not spend his life searching the shallow ponds of the world, just as there is no indication that the Good Samaritan spent the rest of his life wandering the byways of ancient Israel looking for remote strangers in need. Singer aims high in principle but accommodates human frailty in practice. He ends his famous essay with this call to action: "At the very least, though, one can make a start. The philosopher who does so will have to sacrifice some of the benefits of the consumer society, but he can find compensation in the satisfaction of a way of life in which theory and practice, if not yet in harmony, are at least coming together."[59]

Singer himself donates 30 percent of his income to OXFAM and UNICEF. He claims that "[c]omfortably off Americans who give, say, 10 percent of their income to overseas aid organizations are so far ahead of most of their equally comfortable fellow citizens that I wouldn't go out of my way to chastise them for not doing more."[60] Given his own commitment, he admits to "not doing all that I should do; but I could do it, and the fact that I do not does not vitiate the claim that it is what I should do."[61]

Christians share Singer's candid admission that we humans are failing to do what is right even when we do not intentionally will what is evil. Affluent Christians, capable of tremendous compassion in the role of the Good Samaritan, must recognize that we choose to pass by on the other side of the road. Indeed, we are often the robbers on the Jericho road. What does one do with this kind of moral failure? Obvious differences emerge between Christians and secularists in response to this situation, and we reach a point where ethics cannot speak. But that is a story for another day. Until then, Christians might try to follow both the message of the Good Samaritan and of Peter Singer: "Go and do likewise."

---

59. Peter Singer, "Famine, Affluence and Morality," p. 243.

60. Singer, "The Singer Solution to World Poverty," pp. 60-63.

61. Singer, "Outsiders: our obligations to those beyond our borders," in *The Ethics of Assistance: Morality and the Distant Needy,* ed. Deen K. Chatterjee (Cambridge, UK: Cambridge University Press, 2004), p. 29.

CHAPTER 3

Global Poverty and Bono's Celebrity Activism: An Analysis of Moral Imagination and Motivation

Douglas A. Hicks

> *This is the defining moral issue of our time. Two and a half million Africans are going to die next year because they can't get hold of drugs we take for granted. We have these drugs that simply aren't getting to them. If you remember the story of the Good Samaritan, well, when it comes to Africa, we're not just crossing the road to avoid the man who needs help, we're catching a bus in the other direction.*
>
> — BONO, DECEMBER 13, 2003[1]

Introduction

As the chapters by Thomas W. Walker and Eric Gregory have detailed, the parable of the Good Samaritan serves as an important resource for Christian reflection on economic life. This chapter examines one example of a public effort that invokes this parable's expansive view of the neighbor in order to mobilize a movement against severe deprivation in the developing world, particularly Africa. This international initiative, which has been

1. Quoted in David Waters, "Bono Hopes You, Too, Will Care," *Memphis Commercial Appeal*, December 13, 2003, F1.

The author would like to thank Mark Valeri, Beverly Zink-Sawyer, Catherine Bagwell, Thad Williamson, and Betsy Kelly for helpful comments on this chapter. He is also very grateful to Lucretia McCulley and Jessica Scrimale for research assistance. Some of the ideas of this chapter were presented, in much briefer format, in Douglas A. Hicks, "Star Power: The Limits of Celebrity Activism," *Christian Century* 123, no. 6 (March 21, 2006): 23-24.

promoted by celebrities and undergirded by communities of faith across the industrialized world, is known in Britain and Ireland as the Make Poverty History Campaign and in the United States as the ONE Campaign. These campaigns ask for no money, "only" a personal commitment to stand up against poverty. The most visible face of the movement is Bono, the lead singer of the rock band U2. In his concerts, interviews, and speaking appearances, Bono has raised awareness of the most severe forms of global deprivation and urged citizens and political leaders alike to commit to measures aimed at their eradication.

Bono was named, along with Bill and Melinda Gates, as Person of the Year 2005 by *Time* magazine. On its cover, *Time* labeled Bono and the Gateses "The Good Samaritans." But this powerful biblical image misses the point of Bono's significance as a celebrity/leader. Arguably, like the Samaritan, Bono has seen his neighbor in the stranger.[2] But as I argue in this chapter, Bono goes beyond being a high-profile Samaritan to stretch the moral imagination of his musical audience and others so that they, too, see the need to reach out to our global neighbors. Bono frequently invokes directly the image of the Good Samaritan and the duty of neighbor-love as resources for our moral imagination and as sources of motivation to act against poverty.

Many religious and political critics have rightly expressed skepticism about an antipoverty campaign led by celebrity activism, emphasizing that no matter how well intentioned they may be, entertainers like Bono cannot grasp the complexity of the issues and do not have the time or political clout to make lasting change vis-à-vis social problems. After all, analysts agree, the alleviation of global poverty is a matter of justice and economic systems, not the goodwill of even dedicated and super-rich celebrities. Fundraisers such as Live Aid, Farm Aid, and the like provide a drop in the bucket compared to the resources needed to combat the ongoing nature of international deprivation. In addition, debt relief and more direct development aid can actually prop up corrupt regimes instead of helping the poor.

---

2. A number of journalists and religious commentators have also labeled Bono as a Samaritan for his antipoverty work. Prominently, Richard Stearns, president of World Vision, says that "[i]n an updated version of Jesus' parable, the rock star Bono would be cast in the title role of the Good Samaritan." James Traub, "Bono, AIDS, and the Good Samaritan," *Baptist Standard,* June 3, 2002. http://www.baptiststandard.com/2002/6_3/pages/view.html (accessed Aug. 22, 2006).

For his part, Bono has sought to avoid these pitfalls. The degree to which he has succeeded is a matter for critical judgment and a topic of this paper. As many economists and politicians who have met him attest, his understanding encompasses more than individual or collective charity. Through various organizational avenues he has attempted to address the technical issues of development and to work with governments and the international financial organizations to structure assistance in hard-edged, effective ways. Yet critics of Bono, the ONE Campaign, and related efforts raise important issues about the limitations and possible failures of celebrity activism. I will critically review and evaluate Bono's efforts to use his celebrity status and Christian faith to effect socioeconomic and political transformation. After giving an overview of his musical career, faith commitments, and activism, I will present a framework of an effective campaign against poverty, and then will evaluate Bono's work in those terms. The later sections of this chapter examine the role of musical artists in cultivating moral imagination, the challenges and limitations of celebrity activism, and the prospects, limitations, and implications of Bono's activism in the ONE Campaign and similar efforts of celebrity leadership.

Bono as Musician, Christian, and Activist

Bono, né Paul Hewson, is one of the world's most recognizable entertainment figures. U2 is one of the best-known rock bands in the world: the band released its first album, *Boy,* in 1980, and by the mid-1980s it had a broad international audience. Bono's own social and humanitarian efforts began in this early period, with his participation in major benefit concerts, including Live Aid in 1985. By the early 1990s, Bono was widely viewed as a celebrity activist for humanitarian concerns. Indeed, during U2's "Zoo TV" tour, Bono appeared onstage in the personas of a god and a devil, an act that was, in part, a self-reflective parody on his own privileged "do-gooder" image.[3]

In the late 1990s, Bono took on a major role in the public leadership against international debt. He became a visible figure in the Jubilee 2000 campaign, a church-based grassroots effort to promote the cancellation of

---

3. Steven Quinn, "U2 and the Performance of (A Numb) Resistance," *Social Semiotics* 9, no. 1 (1999): 67-83.

debilitating foreign debt that was owed by the poorest countries. In a famous photographic image, Bono appeared alongside Pope John Paul II in the Jubilee campaign. In 2002 he formed the organization DATA (Debt, AIDS, Trade, Africa) to concentrate public efforts for African policy and assistance. During the first half of this decade, he met with world leaders, including U.S. President George Bush, British Prime Minister Tony Blair, and Brazilian President Luiz Inácio Lula Da Silva, in order to raise awareness about poverty, debt, and AIDS, especially in Africa. His high-profile (and somewhat surreal) tour of Africa with the then-U.S. treasury secretary, Paul O'Neill, in 2002 helped establish Bono as more serious than other celebrities in development work. He delivered the senior class day address and received an honorary degree from Harvard University in 2001; he gave another commencement address and received another honorary degree from the University of Pennsylvania three years later.

In 2005, when Make Poverty History was launched in the United Kingdom and Ireland, Bono was the most prominent face of the campaign. During that year the ONE Campaign became the U.S. arm of Make Poverty History, and Bono has been the brightest star in the constellation of stars in the campaign's promotional materials. Bono coordinated with Bob Geldof to arrange, in some six weeks, the Live 8 concerts in July 2006, with significant performances in all eight of the G-8 countries, an extravaganza anchored by major events in London and Philadelphia. At that G-8 summit, the world's most powerful leaders committed to an additional $50 billion in annual debt relief. A number of them met with Bono before and during the summit and credited him publicly for making this agreement happen.

The Christian faith or spirituality of Bono has received significant attention, mostly from appreciative biographers but also from critics.[4] Having grown up with a Catholic father and a Protestant mother in Ireland, Bono expresses a complex relationship with institutional Christianity. He has appealed directly and prominently to his Christian faith, using biblical and theological images in his songs and his antipoverty work. One of the most notable aspects of his social activism has been his ability to mobilize disparate segments of the Christian faith community to support the ONE Campaign and related efforts.

---

4. Steve Stockman, *Walk On: The Spiritual Journey of U2*, rev. ed. (Orlando, FL: Relevant Books, 2005); Mark Allan Powell, "U2," in *Encyclopedia of Contemporary Christian Music* (Peabody, MA: Hendrickson, 2002), pp. 978-83.

Alongside Hollywood's biggest names, ONE has drawn together, in large measure due to Bono's work, a diverse group of religious supporters, from left and right, mainliners and evangelicals, and leaders of many other religious traditions. The campaign has received public support from a disparate list of evangelicals, including author Tony Campolo, evangelist Pat Robertson, social activist Jim Wallis, and musician Michael W. Smith. A host of mainline denominations, as well as social ministries of all theological stripes, have also signed on as partners. Bono and the ONE Campaign have had real success in recruiting younger evangelicals in particular. Church-growth guru Rick Warren issued a public letter and e-mailed hundreds of thousands of pastors urging Christians to join him in signing on to the ONE Campaign. The campaign's list of dozens of nonprofit partners includes as many religious organizations as secular aid groups. Indeed, many of the founding organizations of ONE are religiously based. These range across religious traditions (though most are Christian), from mainline to evangelical theologies, and from established denominational structures to new, independent groups.

The real split between those who support and those who reject Bono's celebrity activism has more to do with age than with religious affiliation. U2's fans range from the late baby boomers to present-day teens; thus it is not surprising that this is the age span most influenced by Bono's social leadership. Older evangelicals tend to reject his rock-star lifestyle, his off-color language, and his criticism of the institutional church. By contrast, many in his own age cohort and the younger generations can relate to his sense of spirituality and a faith-based understanding of justice that are not necessarily attached to church membership. Younger generations can also appreciate Bono's use of the media — video, e-mail, cell phones, the internet — in launching a social movement that is truly international.

On February 2, 2006, Bono addressed President Bush, various senators and representatives, and other political and religious leaders at the National Prayer Breakfast. Drawing on biblical language such as "Jubilee," the "good news for the poor," and the words of Jesus in the Beatitudes, Bono argued that global justice requires the firm commitment of the United States government and other affluent nations to make a significant shift in national priorities. Specifically, he called for a 1 percent increase in the federal budget, from the less than 1 percent presently dedicated to foreign assistance. He called it a "national tithe," and he framed it not as charity but as a move for justice that would also further U.S. national security interests.[5] This National Prayer Breakfast address provided the fullest public exposure to date of how Bono's work against extreme poverty is framed and motivated by Christian faith, and of his call to religious people and organizations, as well as the U.S. government, to join in the effort.

Global Destitution, Morality, and Motivation

What role can a celebrity activist like Bono play in making socioeconomic change? Before we look more closely into Bono's own efforts, it is important to lay out some possible roles, all of which are important elements in effecting change. In this section I would like to outline three roles: 1) providing information; 2) offering moral justification; and 3) fostering motivation to respond to global poverty. In terms of providing information, a baseline or starting point for any action in confronting a problem is understanding its nature and scope. Celebrities have access to information about global poverty and related conditions, and they have the means and access to media to communicate that information to the public. Their role may be largely to convey the same facts and analysis that journalists and development experts can communicate, to be sure. But, as I will discuss below, hearing this information from celebrities can have different effects on the public than hearing it from other news and media sources.

The World Bank estimates that 1.1 billion human beings currently survive on less than one U.S. dollar per day; that is roughly one in six persons alive on the planet.[6] Another way of assessing that level of destitution at the global level is to look at in terms of food security, or undernutrition. The Food and Agricultural Organization of the United Nations estimates that more than 850 million humans are undernourished; these persons lack the dietary consumption required for a healthy life with just the light-

5. "Transcript: Bono Remarks at the National Prayer Breakfast," *USA Today.com,* http://www.usatoday.com/news/washington/2006-02-02-bono-transcript_x.htm (accessed Aug. 22, 2006).

6. The latest World Bank estimates are for 2001 and are adjusted into terms of purchasing power parity (PPP$) across countries. World Bank's Poverty Net, "Overview: Understanding Poverty"; see http://web.worldbank.org/WBSITE/EXTERNAL/TOPICS/EXTPOVERTY/EXTPA/o,,contentMDK:20153855/menuPK:373757~pagePK:148956~piPK:216618~theSitePK:336992,00.html (accessed May 5, 2008).

est of activity.[7] HIV/AIDS is a major focus of the ONE Campaign, and the United Nations joint program organization UNAIDS estimates that, at the end of 2005, 38.6 million people had been infected with HIV. Nearly 25 million of that number were infected in sub-Saharan Africa alone.[8]

Such information about the magnitude of global destitution and illness is widely available to the public via the websites and publications of the organizations noted above. In addition, the Millennium Development Goals and the associated publicity campaign of the United Nations have sought to make the facts and figures of global deprivation as widely available as possible. Journalists have long covered related socioeconomic issues, but the enduring nature of these issues makes them less "interesting" for the daily news cycle than one-time events — whether those events be political, military, sports-related, or otherwise. For example, the widely accepted figure that about thirty thousand people die each day of hunger-related causes is a mundane fact that does not capture headlines. Therefore, the challenge is how to keep the information about the magnitude of this "mundane" problem in the public eye.

Beyond the statistics about poverty is the question of how the facts and figures fit within a broader context for understanding the problem. What are the significant factors contributing to absolute poverty? What kinds of aid could actually be effective in addressing those factors? What political or economic behaviors (e.g., corruption) that contribute to poverty may be exacerbated rather than attenuated by additional aid from the industrialized countries? Economists routinely criticize celebrities (not to mention journalists and even politicians) for not understanding the various dimensions of the issue at hand. Therefore, the question of information focuses not merely on data but on the broader understanding of the dynamics of global poverty. How well celebrities (and other would-be leaders) understand the whole context is a relevant factor for evaluating their information-sharing role.

Yet there is a real difference, of course, between descriptive information and normative commitments. The normative task requires asking what moral sense we are to make of the descriptive reality of poverty. Al-

7. Estimates for the period between 1993 and 2004 all indicate a number higher than 850 million people; see http://www.fao.org/es/ess/faostat/foodsecurity/Files/NumberUnder nourishment.xls (accessed Aug. 29, 2006).

8. See http://data.unaids.org/pub/GlobalReport/2006/2006_GR-ExecutiveSummary _en.pdf (accessed Aug. 29, 2006).

though any description necessarily requires some sort of evaluation of priorities and values, as Rebecca Todd Peters discusses in her chapter later in this volume, the fuller normative exercise of *moral justification* is a different kind of exercise altogether. This is the second role that celebrity activists (or other leaders) can play in mobilizing antipoverty efforts.

It sometimes appears that leaders of international nongovernmental organizations (INGOs) believe that, if they simply communicate the massive magnitude of extreme poverty, people in industrialized settings will realize that they have a moral obligation to respond with generous and effective aid. Many economists, even those doing purely descriptive work, find their raison d'être in a moral commitment to improve economic well-being. For instance, the founder of neoclassical economics, Alfred Marshall, wrote that "the question of whether it is really impossible that all should start in the world with a fair chance of leading a cultured life, free from the pains of poverty . . . [gives] to economic studies their chief and their highest interest."[9] Marshall, like the political economist Adam Smith more than two hundred years before him, took for granted that poverty of this extreme (and nonvoluntary) form is a moral evil. But these assumptions are based on an implicit moral justification.

In Christian theological terms, the basic approach to severe poverty is, I would assert, quite clear: nonvoluntary poverty has the effect of violating a person's inherent human dignity and therefore contradicts God's good purposes for every human being.[10] As the Peruvian theologian Gustavo Gutiérrez might put it, poverty can be so debilitating that people in that condition do not even realize that they are human beings.[11] In a recent press conference, Bono himself cited Christian faith with regard to his work against poverty:

> There are 2,103 verses of Scripture pertaining to the poor. Jesus Christ only speaks of judgment once. It is not all about the things that the church bangs on about. It is not about sexual immorality, and it is not

9. Alfred Marshall, *Principles of Economics*, 8th ed. (London: Macmillan, 1920), "Introduction."

10. For a fuller theological discussion of dignity and economic well-being, see Douglas A. Hicks, *Inequality and Christian Ethics* (Cambridge, UK: Cambridge University Press, 2000), esp. chs. 6-8.

11. Gustavo Gutiérrez, *The Power of the Poor in History*, trans. Robert R. Barr (Maryknoll, NY: Orbis, 1983), p. 193.

about megalomania, or vanity. It is about the poor. "I was naked and you clothed me. I was a stranger and you let me in." This is at the heart of the gospel. Why is it that we have seemed to have forgotten this? Why isn't the church leading this movement? I am here tonight because the church ought to be ready to do that.[12]

When we combine the massive scale and severity of global destitution with the framework of Christian morality, it is not controversial to claim that there are clear Christian *grounds* that call Christians to commit themselves to help in the alleviation of extreme poverty.[13]

Therefore, it is difficult to argue that extreme poverty is a healthy thing, either for individuals or societies as a whole, and it is only slightly easier to argue that we affluent people have no obligation to do something about it. What is often lacking is the *motivation* to act in light of this reality. And this is the third role that leaders, including celebrities, might help fulfill.

To return to the perspective of neoclassical economists, we note that the question of motivation and self-interest comes into play. As Kent Van Til explains in the following chapter, self-interest is viewed by the neoclassical school as the principal motivation for action. Economists, in their modeling, undertake *descriptive* and *predictive* analyses of how people will act; however, they do not mean to make *normative* statements about how people should act. As Amartya Sen has shown, it is possible to incorporate other-regarding (as opposed to merely self-interested) behavior into economic models, either by acknowledging that people may derive their own self-interested satisfaction from helping other persons or by noting that people sometimes willingly override their own interests with behavior motivated by regard for others (or by prior commitments to a cause or a community).[14] Seen from a different angle, a person might well have other-regarding interests that she articulates as important, but it requires an act of will to follow through on those interests in her own actions.

---

12. Bono, press conference, Northeast Christian Church, Louisville, KY; cited on reinform.org website (accessed Aug. 22, 2006).

13. There remains plenty of room for disagreement, of course, at more moderate levels of well-being, causes and dynamics of poverty, etc. The point is simply that, in terms of extreme poverty, few would maintain that there is no moral imperative to respond in some way with assistance.

14. Amartya Sen, "Rational Fools: A Critique of the Behavioural Foundations of Economic Theory," *Philosophy and Public Affairs* 6 (1977): 317-44.

Therefore, it is a significant step from making moral arguments to motivating others to act against poverty, when it is often counter to their narrow conceptions of self-interest. To put it simply, millions (perhaps billions) of people may be convinced that extreme poverty is a moral ill and that they should act against it, but they do not. It is at this point — connecting the roles of moral justification and motivation — that the "moral imagination" comes in. Adam Smith emphasized the need for humans to expand their moral sentiments, their capacity to imagine and understand the reality that other people experience. Smith offered a vivid story to express his meaning:

> Let us suppose that the great empire of China, with all its myriads of inhabitants, was suddenly swallowed up by an earthquake, and let us consider how a man of humanity in Europe, who had no sort of connection with that part of the world, would be affected upon receiving intelligence of this dreadful calamity.[15]

Smith says that the European would be sorry about the situation, but because he was not directly connected to these persons, his own life would not be significantly changed. Smith emphasizes his point by suggesting that if the cultured European were

> to lose his little finger to-morrow, he would not sleep to-night; but, provided he never saw them, he will snore with the most profound security over the ruin of a hundred millions of his brethren. . . .[16]

As Smith observes, without a sense of sympathetic (or empathetic) connection to other people, we simply would not have a proper moral understanding. Through our moral imagination, however, we can develop that understanding and be moved to act according to our moral commitments. Musicians and other artists have the capacity to help spark the moral imagination.[17]

---

15. Adam Smith, *The Theory of Moral Sentiments,* III.I.46. The Library of Economics and Liberty Online, http://www.econlib.org/library/Smith/smMS.html (accessed Aug. 22, 2006).

16. Ibid.

17. Martha Nussbaum, *Poetic Justice: The Literary Imagination in Public Life* (Boston: Beacon Press, 1995).

Bono's Celebrity Activism

In overall terms, celebrities and other leaders seeking to effect social change face the tasks of communicating information about the present reality, articulating a moral argument for change, and cultivating motivation to act for change.[18] I turn now to review and analyze Bono's efforts as a celebrity activist along these lines.

Although the basic statistics on global poverty are available for those who seek them out, Bono is able to communicate the facts to his audience, including young adult fans, who might not otherwise receive much information about poverty. Bono, as a musician who has been an international celebrity for over two decades, now has a following across a broad swath of age groups, from current teenagers to the so-called baby boomers. Even when he simply states figures about poverty, HIV/AIDS, debt relief, and so on, he is likely to be heard in ways that journalists, nonprofit leaders, and even politicians are not.

Beyond a mere stating of statistics, however, Bono is widely respected for his understanding of the contexts and complexities of global poverty. He has collaborated in various ways with renowned economist Jeffrey Sachs (he wrote the foreword to Sachs's book *The End of Poverty*), Bill and Melinda Gates, Bill Clinton, and Jesse Helms. He reportedly convinced Lawrence Summers, the former U.S. treasury secretary and former president of Harvard, about debt relief, and he earned the respect (if not the agreement) of conservative economist Robert J. Barro.[19] Observers frequently note that Bono articulates a more nuanced understanding of development issues than do many of the so-called experts. This consensus of respect affords Bono the legitimacy to communicate information about poverty to the audiences to whom he is more recognizable than most or all of the experts.

---

18. For a fascinating analysis of the grounds of morality with respect to the motivation needed to act for social service, see Jackie Knupp, "Kant's Assessment of Motivation in Fulfillment of Social Obligations," *Penn Bioethics Journal* 2, no. 2 (2006). Knupp argues that Kant's emphasis on actions done from a sense of duty alone overlooks a host of significant questions pertaining to the motivation to act morally.

19. Jeffrey Sachs, *The End of Poverty* (New York: Penguin Press, 2005); Josh Tyrangiel, "The Constant Charmer: The Inside Story of How the World's Biggest Rock Star Mastered the Political Game and Persuaded the World's Leaders to Take on Global Poverty. And He's Not Done Yet," *Time*, December 26, 2006/January 2, 2007, pp. 46-62; Robert J. Barro, *Nothing Is Sacred: Economic Ideas for the New Millennium* (Cambridge, MA: MIT Press, 2002).

Yet, along with many others in the faith community, Bono would argue that the descriptive information only gains its significance from a normative, theological understanding of human well-being. Running throughout the interviews with Bono, throughout his comments during U2 concerts, and throughout his song lyrics is a fundamental moral commitment to the equality of all human beings. Indeed, in nearly every case in which he mentions equality, he grounds his moral claim in the equality of all persons before God, their being created in God's image. For example, in his interview with Michka Assayas, he explained his commitment to social justice as "the journey of equality. Equality is an idea that was first really expressed by the Jews when God told them that everyone was equal in His eyes. . . . I'm not sure we accept that Africans are equal."[20]

Bono's moral argument moves from the status of equality to the expansion of the scope of who our neighbor is. In his own words:

> So the next step in the journey of equality is to get to a place where we accept that you cannot choose your neighbor. In the Global Village, distance no longer decides who is your neighbor, and "Love thy neighbor" is not advice, it's a command.[21]

One important challenge to realizing the global scope of neighbor obligations is to overcome the intense loyalties of nationalism. Rather than strictly oppose national favoritism in the way, for example, that Peter Singer has done,[22] Bono attempts to reappropriate national values to make them truly global. As one notable example, during U2's 2005-06 "Vertigo" world tour, Bono built on the imagery from his song "Pride/In the Name of Love," which is about the American dream of Dr. Martin Luther King, Jr., to extend King's dream to those in extreme poverty around the world:

> Sing for Dr. King, for Dr. King's dream
> For a dream big enough to fit the whole world
> A dream where everyone is created equal under the eyes of God
> Everyone. Everyone.
> Not just an American dream or an Asian dream

20. Michka Assayas, *Bono in Conversation with Michka Assayas* (New York: Riverhead Books/Penguin, 2005), pp. 80-81; cf. National Prayer Breakfast address, 2/2/06.
21. Assayas, *Bono in Conversation*, pp. 81-82.
22. See Eric Gregory's discussion in ch. 2 above.

or a European dream.
Also an *African* dream.
Also an African dream. Africa.
From the bridge at Selma in Mississippi [sic]
To the mouth of the river Nile
From the swamplands of Louisiana
To the high peaks of Kilimanjaro
From Dr. King's America
To Nelson Mandela's Africa
A journey of equality moves on, on, on, on.[23]

In his concert appearances of the 2001-02 "Elevation" tour (including the Super Bowl halftime performance in February 2002) and the "Vertigo" tour, the Irish rocker has softened his critical stance toward various aspects of U.S. policy by prominently displaying the lining of his leather jacket, revealing an American flag. In addition, he has heaped praise on President Bush and Senator Helms (to the dismay of some of his allies on the left) for their domestic political work to provide HIV/AIDS funding for Africa. Seen as a whole, Bono's efforts have embraced a strategy of promoting obligations to "the least of these" around the world while expanding, rather than opposing, the ideals of America. Such a strategy is similar to Martin Luther King's own appropriation of both Christian and American ideals in a struggle for justice.

Bono is self-reflective about the role of storytelling in his musical performances, as well as in motivating his followers toward social change. In an address to a World Bank forum he said:

> What do rock stars like me have to contribute to debates about global poverty, the international debt burden on developing countries, and HIV/AIDS? I think we can help tell the story better. We can help, for instance, in the area of branding, because rocks stars have above all to build their own brands. We need to get much better at branding in the area of poverty. We have to dramatize the story. We have to shape a clear melody line or the public will fall asleep in the comfort of their freedom, as indeed I did for many years. . . . We have a chance to be part of a generation that does not find it acceptable

---

23. *Vertigo 2005, U2 Live from Chicago* DVD (Universal City, CA: Universal Music and Video Distribution Corp, 2005).

that 2.5 million people will die of AIDS next year. I want to be part of that generation.[24]

Bono goes on to say that religious institutions, especially the church, have narratives — the melody line, as he puts it — that can spark the imagination and inspire people to act.

It is precisely at this point that Bono has repeatedly invoked the story of the Good Samaritan and the notion of neighbor-love in the struggle against extreme poverty. The purpose, as his reflection on the story suggests, is to spark the moral imagination of Christians and those familiar with the Christian Gospels to move from religious words to compassionate action. Toward that end, he highlights four dimensions of the parable. First, he emphasizes (like Peter Singer and other moral philosophers and theologians) that the concept of neighbor applies globally in today's interconnected world. In his framework, we are all neighbors in the global village. Bono has said (quoted in this chapter's epigraph): "If you remember the story of the Good Samaritan, well, when it comes to Africa, we're not just crossing the road to avoid the man who needs help, we're catching a bus in the other direction."

Second, Bono criticizes religious inaction, people who express a religious identity but do not live out that faith in practices of justice and compassion. In his words:

We must wake up the sleeping giant of the Church; we must set alarm clocks to rouse our politicians who also slumber. The choice is there before each and every one of us: to stop and tend to the distant pilgrim sick on the side of the road, or, a nervous glance, and we turn away . . . away from the pilgrim, away from God's grace.[25]

Third, and on a related note, Bono is even more critical of religious hypocrisy. The U2 song "Crumbs from Your Table," written by Bono and replete

---

24. Bono, "Challenge for Our Generation," in *Millennium Challenges for Development and Faith Institutions,* ed. Katherine Marshall and Richard Marsh (Washington, DC: The World Bank, 2003), p. 12.

25. Bono, transcript of address for The aWAKE (AIDS: Working towards Awareness, Knowledge, and Engagement) Project: Uniting Against the African AIDS Crisis, 2002. http://www.vanderbilt.edu/AnS/religious_studies/aidsafrica/theawakeproject.html#bono (accessed Aug. 29, 2006).

with biblical imagery,[26] is a stinging attack on Christians who parade their religiosity but do not live out their faith with acts of social justice:

> You speak of signs and wonders
> I need something other
> I would believe if I was able
> But I'm waiting on the crumbs from your table
>
> You were pretty as a picture
> It was all there to see
> Then your face caught up with your psychology
> With a mouth full of teeth
> You ate all your friends
> And you broke every heart thinking every heart mends . . . .
>
> Where you live should not decide
> Whether you live or whether you die
> Three to a bed
> Sister Ann, she said
> Dignity passes by

The final verse included here is a reference to the familiar theme of neighborhoods, human need, and the priest and the Levite in the Good Samaritan parable, those who "pass by" on the other side (Luke 10:31-32).[27]

Fourth, Bono suggests that the people who will respond, as the Samaritan did, might not be the churchgoers or the pious leaders in the world. Though Bono is more subtle in developing this point, he emphasizes in various settings that the coalition he seeks to build will come "from left and right, from churches and casinos."[28] He clearly relishes the fact that he sees God's work taking place in acts of charity and justice far beyond the walls of the institutional church. Indeed, it is reasonable to sug-

---

26. The most direct reference, which forms the title of the song, is from the story of Dives and Lazarus in Luke 16:19-31.

27. In another criticism of religious hypocrisy, in his 2006 National Prayer Breakfast address, Bono says: "Seeing what religious people, in the name of God, did to my native land . . . and in this country, seeing God's second-hand car salesmen on the cable TV channels, offering indulgences for cash . . . in fact, all over the world, seeing the self-righteousness roll down like a mighty stream from certain corners of the religious establishment."

28. Bono, during U2 concert, Charlotte, NC, December 12, 2006.

gest that Bono situates himself as part of the group of outsiders who do God's work without wrapping themselves up in pious garb.

Bono understands himself to be a storyteller who draws on his talents and social position to address social ills, especially absolute poverty. He seeks to move his listeners (and followers) from understanding the descriptive reality and the moral evil of global poverty to engaging willingly in an effective response. This requires telling the story that alleviating the worst of poverty is within reach;[29] that it is a desirable, even "cool," thing to do; and that we will all be proud that we did so.

> I truly believe that when the history books are written, our age will be remembered for three things: the war on terror, the digital revolution, and what we did — or did not do — to put the fire [of severe deprivation] out in Africa.[30]

Critical Analysis: From Imagination to Effective Action

Bono should be seen as more than a "Good Samaritan" or even an educator of Samaritans. He has used his global celebrity to become an organizer, imagination-sparker, and motivator of Samaritans. His efforts at public education, communication, and mobilization are significant, and his challenge to our moral imagination to aid our global neighbor makes for an intriguing case of celebrity leadership.

But do Bono's fans, we must ask, want to be neighbors with the poor or simply neighbors with Bono? It is not clear, of course, that people who respond to Bono (by signing on to the ONE Campaign or in another way) actually do see the global poor as people like themselves. Perhaps they just want to be seen as "in the movement" with Bono — in a sense, to be *his* neighbor. Surely the education piece of the campaign needs to be emphasized, so that even people who join to be like Bono learn to care about poverty and the impoverished. In other words, even if the motives of his followers are different from Bono's intended ones, the ONE Campaign can habituate members, in any case, to cultivate their own commitment against poverty.

29. Bono cites figures from Jeffrey Sachs and other economists to show that the scale of aid needed is, in fact, in the realm of the possible.

30. Bono, National Prayer Breakfast remarks (see n. 5 above).

It is Bono's own role-modeling in his concern for social justice and equality, which is motivated by his faith commitments, that holds together his triple roles of information-sharing, arguing for moral equality, and motivating through the moral imagination. Despite the critique from some Christian circles of Bono's alleged vices, such as his penchant for off-color language and a self-confessed tendency toward a "messianic complex,"[31] he has earned respect from a broad public audience for his dedication. In his life, his fans can see the integration of an understanding about the dynamics of poverty, the faith-grounded belief in moral equality, and the passion to act. Although he has his critics, the consensus is that his genuine commitment, based on his faith, to fight poverty and HIV/AIDS is one of his greatest assets.

Yet the culture of celebrity and affluence, of which a rock star like Bono is necessarily a part, overlooks the question of whether it is morally possible to live with integrity in material comfort in our own industrialized society. That is, does staging a benefit, such as the Live 8 shows in 2006, send more than one message to concertgoers? Fans may learn to show concern about extreme poverty through the spoken, sung, and lived "witness" of musician-activists like Bono. But the audiences, both at the event and on television, may also receive the message that an economically privileged lifestyle, in which they buy CDs (promoted shamelessly by some of the performers) and enjoy expensive iPods (for which Bono's music has been used prominently in marketing), is morally acceptable. Can material excess be as harmful to us spiritually as absolute material poverty can be for the poor physically? Bono cannot lead a campaign against the affluence of U.S. (and European) society, of which we and many of his fans are the beneficiaries.

Bono would claim that his goal, though it is large, does not require a wholesale refutation of Western consumerism. In the grand scheme of things, the relative amount of money needed is small. The United Nations is asking industrialized countries (and their leaders have committed) to give 0.7 percent of their gross national product to fight poverty. This money, some $200 billion annually, would be far more than what is required to meet the basic human needs of the world's poor. The point is that the level of commitment needed to address extreme poverty is not itself extreme.

31. Bono, National Prayer Breakfast remarks.

What is required is a large bloc of citizens willing to express a moral and political commitment to end extreme poverty. During U2's sold-out 2005 concert tour across the continents, Bono declared nightly that the ONE Campaign, then claiming over one million members in the United States, could surpass the 5 million members of the National Rifle Association (NRA) as early as 2008. This comparison is, so to speak, on target. The ONE Campaign's goal is to communicate to political leaders that there is a large bloc of citizens committed to addressing global poverty. It is said that politicians must be concerned, in their public role, not about citizens of other countries, however impoverished those humans might be; rather, political leaders must focus on the wants and needs of their own citizens. By making global poverty a concern of citizens, the ONE Campaign makes it a concern of politicians. Indeed, given our current political climate, even politicians who want to fight global poverty need this public pressure so that they can claim that it is in their own interest to act in such a cause. "Bono made me do it," they can say. As Bono puts it:

> Discussion and debate are helpful, but we must elevate our efforts to involve a wider group of people — people who can enable the politicians to secure higher levels of funding and commitment. Some politicians are interested and anxious to do something. We must enable them to do it.[32]

This issue of political transformation remains a critical point for evaluation of Bono's public leadership. It appears that he has thought more carefully than most celebrities have about the structural, justice-based transformations that need to take place to effect lasting progress against deprivation and disease. It would not be fair to label the ONE Campaign and its sister campaigns around the world as based on charity alone. It is possible that Bono and others will not be able to sustain the momentum to make a political difference. The charismatic celebrity-leader must motivate the citizens to the extent that they, in turn, move their political leaders to policy-based action. Whether the voluntary motivation of citizens to pressure their political leaders to bolster effective aid and increase the fairness of trade systems will work remains to be seen.

32. Bono, "Challenge for Our Generation," pp. 13-14.

Prospects, Limitations, and Implications

Bono may well prove to be the most successful celebrity-leader of our time. He is politically savvy and has used his visibility in North America, Europe, and beyond to leverage a movement that now has our most prominent international leaders paying attention to putting an end to global poverty. He has articulated a vision of global neighbors inspired by appeals, direct and indirect, to the parable of the Good Samaritan. Most significantly and distinctly, I suggest, he has sought to integrate an informed reading of economic realities and a savvy use of international media and communications into the familiar musician's role of fostering the moral imagination of his fans in order to lead to coordinated political action.

Yet celebrity-leadership can take us only so far. What happens, for instance, when the celebrity fades? Although Bono's popularity remains high, a fall from the charts for Bono could decapitate the movement. Leadership scholars have emphasized that the way to insulate a leadership effort from a debilitating loss of the charismatic leader is to create an organizational structure that shares responsibility. That is, Bono's success as a leader will hinge on the extent to which he can create and maintain an enduring institutional and international effort to reduce poverty, through organizations such as DATA and the ONE Campaign and through lasting political changes in foreign development assistance.

Can such an organized effort convince political leaders, not once but over time, to act for debt relief and for human development in Africa and beyond? As Bono himself has acknowledged, the ONE Campaign and others like it should be considered successful if political leaders reshape their understanding of their own responsibilities. Citizens and the movement as a whole must appeal to their leaders' political self-interest and to an enlightened national interest in acting against poverty. Bono's efforts, particularly his appeals to view the global poor as our neighbor, call us to make the relatively modest commitment to combat extreme deprivation. We all too readily praise our globalizing world when we want cheap electronics from East Asia, cheap clothing from Latin America, or cheap oil from anywhere we can find it. We cannot with good reason or in good conscience then state that the global poor are too distant from us. With the power of his privileged access into millions of our homes, Bono tells us that impoverished Africans are in our neighborhood.

Bono has been a public educator about global poverty in ways that

Christian organizations like Bread for the World and World Vision have not been able to accomplish. Star musicians can shape our consciousness and motivate us to think and act creatively. Bono's invocations of the Good Samaritan have sparked the moral imagination of many people and have helped fuel the current global debate about extreme poverty. That is a significant contribution by a highly influential Christian living in the global market. But it is also a call to individual and church-based reflection on Christian faith and the global economy. It is a catalyst to, not a replacement of, coordinated and systematic political actions. Through international mechanisms like the United Nations Millennium Development Goals, the nations of the world have already pledged to act. The bottleneck is the moral and political will to realize those promises. In that context, Bono as celebrity leader makes a notable contribution that stands as a challenge to citizens to press our political leaders into doing their part.

PART II

Christian Witness and Mainstream Economic Theory: Four Critiques

CHAPTER 4

Human Nature and Human Needs
in Recent Economic Theory

Kent Van Til

The previous section's chapters helped us gain an understanding of who our global neighbor is and what our responsibilities toward him or her may be. As we have seen, Jesus' parable of the Good Samaritan stands out in history as a memorable narrative that defines neighbor-love. In this chapter I will take up the question "who is my neighbor?" from the perspective of economics. The dominant economic theory, called "mainstream economics," has a clear and sophisticated view of who human beings are: they are consumers with rationally ordered purchase preferences. This picture of the economic person shapes how we respond to our neighbor when we participate in the global marketplace. The basic question I ask in this chapter is this: Do the anthropological assumptions of mainstream economic anthropology give us a good or accurate basis from which we might respond to the needs of our neighbor?

In my attempt to answer that question, I want to first establish a benchmark of what it means to be human according to Christian Scripture; second, I will present mainstream anthropology; third, I will describe how three contemporary economic theorists, Peruvian political and economic theorist Hernando de Soto, Nobel Prize winner and Chicago School economist Gary Becker, and Nobel Prize-winning economist Amartya Sen, respond to the mainstream understanding of the nature of humans and their needs. In each of the sections on economists I will include a brief appraisal that compares that economist's theory to the biblical viewpoint. By the end of the chapter, the differences and similarities among biblical and economic anthropological perspectives should be clearer. A clearer picture of who our neighbor is, from an economic perspective, may guide us as we attempt to help him or her in time of need.[1]

I. Biblical Anthropology

> Then God said: "Let us make human beings in our image, after our likeness, to have dominion over the fish in the sea, the birds of the air, the cattle, all wild animals on land, and everything that creeps on the earth." God created human beings in his own image; in the image of God he created them; male and female he created them. (Gen. 1:26-27, REB)

And so it began. So, too, began the debates over what it means to be created in "the image and likeness of God." The terms lying behind the biblical anthropology are "image" *(tselem)* and "likeness" *(demut)*. Earlier Christian interpretations of this text often made significant distinctions between the "image" and the "likeness." For example, some early interpreters saw the image as the physical nature of humanity, and the likeness as the spiritual or rational aspect.[2] Others saw the image as the person as created, whereas the likeness referred to the person as glorified.[3]

Today, however, interpreters generally recognize that these two terms are nearly synonymous, and the phrase "image and likeness" is a hendiadys.[4] The terms "image and likeness" do not present a philosophical anthropology; rather, they show that, among all the creatures of the earth, humans are those who are most like God. The similarities between God

---

1. The reader should note that this chapter covers a wide swath of ground, and my attempt to map it will necessarily be incomplete. However, I believe that even this rough sketch can still serve as a useful guide.

2. Gordon J. Wenham, *Genesis 1–15* (Waco, TX: Word, 1987), p. 29.

3. See G. W. Bromiley, "Image of God," in *International Standard Bible Encyclopedia*, ed. G. W. Bromiley (Grand Rapids: Eerdmans, 1986), vol. 2, pp. 803-5, for a brief historical presentation of views on the "image and likeness."

4. A hendiadys is "the use of two words connected by a conjunction to express the same idea as a single word with a qualifier" (*Funk and Wagnalls New Practical Standard Dictionary* [New York: Funk and Wagnalls, 1956], p. 620). From an exegetical viewpoint, Gerhard von Rad says: "One will do well to split the physical from the spiritual as little as possible: the whole man is created in God's image" (*Genesis* [Philadelphia: Westminster Press, 1972], p. 58).

and humankind identified by contemporary exegetes often focus on the particular capabilities that define the essence of humanity.[5] Humans are God's representatives on the earth, and thus they are royalty. As Gerhard von Rad puts it, "Just as powerful earthly kings, to indicate their claim and dominion, erect an image of themselves in the provinces of their empire, so man is placed upon earth in God's image as God's sovereign emblem."[6] To be effective representatives, they must be able to perform certain tasks. The texts that follow in Genesis describe the kinds of tasks these representatives will need to do as they represent God on earth.

The principal task of the bearers of God's image is to "rule and have dominion" over nature (Gen. 1:28). The human ability to rule is derived from the nature of the ultimate ruler and creator — God. Though some commentators see this text as implying a benevolent rule,[7] the actual Hebrew terms used for "rule" and "dominion" are quite strong. Von Rad puts it this way:

> He [mankind] is really God's representative, summoned to maintain and enforce God's claim to dominion over the earth. . . . The expressions for the exercise of this dominion are remarkably strong: *radha,* "tread," "trample" (e.g., winepress); similarly *kabhash,* "stamp."[8]

The softening of, or explanation of, the beneficence of this human rule awaits declaration in Genesis 2, which provides the first "job description" for humankind: God instructs his rulers to "till and keep" the earth that is now in their charge. Before assigning them their tasks, however, God makes provision for his people. God causes moisture to nourish the plants of the earth and provides them with a lovely garden. Then we learn that their task is to "till" (or "work") and "keep" the place they have been given. Tilling *(avad)* is clearly an agricultural term: they were not to leave the creation untouched, but were to develop its potential in such a way that they would unleash its productivity for good. As Christian ethicists Ronald

---

5. Wenham, *Genesis,* p. 32.

6. Von Rad, *Genesis,* p. 60.

7. For example, Gordon Wenham says: "Mankind is here commissioned to rule nature as a benevolent king, acting as God's representative over them and therefore treating them in the same way as God who created them. Thus animals, though subject to man, are viewed as his companions in 2:18-20" (*Genesis,* p. 33).

8. Von Rad, *Genesis,* p. 60.

Sider and Stephen Mott put it, "Just, responsible creation of wealth is one important way persons obey and honor the Creator."[9] The use of the world's resources and the development of the world's potential for the maintenance of life and culture is an explicit desire of God. Humans are asked to do more than catch the fruit that falls from the trees; they are also asked to continue the creative work that God began.[10] The other term, sometimes translated as "guarding" or "keeping," is derived from the Hebrew word *shamar*. Humans are to be the guardians of creation, protecting and watching over it. *Shamar* is used in later sections of Scripture that enjoin Israel to observe proper worship.[11]

This brief picture of human beings in Scripture also shows that humans are relational: together we share in God's image. The image of God is made up of the basic human community — male and female. The text says that God made "them" in his image, not one image-bearer who then shared that image with the other. Like our creator, we are also capable and creative. We are commissioned to cultivate and care for creation as God's official earthly representatives.

Later, after the Flood narrative, God explicitly gives humans the option of providing for their nourishment by eating animal flesh.[12]

> Fear and dread of you will come on all the animals on earth, on all the birds of the air, on everything that moves on the ground and on all fish in the sea; they are made subject to you. Every creature that lives and moves will be food for you; I give them all to you, as I have given you every green plant. (Gen. 9:2-3)

God clearly intended to provide for his creatures, chief among them humankind. He prepared the earth in such a way that it would provide for

---

9. Stephen Mott and Ronald Sider, "Economic Justice: A Biblical Paradigm," in *Toward a Just and Caring Society,* ed. David P. Gushee (Grand Rapids: Baker, 1999), p. 21.

10. For a theology that thoroughly works out this relationship between creation and culture from a Reformed perspective, see Henry Van Til, *A Calvinistic Concept of Culture* (Grand Rapids: Baker, 1999).

11. For example, the command to keep the Sabbath day holy (Exod. 20:8) uses this term.

12. Matthew Scully has recently pointed out that human dominion over animals is excessively cruel in modern meat-processing plants. He argues that killing animals unnecessarily or killing them with unnecessary cruelty is immoral (Scully, *Dominion* [New York: St. Martin's Press, 2002]).

them, and he created humans with the creativity and power they would need to use the earth for their own provision.

II. The Poor in Scripture

The Hebrew words used are: *anawim* (poor, humble, oppressed); *dal* (weak, poor); *rash* (poor, needy); *ebyon* (in want, needy); and *misken* (dependent, socially inferior). All of these words treat various aspects of a similar concept, and they are often used interchangeably (cf., e.g., Ps. 82:3f.).[13] The poor were often seen as the oppressed as well. In some biblical literature (e.g., Ps. 14:6-7; Isa. 3:15; 14:32), the poor are even identified as the people of God, since it is only God who can vindicate them.

In the Septuagint and the New Testament, the Greek words used for the poor are *praus, penas,* and *ptochos.*[14] Outside the Psalms, *praus* is never used; instead, one finds *tapenoi* and *ptoxoi.*[15] According to David Seccombe, these terms for the poor are also used at various places in Scripture to refer to those who are:

1. The pious
2. The needy
3. The nation of Israel
4. People of the land (who don't practice the law, non-Pharisees)
5. Those who have left all for Christ
6. Those who have a disposition to hear the gospel
7. Heirs of salvation

While the various terms for "poor" do take on these wider connotations, a baseline understanding of the terms certainly indicates that the poor are people who suffer lack. And justice in Israel required advocacy for such people. If, for example, a king would be a worthy representative of God himself, he would stand up for the poor (see, e.g., Ps. 72, Prov. 29:14). Josiah, for example, is characterized as a good king because he defended

13. David Holwerda, "Poor," in *International Standard Bible Encyclopedia,* ed. Geoffrey Bromiley (Grand Rapids: Eerdmans, 1986), vol. 3, p. 905.

14. David Peter Seccombe, "Possessions and the Poor in Luke-Acts," *Studien zum Neuen Testament und Seiner Umwelt* 7, no. 5 (1982): 1.

15. Seccombe, "Possessions," p. 2.

the poor (Jer. 22:16). David, the model for Israel's later kings, responds to Nathan's story of a rich man who robs the poor man of his only sheep with absolute fury, condemning the culprit to death (before Nathan turns the tables on David himself, 2 Sam. 12:5-6). In the Wisdom Literature we hear that "God . . . deals out justice to the oppressed. The Lord feeds the hungry and sets the prisoner free" (Ps. 146:5-6). Again, "the righteous care about justice for the poor, but the wicked have no such concern" (Prov. 29:7).

The call to be an advocate for the poor is based on God's own special concern for them. Stephen Mott and Ronald Sider see this concern reflected in Scripture in four ways:

1. The Sovereign of history works to lift up the poor and oppressed (e.g., the Exodus).
2. Sometimes the Lord of history tears down rich and powerful people . . . because the rich sometimes get rich by oppressing the poor.
3. God identifies with the poor so strongly that caring for them is almost like helping God (Prov. 19:17).
4. God commands that his people share his special concern for the poor (e.g., Exod. 22:21-4; Deut. 15:13-15).[16]

Some tithes and offerings were also used for relief of the poor. Craig Blomberg summarizes what these tithes were, and how they were to be used:

> The tithe in Lev. 27:30-33 mandates that a tenth of all the produce of one's land and all of one's flocks should be given to the Lord. . . . In Deut. 14:22-29, a tithe of one's produce and flocks was to be eaten at the central sanctuary. Every third year, however, the tithes would go to the local storehouses so that they could be distributed not just to the Levites but also to other poor and marginalized people: "the aliens, the fatherless and the widows" (Deut. 14:29). Pro-rated annually, these added up to a 23.3% tithe.[17]

---

16. Mott and Sider, "Economic Justice," pp. 27-29.

17. Craig L. Blomberg, *Neither Poverty nor Riches: A Biblical Theology of Material Possessions* (Grand Rapids: Eerdmans, 1999), p. 46. Blomberg also cites J. G. McConville, "Law and Theology in Deuteronomy," *JSOT* (1984): 68-87, as he calculates the overall percentage of the Israelite tithe.

The most thoroughgoing legislation that attempted to restore the poor to their place in Israel was represented in the Sabbatical and Jubilee laws. In the Year of Jubilee (the fiftieth year) most but not all land in Israel was to revert to the heirs of those who received it in the initial distribution under Joshua.[18] This gives us a good picture of the strong restorative intent of the Jubilee command. The land that had been directly assigned by God to each tribe was to remain the possession of that tribe and clan.[19] Again, the basic premise of the Jubilee legislation is that God owns all property and wishes to allocate it in a way that meets the needs of his people.

In a famous passage, Isaiah condemns those who observed rites of worship such as fasting without also performing the corresponding deeds of justice and mercy. Rather than "bowing one's head and fasting in sackcloth and ashes," Isaiah asks:

> Is not this the fast I require?
> to loose the fetters of injustice,
> to untie the knots of the yoke,
> and set free those who are oppressed,
> tearing off every yoke?
> Is it not sharing your food with the hungry,
> taking the homeless poor into your house,
> clothing the naked when you meet them,
> and never evading a duty to your kinsfolk? (Isa. 58:6-7)

As the above passage illustrates, covenant law did not merely require that one do no harm to the neighbor; instead, it required positive, outgoing service to the poor as the practice of justice. Deuteronomy 15:7-11 also requires an open-handed disposition toward the poor: "The poor will always be with you in your land, and that is why I command you to be open-handed towards any of your countrymen there who are in poverty and need."[20]

---

18. For example, a house sold within a walled city is not redeemable by its original owner more than one year after the sale (Lev. 25:29-31).

19. The story of Naboth's vineyard (1 Kings 21:1-19) shows how this notion that land is an inherited gift from God conflicted with King Ahab's view, which was that property is a commodity.

20. For a contemporary commentary on the theological and ethical challenges of Deuteronomy, see J. Gary Millar, *Now Choose Life: Theology and Ethics in Deuteronomy* (Grand Rapids: Eerdmans, 1998).

In the New Testament, and especially the Gospel of Luke, poverty is tied to marginalization. Luke's constellation of terms for the marginalized includes: poor, captive, blind, oppressed (4:18); poor, hungry, mournful, persecuted (6:20); blind, lame, leper, deaf, dead, poor (7:22); poor, maimed, lame, blind (14:13); poor, maimed, blind, lame (14:21); poor, ulcerated, hungry (16:20, 22).[21] Luke contrasts the honor of the rich to the shame and disgrace of the poor. Thus the poor are not only needy physically, but also have social and emotional needs. Joel Green notes that the rich and the teachers of the law are accepted in the important social venues of the day — market, synagogue, and banquet hall — whereas the poor, as we can understand from Luke's many descriptors above, are unwelcome in all.[22] In Luke's Gospel, poverty consists in social marginalization — and the causes that bring it about.

In his book on Christian development work, Bryant Myers summarizes the views of the poor that he has found in Scripture as:

> The poor are those who are for various reasons unable to exercise their creative abilities as image bearers of God.
> The poor are sinners who make bad choices, or are lazy.
> The poor are Christ incarnate, whose suffering was taken up by Christ.
> The poor are oppressed but then delivered by God who sees them as His favorites.
> The poor are the lost, whom the Kingdom of God claims as its own.[23]

It seems clear that poverty is a many-sided thing in Scripture. At its center is certainly a lack of goods; but surrounding this center are oppression, impurity, incapacity, illness, suffering, and so on. It should be clear by now that the poor, as seen in Scripture, do not neatly fit into a modern economic category of poverty, for example, that of a household income of under $12,000 a year. Rather, the poor come in many shapes and sizes, and righteous people like the Samaritan see their needs and reach out to meet them.

21. Joel B. Green, "Good News to Whom? Jesus and the 'Poor' in the Gospel of Luke," in *Jesus of Nazareth,* ed. Max Turner (Grand Rapids: Eerdmans, 1994), p. 68.

22. Green, "Good News to Whom?," p. 67.

23. Bryant Myers, *Walking with the Poor* (Maryknoll, NY: Orbis, 1999), p. 60.

I close this section with a lovely passage from John Calvin, who speaks of the imagination we must exercise when we see even despicable people who need our aid.

> Scripture helps us [not to grow weary in well-doing] in the best way when it teaches that we are not to consider that men merit of themselves but to look upon the image of God in all men, to which we owe all honor and love. . . . Therefore, whatever man you meet who needs your aid, you have no reason to refuse to help him. Say, "He is a stranger"; but the Lord has given him a mark that ought to be familiar to you, by virtue of the fact that he forbids you to "despise your own flesh" [Isa. 58:7]. Say "He is contemptible and worthless"; but the Lord shows him to be one to whom he has deigned to give the beauty of his image. Say that you owe nothing for any service of his; but God, as it were, has put him in his own place in order that you may recognize toward him the many and great benefits with which God has bound you to himself. Say that he does not deserve even your least effort for his sake; but the image of God, which recommends him to you, is worthy of your giving yourself and all your possessions.[24]

III. Anthropology and Need in Mainstream Economics

In the biblical picture presented above, the human being is viewed as a creative and responsible person who images God in her work. A person is not more or less valuable on the basis of her wealth, but she shares in the image of God regardless of economic condition. The mainstream economic view of the human being assumes and even celebrates the fact that humans are creative and responsible. These virtues permit us to become designers, entrepreneurs, skilled laborers, and so forth. But viewed from the side of marketplace, the person is seen first and foremost as a consumer. That is, he has purchasing power that creative businesses can satisfy.

Considered from the perspective of mainstream economic theory, the human being is, first of all, an individual who is rational. He (the consumer) ranks and satisfies his purchase preferences via "instrumental rea-

---

24. John Calvin, *Institutes of the Christian Religion*, Book III, Chapter VII, ed. John T. McNeill, trans. Ford Lewis Battles (Philadelphia: Westminster Press, 1960), p. 696.

son."[25] This "instrumental" rationality is a means-ends style of reasoning in which each individual selects the most efficient means available in order to satisfy his preferences. This "economic way of thinking" assumes that "individuals take those actions they think will yield them the largest net advantage."[26] Economist Wade Hands describes the instrumental view of rational action this way: "[R]ationality is solely a property of the relation between means and ends — being rational simply involves choosing the most efficient means for achieving any given end — and has nothing to do with the nature of the end itself."[27] Mainstream economists take the consumer's purchase preferences as a given: the consumer uses instrumental reason to satisfy those preferences with maximum efficiency.

The individual is also assumed to possess considerable if not complete self-knowledge regarding her preferences. The marketplace then comes to learn of these preferences when she makes a purchase.[28] This view of the rational person who chooses on the grounds of efficiency is the basis for "Rational Choice Theory," which has become normative in mainstream economics.[29]

Rational Choice Theory implies a particular assumption about the nature of humans and their choices.[30] Contemporary political theorists James Caparaso and David Levine put it this way:

25. Economist Shaun Hargreaves Heap says: "The best known of these models [of rational action] embodies an instrumental conception of reason. Individuals on this account have certain objectives (like the satisfaction of preferences or desires or 'passions') that motivate them to act and it is the calculating capacity of instrumental reason which tells them which action will best serve those aims." Shaun Hargreaves Heap, "Rational Choice," in *Handbook of Economic Methodology,* ed. Davis, Hands, Maki (Northampton, MA: Edward Elgar, 1998), p. 400.

26. Paul Heyne, *The Economic Way of Thinking* (Chicago: Science Research Associates, 1987), p. 4.

27. D. Wade Hands, *Reflection without Rules* (Cambridge, UK: Cambridge University Press, 2001), p. 236.

28. James A. Caparaso and David P. Levine, *Theories of Political Economy* (Cambridge, UK: Cambridge University Press, 1992), p. 25.

29. See Hargreaves Heap, "Rational Choice."

30. Social economist John Davis has recently argued that theoretical economists have largely given up or at least avoided the search for a definition of human beings that could serve as a conceptual foundation for mainstream economics. Recognizing that definitions of the individual are value-laden and thus problematic from a scientific viewpoint, many economists have shifted instead to purely formal and mathematical work. That is, rather than attempting to say what economic good is, or how humans might find it, economists instead

The neo-classical [or mainstream economic] theories assume that acts of consumption of different goods all provide a common result: the satisfaction or utility of the consumer. Rational choice, interpreted in this way, requires a foundation in the utilitarian image of persons as agents seeking a single end — subjective satisfaction, utility, or happiness — through alternative means. While the measure of this satisfaction remains unique to each individual, so that we cannot compare or sum satisfaction experienced by different people, within each person the consumption of different goods yields a single result measured by a common unit (usually termed "utility").[31]

Each person thus has the same goal: the satisfaction of his utility. Each person satisfies his utility in the same way: via efficient rational choices. Nevertheless, each person satisfies only his specific preferences, and thus his level of satisfaction is unique. This makes it impossible to compare different individuals' degree of satisfaction.[32]

The reader should also note that it is *individual* wants or preferences that are the starting point for mainstream economic theorizing. Economist Paul Heyne confirms this: "The economic way of thinking definitely does make the individual the ultimate unit of explanation."[33] Society then becomes the composite of its individuals, and societal standards are the composite of their choices. In the mainstream economic picture, society is not viewed as an organism that is centered on certain beliefs, ethnic groups, or customs. Rather, it is seen as the aggregate of individuals with purchasing power who grant some rights to society for their mutual protection and good. All rights originate with, and serve the desires of, the individual — not the tribe, the nation, or humanity.

In summary, the mainstream economic view of the human being is of a rational individual who satisfies her preferences efficiently. She can mentally order her preferences and rationally choose the most effective

---

focus on developing sophisticated mathematical models that attempt to explain narrowly defined functions within the market. Instead of the "political economy" of Adam Smith, they have turned to game theory, calculus, etc. Their models operate without reference to, or perhaps even awareness of, the anthropological theory latent within them (Davis, "The Emperor's Clothes," *Journal of the History of Economic Thought* 24, no. 2 [2002]).

31. Caparaso and Levine, *Theories of Political Economy*, p. 80.

32. This is described as the "problem of interpersonal utility comparisons."

33. Heyne, *The Economic Way of Thinking*, p. 8.

way of satisfying those preferences. Let's briefly compare this picture of the person with Scripture's picture. The person in Scripture is created in relationship to God, to other persons, and to creation. Each person has the task of caring for the world and developing its potential in various ways. In mainstream economic theory, however, the human being is an individual who uses her reason to satisfy preferences as efficiently as possible. There is little connection to other persons or to the created world except inasmuch as they serve as means to satisfy the individual's preferences.

IV. The Poor in Mainstream Economics

Let's now consider mainstream economic theory's desired outcome for those individual preferences and actions. As I have observed above, the composite total of each individual's preferences is the desired state of affairs. This desired outcome for economic actions is called "Pareto optimality." Economic historian Ingrid Hahne Rima describes Pareto optimality in this way:

> Pareto optimality holds when we have a state in which there is no alternative distribution of commodities that can improve the position of anyone without making someone else worse off. Nor is there an alternative allocation of factors that can yield a larger output given the distribution of income and the supply of resources.[34]

This is not to say that everyone gets whatever he or she wants. Rather, it is the condition that occurs when no one is able to, or wishes to, make more trades. When desired trades have been completed, we have a Pareto optimal condition. This situation is assumed to be optimal since economists believe that people only trade when it is in their best interests to do so. In other words, people trade in order to make themselves better off. If people have made all the trades they wish to make, it follows that they will be as well off as possible under the circumstances.

By using the conceptual standard of Pareto optimality as a desired outcome, economists steer clear of moral judgments about the nature of the preferences themselves. For example, a free market will satisfy prefer-

34. I. H. Rima, *Development of Economic Analysis* (Homewood, IL: R. D. Irwin, 1967), p. 360.

ences for hard liquor, pornography, and guns just as readily as it will satisfy preferences for bread, symphony tickets, and charitable contributions. Regardless of *which* preferences are actually fulfilled, Pareto optimality occurs when as many of them as possible are satisfied. While economists as individuals certainly may hold private opinions on the moral goodness of particular preferences, the moral standing of others' preferences do not enter into economic calculations. The preferences of the individual are taken as a given, and greater degrees of preference satisfaction are taken to be greater goods.

From this brief description, we see that phrases such as "basic human needs" or even terms such as "poverty" typically do not arise in mainstream economic discourse. Instead, terms such as "sub-optimal" describe what most of us recognize as poverty. Mainstream economic theory uses terms such as "preferences," "satisfaction," and "utility" when it describes the process by which humans choose material goods. When it addresses human need, it assesses it in monetary terms. Government authorities, not economists, set a monetary baseline for poverty; those below the established line are the poor. The economists may provide the data to the decision-makers, but the definition of poverty is seen as a normative one, left to policy-makers.

In this definition of poverty, the difference between Scripture and economic theory is also significant. Mainstream economists deal with market interactions: they measure market expenditures, and so forth. They do not make judgments about purchases that individuals make, nor about what constitutes poverty. Those decisions are left to policy-makers, who set the definition in monetary terms as a particular level of income. Scripture, on the other hand, is rich in its description of poverty. It describes the poor as not only those who lack physical things, but those who experience social alienation, uncleanness, spiritual and social oppression, illness, and so on.

V. Hernando de Soto

The anthropology derived from mainstream economic theory is assumed in most schools of economics today. Peruvian social theorist Hernando de Soto assumes that anthropology: in his work he does not propose a redefinition of rationality, preferences, or needs. However, he is deeply concerned about poverty in his native country, and he has proposed a partial solution for the alleviation of poverty and hunger there and in other developing nations.[35] He does not see a problem in the market itself; rather, he sees the problem in the fact that the poor cannot participate in the global marketplace. Via his proposal for the "capitalization of assets," he hopes to enable the poor to participate in the market so that they can provide for their own basic needs.

De Soto notes that previous attempts to introduce capitalism in the Third World have met with disappointing results. Various countries in Latin America, for example, have tried to adopt capitalism at least four times since their independence from Spain (*Mystery*, p. 3). The problem, according to de Soto, cannot be explained by lack of talent or initiative, nor on the basis of faulty religious underpinnings that do not create the necessary "spirit of capitalism." Instead, he says:

> The major stumbling block that keeps the rest of the world from benefiting from capitalism is its inability to produce capital. Capital is the force that raises the productivity of labor and creates the wealth of nations. It is the lifeblood of the capitalist system, the foundation of progress, and the one thing that the poor countries of the world cannot seem to produce for themselves, no matter how eagerly their people engage in all the other activities that characterize a capitalist economy. (*Mystery*, p. 5)

De Soto believes that, whereas even the poorest people have *some* assets, the problem remains that those assets are not convertible into "capital." And an asset is not the same as capital: capital is an asset with legal and economic status. An asset that is not capital is not fungible until it is legally registered. Thus it cannot serve as collateral or be exchanged in market transactions. This literal failure to capitalize, de Soto argues, is the source of much of Latin America's poverty.

In contrast, the West injects legal and economic life into its physical assets, making them into capital, which in turn permits them to generate further capital. Each physical asset has a parallel life as capital, which is legally recognized and documented. "This explains why people who have adopted

---

35. Hernando de Soto, *The Mystery of Capital: Why Capitalism Triumphs in the West and Fails Everywhere Else* (New York: Basic Books, 2000); see also his earlier work, *The Other Path: The Invisible Revolution in the Third World* (New York: Harper and Row, 1989).

every other Western invention, from the paper clip to the nuclear reactor, have not been able to produce sufficient capital to make their domestic capitalism work" (*Mystery*, p. 7). This is the crux of the problem: only in the West are visible assets converted into invisible conveyors of capital.

Why is this capital "missing" from Third World countries? De Soto gives five reasons.

1. Developing nations are missing important information regarding who actually owns properties (pp. 15-38).
2. Physical things have parallel lives as capital/assets in the West, but in undeveloped nations they do not, as they are not titled or recorded (pp. 39-68).[36]
3. The political systems in undeveloped nations have not kept up. Underground or unofficial markets account for as much as half the production in many nations, and bribes often take the place of trade (pp. 69-104).
4. The laws of property ownership have not adapted to the reality of who actually possesses things (pp. 105-52).[37]
5. The legal system inhibits attempts by the poor to capitalize properties they have accumulated such as long-held squatters dwellings, defending traditional landholdings instead (pp. 153-206).

In light of all this, de Soto believes that, while many of the poor in Latin America have some resources, these uncapitalized resources are of no value in the market. According to de Soto, however, some steps can be taken to prepare for a market economy. They include the need to:

1. Document the actual economic situation and potential of the poor.
2. Recognize that all people are capable of saving.
3. Recognize that what the poor are missing are the legally integrated property systems that can convert their work and savings into capital.
4. Recognize that the poor are not the problem but the solution. They can produce, and they are working, but they are not part of the formal system (pp. 207-28).

36. For example, in the West, one's house is not only a place to live, but also a legal asset that can be used as capital.
37. In the U.S. this legal technique was known as "pre-emption."

Until these changes are made, the poor will not gain by any global expansion of the market. Proponents of globalization falsely assume that these poor populations are actually integrated into the legitimate economy, and will thus profit from trade. In fact, however, they have little or no access to legal markets, living as they do within the underground or black market. As a result, they are untouched by expansions of the legal market. Capital remains concentrated in the hands of the few who can access formally titled property. Therefore, "[i]t makes no sense continuing to call for open economies without facing the fact that the economic reforms underway open the doors only for small and globalized elites and leave out most of humanity" (p. 227).

De Soto raises interesting and important issues. I have lived in the Third World and can agree that much of what de Soto says makes great sense. The gross inefficiencies of governments, numerous silly regulations, and "off the books" accounting methods are notorious. De Soto has put his finger on a real problem, and the last quote shows that he clearly recognizes that international trade as currently practiced is not the solution. Changes in the legal/social structure must occur in many nations before international trade can have a positive effect on reducing poverty.

If de Soto's program were enacted in many underdeveloped nations, might it overcome problems in meeting human needs? De Soto realizes that an expanding market will not necessarily result in more well-being for all (p. 136, point I, 1), because small and poor communities do not participate in the global economy. Instead, movement of capital transcends national borders among those whom de Soto calls the "globalized elites," leaving those without goods to exchange outside the system altogether. De Soto's plea to capitalize the property of the poor as a response to this problem provides some hope. If people in developing nations *do* in fact have property to exchange, they might be able to participate in the market if their legal rights to this property were formalized. If de Soto's statistics are correct, this formalization would provide a tremendous boost in available capital in the Two-Thirds World, and thus potentially reduce poverty. Enactment of de Soto's plan would then help many who have unrecognized assets become a part of local and world markets.

At the same time, of course, it would subject these people to the risks inherent in the marketplace. As an example of risks that arise when some goods are privatized, consider water rights. In 1999 the Bolivian government sold the water system of its third largest city, Cochabamba, to a multinational consortium. This private company immediately asserted its property rights over the water, and it raised prices so that many residents could not afford both food and water. Protests and confrontations occurred until the government relented and cancelled the contract for privatization. The exclusive nature of property rights can be a double-edged sword.[38]

De Soto's proposal to formalize/capitalize the underground economies of the Two-Thirds World may help alleviate this one important practical problem involved in the expansion of the market, and as such it is most welcome.[39] Nevertheless, DeSoto's solution to poverty does address only one factor: the need for the poor to capitalize resources. His proposal thus does not address other social, emotional, spiritual, or political causes of poverty. His proposal also continues to use the narrowly focused view of humans and human need derived from mainstream theory. Instead of the biblical view of poverty as a many-faceted condition, de Soto sees poverty as low income, and thus the capitalization of property as its solution.

VI. Gary Becker

As I have noted above, mainstream economic theory takes an individual's ordered preferences and uses them as the basic "given" in economic decision-making. Purchasing decisions are then assumed to reflect the most rational pursuit of these ordered preferences. In short, preferences are revealed by purchases. For Becker, this approach to preferences is problematic. "The weakness," he says, "in the received theory of choice (preferences), then, is the extent to which it relies on differences in tastes to ex-

---

38. Reported in the *New York Times,* April 23, 2001, section A5, as part of an advertisement for the "Goldman Environmental Prize."

39. A recent report in the *New York Times* suggests that de Soto's proposal may provide a pleasant unintended consequence: when properties were titled, squatters who previously felt that someone always needed to stay home and protect the property now felt themselves at liberty to go out and seek employment. However, the report noted that, as of its writing, few families have been able to use their newly titled properties as collateral. Alan B. Kreuger, "A Study looks at squatters and land titles in Peru," *New York Times,* C2, Thursday, January 9, 2003. The article is based on the doctoral dissertation of Erica Field, which can be found at www.irs.princeton.edu.

plain behavior, when it can neither explain how tastes are formed nor predict their effects."[40] The circularity of this position is clear: preferences are observed through purchasing behavior, and purchasing behavior reveals preferences. Therefore, preferences are of little use as predictors or descriptors of economic behavior.

Becker also notes that "basic needs" have little real applicability in modern economies. While it may hold true that people in very poor countries must first satisfy their basic needs, Becker says, "it should be obvious that basic needs for food, shelter, and rest have little to do with the average person's choice of consumption and other activities in modern economies." The behavior of those who have satisfied their basic needs is better described, in Becker's judgment, on the basis of their past experiences, cultural interactions, and so on.[41] In light of these kinds of difficulties with the mainstream perspective, Becker argues that our preferences, including what we consider basic needs, are in fact "stable," or unchanging. They are stable since they include not only immediate purchase choices but also past experiences and social influences.

Rather than viewing the individual as one who makes instant choices based on changing preferences, Becker views the person as a business that attempts to increase its capital. Like a business, consumers make choices on the basis of their ability to increase future capital. All people have the same set of stable lifelong preferences. Differences in each person's efficiency, social conditions, and initial endowments explain the variety of actual choices consumers make.

According to Becker, all behavior can be explained via this business model. For example, if you get an advanced academic degree, it will likely contribute to your ability to earn more income. Or, as a parent you may influence your children in such a way that their own ability to earn income increases. "They [parents] may try to protect themselves against ill health, unemployment, and other hazards of old age by instilling in their children a willingness to help out if that becomes necessary."[42] For Becker, even religious altruism may be understood in this way. While altruism is sometimes seen as the reason for church attendance, the attendees do in fact re-

40. Gary Becker, *The Economic Approach to Human Behavior* (Chicago: University of Chicago Press, 1976), p. 51.

41. Gary Becker, "Preferences and Values," in *Accounting for Tastes* (Cambridge, MA: Harvard University Press, 1996), p. 3.

42. Becker, "The Economic Way of Looking at Life," in *Accounting for Tastes*, p. 153.

ceive long-term benefits from their churches: they find friends, they are comforted during times of family deaths, and so on. In addition, church attendance has been shown to have a strong relationship to socially responsible behavior. And socially responsible behavior is particularly beneficial to the upper classes, since it provides the necessary social and economic stability they desire. Thus, well-to-do individuals often give large sums of money to churches, and the churches, in turn, establish norms and values that benefit the well-to-do in the long term.[43] Therefore, charity is actually a long-term investment.

Becker does not directly address the question of what poverty is in his explanation of human behavior, but Alexander Rosenberg has fleshed out the significance of Becker's proposal on this issue.[44] Rosenberg says: "I shall argue that these 'stable preferences' need to be interpreted as human needs, if they are to do the work Becker wants them to do."[45] Following Becker, Rosenberg argues that all humans are known to have the same basic and stable set of preferences: shelter, nutrition, warmth, amusement, and so forth.[46] Unlike the mainstream economic theory of "tastes," or preferences, these "stable" preferences are comparable among people, thus eliminating the problem of interpersonal utility comparisons. These basic and stable preferences must, in Rosenberg's view, be thought of as *needs* rather than preferences. Rosenberg says: "To implement the new theory beyond the limits of the conventional one, we shall have to identify a fairly large, variegated, but manageable number of universally desired household commodities. Their amounts must be measurable and independent of one another in their effects on utility" (p. 58). Rosenberg believes this may permit us to overcome the problem of the incompatibility of personal utility comparisons, and enable us to make normative decisions regarding the distribution of some goods.

43. Becker, "Norms and the Formation of Preferences," in *Accounting for Tastes*, p. 227.

44. Alexander Rosenberg, "Prospects for the Elimination of Tastes from Economics and Ethics," in *Ethics and Economics*, ed. Ellen Frankel Paul, Fred D. Miller, Jr., and Jeffrey Paul (Oxford: Basil Blackwell, 1985).

45. Rosenberg, "Prospects for the Elimination," p. 50.

46. The list is in Rosenberg, "Prospects for the Elimination," p. 63. He earlier follows Hobbes's example and uses "safety, gain, and reputation." Becker uses the phrase "basic pleasures" (Rosenberg, p. 56).

Thus, with respect to some household commodities like nutrition, we can transcend the limits of Pareto-optimality because we can make specific interpersonal comparisons of the attainment of biologically specified needs, instead of psychologically indeterminate satisfactions. Other goals and ends of individuals we may wish to leave unadjudicated beyond the requirement that satisfying them pass the Pareto test. (p. 63)

In summary, Becker attempts to solve the problem of "preferences" in market economies. He notes that basic needs for food, shelter, and so forth have little to do with the purchases most people make in advanced economies. He proposes that "stable preferences" exist and are common among all people. These stable preferences are shaped by our past behaviors and social influences. Therefore, people do not make market choices on the basis of constantly changing preferences but on the basis of their long-term desire to increase their future capital.

How does this view of "stable preferences" relate to the scriptural picture? First, let us note that the economic person for Becker is still the rational individual who seeks to satisfy his preferences; it just happens that some of his preferences are held in common with all other people. For Becker, needs may no longer be just some among many preferences that different people hold, as they are in mainstream theory. But Becker's proposal seems to suggest two different views of human nature: one that addresses people in advanced countries with preferences that are really secondary wants, and another that addresses people in poor nations with real needs. Or perhaps Becker's position may indicate two economic theories and systems, one that works in advanced market economies where people have satisfied their stable preferences, and another that works in poor nations in which stable preferences are not met. It does not seem that Becker has successfully distinguished among wants, needs, and preferences. Other problems also arise. If, for example, stable preferences are equal to basic human needs, who will determine which of our preferences are stable (and how will they do so)? The market itself will not do so.

In addition to these problems of economic definitions, Becker's proposal, like its mainstream protagonist, begins and ends with an individual and his or her ordered preferences. It does not address our incorporation into community with others and creation; and it does not treat poverty as marginalization in its various forms. Overall, I doubt that Becker's proposal regarding "stable preferences" helps us escape the problems of distinguishing among needs and wants, or of understanding and comparing what poverty is across cultures.

VI. Amartya Sen

Like de Soto, Nobel laureate Amartya Sen was raised in the Two-Thirds World. But unlike de Soto, he has thoroughly critiqued the underlying premises of mainstream economics.[47] He challenges the limitations of the mainstream view of well-being based on the satisfaction of an individual's preferences, as well as the belief that societal good equals the aggregate of individual goods, noting that even conditions of Pareto optimality allow great misery for many. He says: "If the utility of the deprived cannot be raised without cutting into the utility of the rich, the situation can be Pareto optimal but truly awful."[48] These problems cause Sen to propose another standard for measuring economic success: the provision of "basic capabilities." By basic capabilities Sen means "the ability to do valuable acts or reach valuable states of being."[49] Sen's focus is the capability of humans to function freely. A person is an agent, and the agent must be able to act. Sen puts it this way: "This 'agency aspect' takes a wider view of the person [than merely 'well-being"], including valuing the various things he or she would want to see happen, and the ability to form such objectives and to have them realized."[50] I believe, and will show, that this "agency aspect" also brings us closer to the biblical portrayal of human nature and human need.

Sen proposes that the standard by which economic systems be judged is their success in providing humans with the capability of achieving crucial "functionings."[51] These functionings may include basic physical things, such as being nourished and sheltered, breathing clean air, and so on; but they may also include more abstract notions, such as possessing

47. See, e.g., Amartya Sen, "Rational Fools: A Critique of the Behavioural Foundations of Economic Theory," *Philosophy and Public Affairs* 6 (1977): 317-44.
48. Sen, "The Moral Standing of the Market," in *Ethics and Economics*, p. 10.
49. Sen, "Capability and Well-Being," in *The Quality of Life*, ed. Martha Nussbaum and Amartya Sen (Oxford: Clarendon Press, 1997), p. 30.
50. Sen, *On Ethics and Economics* (Oxford: Basil Blackwell, 1987), p. 59.
51. Sen, "Capability and Well-Being," pp. 30-53.

self-respect and dignity, participating in the life of community, and being able to appear in public without shame.

Sen recognizes that an unrefined definition of functioning might lead to absurd conclusions. For example, a wealthy person may choose to fast for health or religious reasons at the same time that a poor person does not eat because she has no food. Both are functioning in the same way, but their capabilities are clearly very different: one fasts out of choice, the other is compelled to starve.[52] Therefore, the *capability* and decision-making power to achieve a particular functioning, rather than the particular function itself, is Sen's standard of judgment. Moreover, the capability of achieving functions does not require that all people have an absolute equality of goods. Rather, we can recognize differences based on cultural and personal diversity.

Douglas Hicks, who has used Sen's work extensively, addresses this question of equality, showing that equality does not mean that we must all have the same things. Hicks says: "Equality and difference is a false dichotomy; it is preferable to speak of basic equalities that enable genuine complex differences." He goes on to say that "equality of basic capability is a necessary condition for the expression of genuine differences."[53] In this way basic equality is not a leveler that makes all alike, but the basis that provides each person with the potential to develop as a distinct individual.

For Sen, then, poverty means not only that one has a low income (as in mainstream theory), but that a person cannot function in her community. A low income may be but one cause of her incapacity. On the other hand, someone could function well at one income level, while another would be destitute if he had to live at that same level of income. Factors such as pregnancy, the ability to work, or household roles may make it more difficult for women to convert a basic capability into a functioning than it is for men. Being able to "convert" a capability into a function is the issue that an income-based definition of poverty does not address. Sen says:

> The conversion of income into basic capabilities may vary greatly between individuals and also between different societies, so that the abil-

---

52. This example is from Sen, "Capability and Well-Being," p. 45.

53. Douglas Hicks, *Inequality and Christian Ethics* (Cambridge: Cambridge University Press, 2000), p. 35.

ity to reach minimally acceptable levels of basic capabilities can go with varying levels of minimally adequate incomes. The income-centred view of poverty, based on specifying an interpersonally invariant "poverty line" income, may be very misleading in the identification and evaluation of poverty.[54]

Sen also challenges the mainstream assumption that the satisfaction of an individual's preferences leads to personal well-being. Social factors, he suggests, must also play a part if people are to possess basic capabilities: "A person's ability to achieve various valuable functionings may be greatly enhanced by public action and policy. . . ."[55] Policies set in place by government may give us the freedom to choose a life, for example, without malaria or polluted water, or the freedom to receive a challenging education, equal opportunities in the labor market, and so on. These public and social goods then become part of an economic system dedicated to enabling people to function within that particular society, bringing about their well-being.

The reader can see in this brief presentation that Sen has moved away from mainstream economic theory. Mainstream economics seeks each individual's well-being, and defines that well-being as the satisfaction of personal, rationally ordered preferences. On the other hand, Sen seeks a person's capability to function as a human agent in a particular society, and he wants to provide the resources that make this possible. Mainstream economics sees the goal as a Pareto-optimal trading situation in which the poorest cannot be made better off if others are made worse off. Sen sees optimality as a situation in which all people have the capability to achieve basic functionings, and to perform as human agents within their particular community. For Sen, the question of whether a person has the ability to function as a human being is both a moral and an economic one. The issue of good or bad preferences is also of interest to Sen and his followers.

A further virtue of Sen's proposal is that it may be used to address gender-equity issues. Hicks shows how Sen's approach can be used to understand discrimination against women (especially in the Two-Thirds World).[56] Sen's approach recognizes that women may be hindered by discrimination in their abilities to function. Medical attention, educational

---

54. Sen, "Capability and Well-Being," p. 41.

55. Sen, "Capability and Well-Being," p. 44.

56. Douglas A. Hicks, "Gender, Discrimination and Capability," *Journal of Religious Ethics* 30, no. 1 (2002): 137-54.

opportunities, and even life itself are often denied to females, something a purely income-based definition of poverty will not necessarily note (Hicks, p. 142).

Christian ethicist Harlan Beckley also shows that Sen's approach may correct deficiencies in the common conception of "equal opportunity."[57] The political notion of equal opportunity is often contrasted with that of an "equality of results" (Beckley, p. 107). Beckley notes that an equality of opportunity may not, for various reasons, yield equal capability. He argues that Sen's approach can be successfully used in contemporary political, as well as theological, reflection on equality. He sees that Sen's capability approach will require more of society than merely the provision of equal opportunity. He believes that Sen's approach recognizes the human agent's freedom and responsibility, and that it is amenable to the Christian doctrines of love and grace for those who falter (Beckley, p. 108).

Given all of this, it seems that Amartya Sen's understanding of human nature and human need is closer to the Bible's understanding than what is found in mainstream theory, Hernando de Soto, or Becker. Sen's perspective is more relational and communal than individualistic: it allows us to challenge the legitimacy of an individual's preferences. It sees poverty in terms that are broader than simply having low income. Sen's perspective, it seems, is also open to the view of the poor as the marginalized, those whom society has rejected.

Who is our neighbor, and when is he or she in need? Mainstream economics, the dominant theory, responds to these questions only indirectly with its anthropological assumptions about preferences, utility and optimality, and so forth. It also makes assumptions that do not necessarily match the biblical picture of the needy neighbor. If we, as Christians, wish to address poverty, we need a better model of the human being and of needs. In my judgment, the capabilities perspective of Sen seems closer to the biblical picture than those derived from mainstream theory, and thus Sen's approach may provide us with a more realistic way of addressing the needs of our neighbors.

---

57. Harlan Beckley, "Capability as Opportunity: How Amartya Sen Revises Equal Opportunity," *Journal of Religious Ethics* 30, no. 1 (2002): 107-35.

CHAPTER 5

Economic Justice Requires More than the Kindness of Strangers

Rebecca Todd Peters

Every day of our lives we are forced to make dozens of moral decisions that impact the health and well-being of our neighbors, many of whom we do not know and *can never know.* This is true in my own actions as a consumer when I choose to purchase locally produced organic food rather than conventional products shipped in from Chile, Argentina, or even California; when I use cloth diapers on my infant rather than disposable diapers; or when I ride my bike to work rather than drive my car. This is true in my actions as a professor and scholar when I have my students submit their work electronically rather than print out reams of paper to hand in; when I design my classes in ways that prompt students to examine their own consumer habits and behaviors; when I edit my own work electronically rather than on hard copies. This is true in my actions as parent and a spouse when my husband and I choose to prepare dinner from fresh ingredients rather than processed and prepared foods; when I take my daughter to the farmer's market and help her build relationships with the people who grow our food; when I buy clothes for her from resale stores or sweat-free clothing brands and teach her why it is important to know where our clothes come from.

Every day we are called on to make seemingly insignificant decisions that are, in fact, morally significant. Each of our decisions is important because those decisions can build up our local economies, reduce our environmental footprint, and contribute to our own health and well-being in the process. Or they can build up the profit margins of corporations, create more waste and pollution in our world, and contribute to our participation in the problem of obesity in our country.

Having said that, however, I must add that the health and well-being of our world is not my *individual* responsibility. While my individual behavior is important, I cannot solve the problems of poverty, environmental degradation, and inequality in our world simply by the individual lifestyle choices I make. More importantly, as a privileged member of a First World country, I have the material resources to buy organic food, prepare healthy meals with my family, and buy sweat-shop-free clothing. Many working-class and working-poor people in the First World — and many more people in general in the developing world — do not have the privilege of making the choices I do. As a human community we must recognize the fact that economic justice requires more than individual behavioral change. As long as children born in the United States require eight to nine times more of the world's resources that do children born in India, Cambodia, Zimbabwe, and dozens of other countries around the world,[1] we must recognize that inequality is built into the structures of our society, including our economic structures. It is essential for us to recognize that the larger challenges that face us as a human community will require a concerted effort at systemic transformation. While the choices that each of us makes as individual consumers are important, we must examine our individual consumer behavior within the context of the global market economy in which it is exercised. Economic justice is, at its heart, an issue of systemic transformation that requires us to look more carefully at how we have theorized and structured our economies.

Traditional economic theory assumes that I will make the kinds of moral decisions identified earlier based solely on what is in my best interest, but many people today challenge this foundational principle of economics: that individuals function primarily as *homo economicus* ("economic man"), making decisions solely on the basis of how they maximize their own personal well-being. I have named just a few of the many decisions that I make on a daily basis, decisions that impact the lives of others and the health of our planet. Were I to make these decisions thinking only of myself and what is easiest or most convenient for me, it is quite possible that I would use disposable diapers, open a jar of Ragu for dinner, and buy my daughter's clothes at Wal-Mart, where they are the least expensive. Indeed, many people do opt for these choices on a daily basis. However, some

---

1. Ecological Footprint of Nations 2004, http://www.rprogress.org/newpubs/2004/footprintnations2004.pdf.

people are choosing to make different decisions that are based on different assumptions about relationships, transactions, and community — in short, decisions that are based on a different value system.

The issue of "values" has become a national debate in recent years. In this chapter I want to raise the question of what we mean by the term "values" when it comes to our economic behavior and our economic systems. The question is more complex than simply what values impact our individual decision-making. Traditional economic theory holds that economics is a "science" and thus is "value-free." This position allows economists and businesspeople to make decisions that they claim are simply "rational" and "efficient" from a practical viewpoint that they claim exists outside of values and moral concerns. It is my observation that economic models and theories are human creations based on assumptions and priorities that do reflect particular moral concerns and agendas and, as such, they do exhibit and support particular, often unacknowledged, value systems.

I will argue that it is important to incorporate values in descriptive and normative economic models because this allows for the creation of an economic system that self-consciously acknowledges its moral framework. It also allows for the creation of economic models that balance profit with social accountability — or economic justice, if you will. My argument begins by examining the ways in which Adam Smith's work on economy, which modern economic theorists take as a basis for their assumptions, was rooted in a well-developed set of moral-philosophical ideas. We will see that, by abstracting Smith's economic theory from his moral framework, modern economists change the meaning of his work in ways that have important negative consequences in application. From there we will move to examine how these abstractions translate into negative practical outcomes by using the example of Robert McNamara, specifically his actions during his time as president of the World Bank. Based on this analysis of the current state of economics, I will argue for a greater intentionality in determining the values that will influence our economic models and behaviors as a human community, rather than simply focusing on what our values are as individual economic actors.[2] Like Janet Parker's chapter later in this volume, my chapter recognizes the multiplicity of opportunities for ordering economic behavior and activity and argues for

---

2. I am indebted to Rob Austin and Bill Goettler, who provided substantive feedback on an early draft of this paper that helped me to focus and clarify my argument.

more intentional discussion about the moral frameworks of differing economic models and what vision of the good life they offer to the human community.[3]

Remembering Adam Smith

It is important, when we examine the deficiencies of neoclassical economic theory, to root economic ideas and theoretical models in their historical context. Neoclassical economic theory traces its own roots to two important aspects of Adam Smith's work: Smith's concept of the invisible hand and his description of human behavior. Over the past two hundred years, Smith's own understanding of these concepts has been eclipsed by later interpretations of his work. A misreading of these key Smithian concepts has led to the development of a reigning model of economics that considers itself to be both "scientific" and "value-free," two assessments that Smith himself would not have endorsed. This misreading of Smith is particularly important because the contemporary capitalist followers of neoclassical economic theory who understand their work to be scientific and value-free promote their theory not as a *theory*, but as a factual "description" of the way markets and capitalism work. This mystification of the ideology that undergirds neoclassical economics functions to alienate and marginalize nonspecialists (i.e., people who are not formally trained in economics) and to mask the very concrete values that guide this system. Let us examine Smith's understanding of anthropology and the invisible hand in an attempt to clarify for contemporary readers how Smith understood these concepts to relate to his economic thought.

Adam Smith was not an economist by profession; rather, he was a moral philosopher, and he wrote a volume of moral philosophy entitled *Theory of Moral Sentiments,* a work that is virtually unknown by many who praise Smith's economic work.[4] As a moral philosopher, Adam Smith

---

3. For a more detailed discussion of the moral worldviews of four competing theories of economic globalization, see Rebecca Todd Peters, *In Search of the Good Life: The Ethics of Globalization* (New York: Continuum, 2004).

4. Herman Daly and John Cobb, in their book *For the Common Good: Redirecting the Economy Toward Community, the Environment and a Sustainable Future* (Boston: Beacon Press, 1989), attribute this separation of Smith's economic work from his work on moral sentiments to the creation of academic disciplines, which viewed different subject matters as

can best be understood as a natural-law deist. His theory of moral sentiments is rooted firmly in two complementary tenets: that the natural
world, particularly humanity, is governed by a set of innate or intrinsic
principles (he calls them natural laws) and that there is a divine Being who
watches over and cares for the universe. A close look at *Wealth of Nations*
alongside *Theory of Moral Sentiments* illustrates that much of Smith's economic theory is based on particular understandings or assumptions about
how people live, work, and interact that he outlined in *Theory of Moral
Sentiments*. Smith's moral framework is an essential part of his economic
theory, and yet many economists and businesspeople have systematically
ignored it. In Smith's moral framework, certain principles of natural law
are foundational to understanding human behavior. The opening line of
Theory of Moral Sentiments introduces the most important of these principles for Smith — compassion — which he defines as a principle of humanity's nature. Compassion enables people to feel the miseries and joys
of others: it includes sympathy and empathy in Smith's thought and serves
as a foundation for human social interaction. As the core of Smith's moral
framework, compassion makes possible a relationship between people that
makes for a caring and connected community. It is because nature has provided humanity with compassion that we do not live our lives as isolated
individuals who are concerned only for our own self-interest.

Smith connects humanity's sense of ethical behavior, or learning to
distinguish right from wrong, with this principle of compassion or
"fellow-feeling." He argues that we learn to approve of or disapprove of
our own behavior by imagining our reaction to the same behavior if engaged in by someone else. Smith likens the assessment of our own moral
character or actions to our assessment of our appearance. When judging
our appearance, we look into a mirror and try to see ourselves as others
will see us. When we are judging our moral behavior, we try to imagine
how others see our behavior and whether or not they would empathize
with our situation and our action. In other words, our assessment of the
morality of our own behavior is determined by thinking about how other
people would judge it. Our moral judgment — what Smith refers to as our

---

separate and discrete modes of intellectual inquiry. This isolationism has prevented subsequent generations of scholars from understanding the comprehensive approach to scholarship that people like Adam Smith took. As Daly and Cobb point out, "The early economists
studied the economy as an aspect of the whole of social life" (p. 33).

"sense of duty" — is thus forged by our observation of what is accepted as prudent and what is labeled as aberrant by society. Within Smith's moral framework, these judgments are made by people who are exercising empathy or compassion in evaluating their neighbors' behavior.

> Our continual observations upon the conduct of others, insensibly lead us to form to ourselves certain general rules concerning what is fit and proper either to be done or to be avoided . . . the general rules of morality are formed . . . upon experience of what, in particular instances, our moral faculties, our natural sense of merit and propriety, approve or disapprove of.[5]

Adam Smith presented a model of human behavior in which people made economic decisions based on self-interest (the most common interpretation of Smith), but they did so within a moral context of obligations that included the family, community, and nation. Smith's descriptions of people's actions in the marketplace are rooted in his reflection on characteristic "moral sentiments" that inform their decision-making, which is the subject of *Theory of Moral Sentiments*.

A classic example of Smith's description of the rational economic individual is the butcher who provides his merchandise out of his own self-interest rather than as a benevolent act: that is, the butcher is *selling* his meat to make a profit; he is not giving it away. What many readers of Smith have forgotten is that Smith conceived of his rational individual as existing within a moral framework bound together by compassion.[6] Therefore, while the butcher's choice of profession might not be guided by the wants or needs of others (i.e., he becomes a butcher because he wants to or because he has an entry into the trade, not necessarily because the community wants him to become a butcher), his behavior within that profession will be based on the principle of compassion or "fellow-feeling" that he has for others. As he is understood within Smith's moral framework, the butcher is not likely to serve bad meat or to cheat his customers, not only because his individual self-interest dictates that he is likely to lose his cus-

5. Adam Smith, *Theory of Moral Sentiments* (1759), ed. D. D. Raphael and A. L. Macfie (Oxford: Oxford University Press, 1976; repr., Indianapolis: Liberty Fund, 1982), III.4.7-8.

6. Adam Smith, *An Inquiry into the Nature and Causes of the Wealth of Nations*, Vols. I and II (1775), ed. R. H. Campbell and A. S. Skinner (Oxford: Clarendon Press, 1979; repr., Indianapolis: Liberty Fund, 1981), I.ii.

tomers if he treats them poorly, but also because he recognizes through his empathetic/sympathetic faculties that he would not like bad meat or price cheating to happen to him.

In addition to compassion, nature endows humanity with mutual kindness, another essential element of society's moral framework that has implications for behavior within the economic realm (*Theory*, VI.ii.1.19). If people act in beneficent ways toward others, even if it is motivated by their own desire for happiness, these acts of mutual kindness will also be operative within the business world. Consequently, economic activity will be played out within a moral framework where people desire to act kindly toward others, even if it is prompted by their expectation of reciprocal behavior. Smith believed that natural law also assures that humanity is endowed with "an original desire to please, and an original aversion to offend his brethren" (*Theory*, III.ii.6). Natural law has endowed humanity, "not only with a desire of being approved of, but with a desire of being what ought to be approved of; or of being what he himself approves of in other men" (*Theory*, III.ii.7). By focusing on mutual kindness as necessary for happiness and on the desire to please and be approved of by others, Smith's moral framework is even more intricately woven together by the element of human relationship and interaction. Once again, we are reminded of the ways in which our butcher's desire for happiness and his sense of fellow-feeling for others are likely to impact the way he runs his business, the care he takes with his craft, and the way he interacts with his customers. While our butcher desires wealth, in Smith's world, he also desires to be loved and respected (*Theory*, III.iv.8).

In addition to the natural laws that are embedded in the universe, for Smith there exists a "divine Being," a great judge, a deity who interacts with humanity and creation and helps to maintain society's moral framework. This deity shows up in numerous places in *Theory of Moral Sentiments* as a caretaker and a judge of humanity. Smith says:

> The idea of that divine Being, whose benevolence and wisdom have, from all eternity, contrived and conducted the immense machine of the universe, so as at all times to produce the greatest possible quantity of happiness, is certainly of all the objects of human contemplation by far the most sublime . . . . The administration of the great system of the universe, however, the care of the universal happiness of all rational and sensible beings, is the business of God and not of man. (VI.ii.3.5-6)

Smith's deism is integrally connected to his moral framework of the world. The divine being is intimately involved in the life and work of the universe. Smith's references to an "invisible hand" clearly must be read in the context of his deism. In *Theory of Moral Sentiments*, Smith refers to an "invisible hand" that leads the rich to make an equitable distribution of the "necessaries of life," which he defines primarily as happiness (IV.i.10). When read in the context of Smith's deism, his reference to an "invisible hand" in *Theory of Moral Sentiments* and his reference to it in *Wealth of Nations* can be read as meaning a divine being who watches over not only humanity but also the economic realm (*Wealth*, IV.ii.9).

While Smith has relegated the "universal happiness of all rational and sensible beings" to the realm of God, he states very clearly that humanity's much humbler task is to care for our own happiness, and that of our friends, family, and country (*Theory*, VI.ii.3.6). Smith's description of happiness is decidedly Aristotelian in its emphasis on happiness as the good life, as the ability to live and act well in society. Smith believes that the real happiness of human life is to be found in "the consciousness of being beloved" (*Theory*, I.ii.5.1) and in the "ease of body and peace of mind" (*Theory*, IV.i.10) to which rich and poor alike have access. In *Theory of Moral Sentiments*, Smith says very clearly that the good life is marked by the joy, company, and the respect of friends and family and by a certain pleasure that comes from enjoying simple experiences, such as a good meal. He even sees aspects of the good life in the fact that "the beggar who suns himself by the side of the highway possesses that security which kings are fighting for."[7] Smith also says that, except for the case of exacting justice, people should refrain from harming others so as not to interfere with their happiness.[8]

---

7. Smith's class bias blinds him to the struggles and difficulties of a life of poverty. While it is honorable that he believes true happiness is not based on material possessions, his disconnection with the hardships of the life of the poor and their experience of material deprivation lends a hollow ring to his notions of equal access to happiness. It also provides Smith with a tendency toward a romanticization of poverty as exemplified in this description of the beggar (*Theory*, IV.i.10).

8. "Proper resentment for injustice attempted, or actually committed, is the only motive which, in the eyes of the impartial spectator, can justify our hurting or disturbing in any respect the happiness of our neighbour. To do so from any other motive is itself a violation of the laws of justice, which force ought to be employed either to restrain or to punish" (*Theory*, VI.ii.intro.2).

This way of conceptualizing happiness has profound implications for understanding *Wealth of Nations* and Smith's economic theory. Smith has defined the care of one's own happiness as an important aspect of life in *Theory of Moral Sentiments,* and he has defined happiness in relational and psychological terms. He has even explicitly declared that happiness is not defined by material possessions or social rank or status. In order to accurately understand Smith's own economic theory, we must read *Wealth of Nations* in this context. While that work focuses exclusively on the economic realm of life, it does not follow that the economic realm is the most important aspect of life; indeed, we have already seen that this is not true for Smith.

In *Wealth of Nations,* Smith describes the workings of markets and the way economic interactions take place within society. In that work Smith chose to root his economic theory in the principles of growth and productivity. These two principles necessarily put people in competition with each other, and *Wealth of Nations* describes that competition: between landowners, between mercantilists, between workers and landowners and mercantilists, and between countries. Smith's work was important because of its comprehensive and systematic approach to economics. He observed the growing capitalist world around him and synthesized it into a coherent theory of economic activity. What we must remember is that this work was accomplished by a moral philosopher who was also a natural law deist. Undergirding *Wealth of Nations* is an elaborate moral framework out of which people function in the economic realm. Therefore, while the individualism and self-interest that Smith so strongly articulates in *Wealth of Nations* as motivating the economic activity of all people is surely present, it is tempered by the principle of compassion that Smith defines as part of the natural law of the universe. In short, Smith's vision of the economic person is one of an individual who functions in and is responsible to society, a society that shares a moral framework of compassion and that is watched over by a benevolent deity.

Adam Smith's descriptions of economic behavior are reflective of two things: the moral sentiments that he argues guide individual behavior and the economic structures of eighteenth-century Europe. Smith believed that the power of our common moral sentiments would function to mediate against any ill treatment of our neighbors and countrymen and -women. The butcher lives in a community where he knows his customers and is known by them; the fact that he is in relationship with them beyond his economic transactions affects his behavior. If we understand human behavior in a holistic way, then we must acknowledge that many things, including relationships and moral sentiments, affect economic decisions. Some of the structures that Smith fought to break down were the hierarchical structures of society that had marked much of human history. Belief in the hard-working sensibilities of craftsmen and laborers who only needed access to avenues of trade prompted Smith and his cohorts to fight against the monopolistic power of the strict guild structures of their day.

Smith's observations in *Wealth of Nations* about human nature in eighteenth-century Scotland have been transformed into the foundational principles of the neoclassical economic theory that shape contemporary markets and global international business and development. As a moral philosopher who was deeply engaged in Enlightenment discourse and rhetoric, Smith applied the themes of rationality and natural law to the emerging "public" sphere that came to be known as "political economy." In so doing, he pioneered the development of contemporary notions of human economic behavior as rooted in rational self-interest. Very simply put, Smith observed that the self-interested economic decisions of individual actors (producers, consumers, and workers) worked together to create market mechanisms that proved to be the most efficient for society as a whole. While Smith characterized his observations of human behavior as "natural laws," they have been characterized within neoclassical economic theory as the "laws of the market," which function to establish a scientific basis for the efficacy of the theory itself. Smith's ideas about the primacy of economic growth as the single most important goal of the economy is the driving force behind the contemporary models of capitalism and development that dominate the global economy.

What Smith described in *Wealth of Nations* is a rational approach to economic theory that is based on a presumed set of behaviors that individuals will exhibit when placed in the situations he describes. This presumed set of behaviors, including compassion and duty, can also be understood as his moral framework, a framework that he developed and discussed in great detail in his earlier work, *Theory of Moral Sentiments*. The problem with the economic theorists who claim to have built on Smith's work is that many have in fact abstracted Smith's rational economic theory from the moral framework in which he had situated it. When the two are torn apart, neither part continues to function in the same way. To maintain the integrity of Smith's economic theory as he understood it, we must read the discussion of human self-interest in *Wealth of Nations* in the light of the moral framework he develops in *Theory of Moral Sentiments*. Those who abstract Smith's economic theory from his moral framework attempt to view economic behavior in a mechanistic, rational, and amoral way that is contrary to Smith's intention. In order to see how this abstraction of economic theory impacts economic decision-making, let us turn to a contemporary example of the neoclassical model in action in the workings of the World Bank and its former president, Robert S. McNamara.

McNamara's Moral Obligation and View of Economics

Robert Strange McNamara became president of the World Bank in April 1968 at the age of fifty-one. While previous World Bank presidents had come from the realms of business, law, and banking, McNamara was chosen for his managerial expertise, which he had honed as president of Ford Motor Company and as U.S. Secretary of Defense during the Vietnam War. He was a decisive leader and a man of action. At Ford he had modernized the automobile industry, and in Washington he had streamlined the Pentagon bureaucracy.[9] He had studied at Harvard Business School in an emerging field of studies that has alternatively been called "financial control," "management control," "statistical control," or "accounting control."[10] What McNamara had definitely learned at Harvard and had applied throughout his career was an emphasis on control.

He entered a World Bank that was in a deeply ambiguous position. Many borrower countries in the Two-Thirds World were sinking deeper and deeper into poverty while continuing to amass enormous debt burdens.[11] The Bank's donor countries were disillusioned with an idea of development that didn't seem to be working, and they were reducing their contributions to the Bank's coffers. The former president, James Woods,

9. Catherine Caufield, *Masters of Illusion: The World Bank and the Poverty of Nations* (New York: Henry Holt and Company, 1996), p. 96.

10. Deborah Shapley, *Promise and Power: The Life and Times of Robert McNamara* (Boston: Little, Brown, and Co., 1993), p. 21.

11. I will use the phrase "Two-Thirds World" instead of the more traditional but marginalizing phrase "Third World," recognizing that the overwhelming majority of the world's population lives there.

had even called for a reassessment of the World Bank's work and of the development process in general.[12]

When Robert McNamara came to the World Bank, he was deeply troubled by his experience of the Vietnam War (a war that he knew was unwinnable) and motivated to do something to help people. His awareness of the injustices associated with poverty had led him, as secretary of defense, to implement a program to help people from poverty-stricken backgrounds gain admittance to the military, even when they had flunked the military entrance exam. McNamara implemented this program because of his beliefs about the scourge of poverty:

> Poverty is a social and political paralysis that atrophies ambition and drains away hope. It saps the strength of nations . . . because it withers and weakens the human potential necessary to development.[13]

These words also typify McNamara's opinion of poverty during his tenure at the World Bank. In speaking of his vision for that institution, McNamara said: "Our ultimate goal is to help . . . create a political, social and economic environment in which individual men and women can more freely develop their own highest potential" (Caufield, p. 97). McNamara's presidency at the World Bank was marked by this deep personal compassion that he felt for the poor. He once observed:

> We have come to see our planet as "spaceship earth." But what we must not forget is that one-quarter of the passengers on that ship have luxurious first-class accommodations and the remaining three-quarters are traveling in steerage. That does not make for a happy ship. (Caufield, p. 105)

He was aware of his own privileged position as one of the "first-class" passengers, and he felt a moral obligation to help those in need. He brought these moral convictions to his leadership of the World Bank, and he worked to redefine its agenda as helping the poor and marginalized. His moral agenda for the World Bank was clear in a famous speech to its board of governors in Nairobi, Kenya, in 1973: "The whole of human history has recognized the principle — at least in the abstract — that the rich and the

12. Caufield, *Masters of Illusion*, pp. 95-96.
13. Shapley, *Promise and Power*, p. 384.

powerful have a moral obligation to assist the poor and the weak" (Shapley, p. 512). McNamara's biographer, Deborah Shapley, argues that McNamara believed that, once the industrialized nations were presented with the "facts" of how desperately low the levels of foreign aid were, they would respond with the same moral conviction that had characterized his response. He closed the Nairobi speech with these words:

> All the great religions teach the value of each human life. In a way that was never true in the past, we now have the power to create a decent life for all men and women. Should we not make the moral precept our guide to action? . . . You and I — and all of us in the international community — share that responsibility. (Shapley, p. 512)

McNamara spoke passionately about his experiences of meeting people "out in the field" whose lives had been changed by the World Bank and of how he knew that all people were linked together by our common humanity. He was unwavering about committing the World Bank to a moral agenda of compassion, empowerment, and growth. This attitude was typical of McNamara, a deeply religious and ethical man whose life was marked by an ongoing struggle to figure out how to do the right thing — at Ford, in Vietnam, and finally at the World Bank. He was explicit in his articulation of this moral agenda for the World Bank, repeatedly making it clear in speeches, meetings, and work with colleagues, that he intended to alleviate the poverty that was crushing millions of people's lives.

McNamara heeded his predecessor's words that there needed to be a reassessment of the World Bank and of development in general, and he resolutely offered a new vision for that institution's role in development. Not only did he offer a new vision, he also brought with him new ideas about the size and scope of the World Bank's role in the development community. Coming from the Department of Defense, McNamara was used to working with a budget of billions of dollars, not the millions that flowed through the World Bank. As Shapley put it, "McNamara knew he wanted a big Bank before he knew for certain what to do with it" (p. 471). Within his first week at the Bank, McNamara decided that it should be lending far more than it was and he instructed his senior managers to "create a list of every project the Bank would consider funding if money were no object" (Caufield, p. 98). McNamara's first five-year plan projected lending $11.6 billion, more money than had been lent in the entire first twenty years of the World Bank's existence (Caufield, p. 98). His plan for managing the World Bank emphasized growth and efficiency in a way that is wholly rational within a neoclassical model of development, namely, that growth leads to increased capital accumulation. He believed that this capital accumulation was the solution to poverty. McNamara believed that more money, dispersed more broadly, would ease the burden of poverty more rapidly.

Unfortunately, McNamara and the World Bank were not nearly as successful at eliminating poverty as he had hoped they would be. While McNamara's personal commitment to alleviating poverty is not in question, the adequacy of his reliance on neoclassical economic theory as the basis for his model of development is. McNamara wanted to help people raise themselves out of poverty, but he relied on capitalist economic models of growth that had "worked" to develop the First World without questioning whether or not "growth" was really what was needed. Because the neoclassical economic model has abstracted itself from the social relationships within which economic behavior takes place, its ability to effectively eliminate poverty is seriously compromised by its adherence to the capitalist values of growth and profit over alternative values such as education, democratic participation, and sustainability. A neoclassical system that values profit, efficiency, and growth as the primary indicators of well-being and success was unable to adequately respond to the needs of the poor in the Two-Thirds World. The poor, his targeted group, were often not even included in the development of projects that were funded by the World Bank.

A Comparison of Adam Smith and Robert McNamara

While Robert McNamara exhibits in some ways the very kind of "moral sentiments" that Adam Smith describes as guiding people's behavior in his *Theory of Moral Sentiments,* there is a distinct difference between the individual actions of McNamara as the president of the World Bank and the relational community in which Smith described the behavior of citizens in *Moral Sentiments* and *Wealth of Nations.* McNamara cared about the health, safety, and security of millions of the world's people in the abstract; his moral sentiments led him to work tirelessly toward alleviating poverty with the only means he knew — through promoting capitalist development that would "raise" people out of poverty. But McNamara expressed a rather peculiar disdain for actual people. Shapley tells the story of his first visit to western Pakistan, where McNamara was visiting a remote dam site. "During the ride, he was subjected to hours of monologue by one of his hosts. Afterward, he instructed his staff to never again put him in a position where he could not control his time" (Shapley, p. 528). This effectively meant that his extensive travel schedule was characterized by "instantaneous arrivals, and rushed departures," which left many World Bank staffers and observers wondering whether his trips enabled him to understand the complexities of the real problems that people and their communities faced. His aloof and detached managerial style, which was often criticized by World Bank employees, represented his 1930s Harvard Business School training, where the prevailing wisdom was that the most efficient way to manage a business was to treat workers as "cogs" in a machine (Shapley, p. 608).

The main difference between these two men's usage of the concept of what Smith terms "moral sentiments" and McNamara terms "moral obligation" is found in their understanding of economics. Smith's concept of economics is inherently social and relational, which allows for some attention to the good of the society as a whole, and which assumes an ethical framework. McNamara's concept of economics is based on the assumption that economic activity and behavior is essentially value-free and that people make economic decisions based on individual self-interest.[14] When we look at Smith's understanding of anthropology and human behavior, we see a model of rational self-interest that is mediated by our context within a community that exercises a particular set of moral sentiments. Smith's model, which has been misread by utilitarians and others who would argue for an atomistic interpretation of individualism, can offer us a new way of thinking about economic behavior and "rationality" by challenging us to reconstruct our economic models in ways that retain the balanced tension between the individual and the community that was present in Smith's day.

---

14. Ironically, McNamara's individualistic approach to economic activity and moral behavior is rooted in the intellectual legacy of Adam Smith. Nevertheless, I argue in this chapter that Smith's emphasis on individualism has been misread and developed into a form of atomistic individualism that is not representative of Smith's own anthropological sentiments nor his understanding of economic behavior.

103

So Where Does This Leave Us?

While Smith may have misjudged the way human moral sentiments might function as a check on human avarice and greed, the accuracy of his anthropology is not nearly as important as examining his system from a meta-ethical perspective. Stepping back to get a longer view of Adam Smith's thought, we see a holistic and social approach to thinking about political economy and human behavior. Smith understood that the economic behavior of individual actors always and necessarily took place *within* the commonly held moral framework of a society; and he *assumed* that moral framework as he developed his ideas in *Wealth of Nations.* Subsequent theorists who have drawn on Smith's work by focusing solely on his description of self-love and self-interest, and have defined economic behavior and rationality based on that model, have fundamentally misunderstood Adam Smith. Furthermore, while these theories may accurately describe the economic behavior of some privileged (i.e., educated, wealthy, white, and male) actors,[15] they do not accurately describe the economic rationality and behavior of marginalized economic actors who often make economic decisions based on the well-being of others (children, the sick, the community, etc.) rather than on personal self-interest.[16]

Smith promoted growth and trade *within* a moral framework in which people lived in a community that served to place functional moral limits on individual behavior. He could not have envisioned the world we live in. The globalized economy of the twenty-first century means that people often have no knowledge of where the products they are purchasing came from, who produced them, or under what conditions. This mystification of production often allows for scandalously low prices that do not reflect either the cost to the environment or adequate compensation for the value-added labor that produced them. The further production becomes removed from consumption for any product, the less likely our

---

15. Recent studies have shown that the people who behave in a way that is most true to the abstract model of rational self-interest are students and professors in economics departments. See Robert H. Frank, Thomas Gilovich, and Dennis T. Ragan, "Does Studying Economics Inhibit Cooperation?" *The Journal of Economic Perspectives 7*, no. 2 (Spring 1993).

16. For a detailed examination of how the concept of "rational man" negatively impacted welfare reform policies in the United States, see Carol Robb, "Rational Man and Feminist Economics on Welfare Reform," in *Welfare Policy: Feminist Critiques,* (Cleveland: Pilgrim Press, 1999).

moral sentiments of compassion and empathy will be engaged. If we don't know how our consumer goods are being produced, and if consumers don't demand transparency and accountability, our moral sensibilities lie dormant as we revel in the "good deals" we have acquired at Wal-Mart and Sam's Club.

Another difference between Smith's world and ours is that economic development models that promote export-oriented growth and trade before a country is capable of feeding and caring for its own citizens is antithetical to Smith's vision of growth and trade. He advocated that nations should begin their development with domestic agriculture and then move on to domestic manufacturing for domestic consumption. Only after these basic needs were met would a country move on to engage in trade with any surplus goods.[17]

Our economic and social world is quite different from the world of Adam Smith. Technology has virtually eliminated many kinds of barriers that hampered international trade in the eighteenth century. Multiple modes of rapid transit have broken down many of the physical barriers that separated people and countries. What Smith assumed as self-evident regarding development and trade (that a country's economy would develop domestically and then progress to international trade) is no longer an assumption for most contemporary economists and businesspeople. While Smith's model may still be the most sustainable model in terms of caring for the planet and for the social well-being of people, many economists, environmentalists, and ethicists are now forced to develop sophisticated arguments to demonstrate why sustainability is an important value that should mediate against maximizing profit.

And herein lies the rub. While comparing a theoretician (Smith) and a practioner (McNamara) may seem like comparing apples and oranges, examining the actions of a leader in the field of business and international development offers us a lens to view the moral implications of the dominant economic theory on addressing the presenting problem of poverty. Through McNamara's words and deeds we can get a glimpse into the functional reality of the claim of neoclassical economic theorists that the contemporary discipline of economics has no allegiance to values. That it is, in fact, "value-free." Given the fact that economists — and their capitalist

---

17. Carol Johnston, *The Wealth or Health of Nations: Transforming Capitalism from Within* (Cleveland: Pilgrim Press, 1998), p. 14.

business protégés — argue that the maximization of profit is their sole concern, it is clear that economics does have a set of values. I would name the top three as profit, efficiency, and growth. To the extent that these three issues mediate and shape economic decisions and activity, they are functioning as "values." McNamara's desire for a "big Bank," his commitment to the belief that increased growth leads to capital accumulation, and his belief that capital accumulation is the solution to poverty are obvious expressions of his neoclassical commitment to profit, efficiency, and growth.

We have seen two approaches to the issue of values or moral sentiments. In one instance, Robert McNamara relied on a model of economic theory that did not recognize any of its economic decisions or behaviors as inherently value-laden activities. While McNamara felt personally obligated to work to alleviate poverty and attempted to do so through a capitalist managerial approach to the problem, the economic theory that undergirded his actions holds that the economic processes of quantification of success and prioritization of projects is value-free. In the other instance, Adam Smith articulated a theory of economic behavior that took place in the midst of a particular moral framework. In this instance, it was understood that while individuals made their own economic choices, they exercised them within a moral framework that would mediate their behavior. What is clear is that when it comes to addressing issues of social injustice such as the rampant poverty of the Two-Thirds World, we simply cannot rely on the moral obligation of an individual business leader like Robert McNamara. When we are able to establish the moral failings and biases of neoclassical economic theory, it becomes evident that what we need is systemic reform.

A Proposal for the Future

The failure is not McNamara's alone. Rather, it is a failure of our society to recognize that the economic model on which we rely is not a value-free system, but that it is one laden with values that favor profit and economic gain over other priorities — such as sustainability and economic justice. What we need is a new economic model that self-consciously understands the ways in which values are embedded in political economy, a model that is rooted in a moral framework of compassion and the elimination of poverty. We need an economic model that does not focus on growth and trade as its primary indicators of success, but a model that focuses on the health and well-being of workers and the environment, the reduction of infant mortality, starvation relief, healthcare delivery, the feeding of the most impoverished people, and the control of HIV/AIDS for all people, rich and poor. This new economic model need not eschew profit, or growth, or efficiency, but it should recognize the ways in which it values these goals. And it will balance them with other moral considerations, such as sustainability, justice, and the social well-being of people and communities.

Economic activity and the theory that undergirds it is a human creation that is intended to serve the needs of human societies. As a reflection of the actions of the human community in attending to the necessity of trade and economic transactions for human survival, economic activity is inherently an expression of moral behavior precisely because it is human behavior. From an ethical perspective that seeks to promote justice and human well-being, the human community can no longer continue to follow a model of economic theory that does not incorporate these values into its economic rationality. I do not wish to imply that markets and trade are causing the problems of social unrest and injustice that we see in the majority of the Two-Thirds World today. Markets are tools that are used by human communities to trade goods and services and, as such, are necessary. However, we do have a moral responsibility for the ways we structure markets and trade, and we must begin to consider what values are embedded in these structures. We need to rethink the moral frameworks within which our economic theory exists, and we must create economic models that incorporate justice *into* their rationality.

Remembering the work of Adam Smith helps us perceive how economic theory has been grounded in a solid moral framework in the past. The point is not to try to revive an eighteenth-century British worldview or morality, but to see how economics and economic behavior is rooted in particular human communities with particular moral values. There are at least two reasons why we, as the economic heirs to Adam Smith, need to incorporate values into new economic models. First, the moral framework that Smith assumed as background for his economic theory is not an accurate description of human behavior in the twenty-first century. Smith's model assumed that values such as compassion and duty were universally embraced and exercised within the economic sphere; in fact, his description of economic behavior is predicated on these values. Regardless of whether or not Smith's anthropology was universally applicable in his own day (or even if it was an accurate representation of eighteenth-century Britain), his economic theories presume a particular moral framework. As it becomes clear that the twenty-first-century global economy does not possess a shared moral framework, it becomes even more important that the values that shape our economic theory be explicitly acknowledged and mutually agreed on. Rather than simply accepting profit, efficiency, and growth as our ultimate values, we need to have rigorous public debate regarding the values that *should* guide our economic interactions, and we need to build economic theories that reflect the broader values of the human community.

Second, capitalism itself has changed a great deal from Smith's day. While Smith believed that the behavior of individual economic actors would be mediated by their close contact with one another (buyers and sellers and owners and workers all knew one another), this is no longer the case in the context of the twenty-first-century capitalism. The anonymity of the global marketplace requires an explicit integration of moral commitments and boundaries to mediate human behavior that might otherwise tend toward greed, avarice, and exploitation.

We need economic models that allow for us to take care of the planet and to attend to the social well-being of people — *as well as* allowing for profits to be made. Profit, in and of itself, is not the enemy. But we, as a world community, must engage in a deep critique of the moral accountability of corporations and the means by which profits are made in our society. Just as Adam Smith rooted his own economic theory within a complex moral framework, it is incumbent on us as ethicists, economists, businesspeople, laborers, and citizens to work together to create new economic theories and models of economic behavior that will allow for a more compassionate and just human existence.

CHAPTER 6

Free Markets and the Reign of God: Identifying Potential Conflicts

Jeff Van Duzer

Given that the fundamental philosophical assumptions that undergird a free market economy (e.g., individual decision-makers acting from self-interest without explicit regard for the welfare of weaker market participants) are not wholly consistent with Christian principles of ethics, one would expect Christians in business to experience many occasions when procompetitive behavior is at odds with kingdom values. In fact, however, many Christian businesswomen and -men report experiencing few such conflicts. In this chapter I explore, at a conceptual level, possible explanations of why so few conflicts are identified. Specifically, the chapter examines the possibility of market participants' insensitivity to conflicts that actually do exist, the possibility of overlapping market and kingdom values ("good ethics is good business"), and the possibility that anticompetitive ethical behavior can hide in market imperfections. I conclude the chapter with a discussion of whether the number of market-kingdom conflicts is likely to increase in the future, and, if so, whether there are possible strategies that could be pursued to minimize the incidence of such future conflicts.

Free-Market Principles and Christian Ethics

As Rebecca Todd Peters has argued in the preceding chapter, a society's determination to rely on the market system for the distribution of its goods and services is not a value-free decision. The decision to use such a system may represent a choice to promote efficiency at the expense of justice; it may amount to a choice for more aggregate growth and less equality in wealth distribution; and it may mean a choice to favor the individual over the collective. In any case, it is a decision that favors some values over others, and there is certainly no reason to assume, *ab initio*, that these favored values will line up in all cases with the values desired by God. Indeed, there is reason to suspect the opposite.

A competitive market model assumes that individual actors operate out of self-interest. As Adam Smith so famously suggested: "[I]t is not from the benevolence of the butcher, the brewer or the baker, that we expect our dinner, but from their regard to their own interest. We address ourselves not to their humanity but to their self-love, and never talk to them of our own necessities but of their advantage."[1] The model also assumes that decision-making will be made at an individual level, that the system will be value-neutral with respect to these individual choices, and that better or worse can be measured by the metric of "more" or "less."

It is also fundamentally premised on a quid pro quo arrangement: one gets out of the market only what one puts in or, more accurately, only what one offers to sell that others are willing to purchase. The ability to direct the market toward the production of certain goods and not others is proportional to the assets and other resources available to purchasers. The market is not a one-person, one-vote system; rather, it is a one-dollar, one-vote system. As such, the free market tends to aggravate inequalities rather than narrow the gap between rich and poor. "In its distribution of cooperatively produced goods and services, the market system serves the needs or wants of some people far more than others, at an extreme leaving many millions without . . . elementary requirements of the good life. . . ."[2]

Competitive markets are effective only if one is willing to embrace the notion of "creative destruction," which, for the sake of increasing wealth and efficiency, destroys industries, jobs, and, from time to time, people along the way. To put it another way, market changes are not always marked by gradual slopes but often by sudden breaks. While there are many government programs designed to soften the blow of market transitions, the market itself has no room for such comfort. Unless an individual has a good or service that the market wants to buy, the market will pass her by.

1. Adam Smith, *Wealth of Nations* (New York: The Modern Library, 2000), p. 15.
2. Charles Lindblom, *The Market System* (New Haven: Yale University Press, 2001), p. 164.

Obviously, in many respects these underlying premises of the free-market system are at odds with Christian ethics. The Christian ethic begins with the understanding that each human being has been created "in the image of God" and that, consequently, a certain dignity inheres in that individual. Therefore, each individual's value is established independent of a quid pro quo calculation: even those with nothing to sell are to be treated as children of God.

> All people have a right to participate in the economic life of society. Basic justice demands that people be assured a minimum level of participation in the economy. . . . As Pope John XXIII declared, "all people have a right to life, food, clothing, shelter, rest, medical care, education, and employment." This means that when people are without a chance to earn a living, and must go hungry and homeless, they are being denied basic rights.[3]

In contrast to a market system that depends on individualized decision-making, a Christian ethic calls people into community with each other. In contrast to a market system that is built on the assumption that each person acts in his or her self-interest, a Christian ethic calls on Christians to "love your neighbor as yourself." Whereas the market system affirms that more choices are better and that each individual choice is morally neutral, a Christian ethic directly challenges the "more is better" assumption, particularly when it is applied to the acquisition of material wealth, and denies that all choices are equal. For example, the market will respond to the consumer demand for pornography and, if freed from governmental interference, would produce it "efficiently." Proponents of the market system would argue that this is good; a Christian ethic would insist that it is not.

None of this should be particularly surprising, nor is it intended to suggest that, given the available alternatives, a market system isn't the best choice for society to use in allocating resources. It is simply that even the most vigorous proponents of the market system argue only that it enhances freedom and a particular form of efficiency. A free market, they claim, will maximize the ratio of valued outputs to valued inputs and will most efficiently allocate productive resources based on the asset-backed

---

3. National Conference of Catholic Bishops, *Economic Justice for All: Pastoral Letter on Catholic Social Teaching and the U.S. Economy* (Washington: United States Catholic Conference, 1986), paragraphs 15, 17.

desires of consumers without centralized control. No economist has ever claimed that an individual's strict obedience to the dictates of a free-market system will necessarily contribute to ushering in the reign of God. The invisible hand of Adam Smith is, simply put, not the hand of God, and one should expect from time to time that these hands will point in opposite directions. Even some of capitalism's biggest supporters within the church concede as much. For example, Michael Novak, a leading Catholic apologist for capitalism, notes that

> [c]apitalism itself is not even close to being the kingdom of God. . . . The presuppositions, ethos, moral habits, and way of life required for the smooth functioning of democratic and capitalist institutions are not a full expression of Christian or Jewish faith, and are indeed partially in conflict with the full transcendent demands of Christian and Jewish faith.[4]

In short, Christians in business should expect that their call to a Christian ethic will at times be at odds with what it will take to remain competitive in a marketplace operating on contrary underlying principles.

However, based on anecdotal evidence (and certainly worthy of a more systematic study), it appears that most Christians who are successful in business simply do not experience significant tensions between the ethics of the marketplace and the ethics of the gospel. Remarkably, many Christians in business find it difficult to identify even a single instance where their Christian convictions have caused them to act in a manner that was contrary to their businesses' financial interests. When presented with hypothetical situations that seem to crystallize such tensions, they will acknowledge the apparent conflict but then explain it away by referring to the time frame: "While there may be a short-term cost, in the long-term. . . ."

Insensitivity to Conflicts

How can we account for this lack of tension? There may be several possible explanations. For one thing, Christians active in business may simply fail to recognize conflicts that do exist. In her research on interactions between

---

4. Michael Novak, *The Catholic Ethic and the Spirit of Capitalism* (New York: The Free Press, 1993), pp. 227-28.

believers in business and church leaders, Laura Nash, a senior research fellow at Harvard Business School, identified what she referred to as "a disheartening pattern."[5] Christians in business engage in "a kind of dead-end thinking by posing limiting constraints on one's ability to entertain sustained attention to inherent conflicts in the foundational value of one's corporation and religion" (p. 59). Some of this insensitivity may be rooted in personality characteristics that typically characterize the businessperson. As Nash suggests, successful businesspeople are often optimistic pragmatists (pp. 139, 143, 190). They tend to be disinclined to reflect and ask questions in situations where such reflections aren't likely to lead to conclusions that can be readily implemented "on the ground" (pp. 141, 142). As a corollary, they have a tendency to find meaning in concrete factors within their control (pp. 191, 193), and they are less likely to see value in musing about systemic issues beyond their individual horizons.

The market tends to reward these characteristics. Pragmatists take action. Optimists persist in the face of great challenges. Those who focus on what they can change rather than musing on factors beyond their control stay committed to implementing strategies that can yield financial success. Jim Collins, in his best-selling book *Good to Great*, identifies a number of characteristics that seem to characterize companies with financial results that are far above average. According to his research, companies are more likely to excel if they confront the "brutal facts" about their situation (i.e., pragmatists) but at the same time retain unwavering faith in their capacity to overcome the challenges they face (i.e., optimists).[6] In addition, highly successful companies tend to take a complex world and simplify it (i.e., focus on factors within their control): "It doesn't matter how complex the world, [a great company] reduces all challenges and dilemmas to simple — indeed almost simplistic — hedgehog ideas. For a hedgehog, anything that does not somehow relate to the hedgehog idea holds no relevance" (p. 91).

Of course, these same factors make it likely that many in business will miss more high-level and more theoretical conflicts between the underlying precepts of Christianity and global capitalism. They are not conditioned to consider whether their efforts to get the best price from a sup-

---

5. Laura Nash and Scotty McLennan, *Church on Sunday, Work on Monday* (San Francisco: Jossey-Bass, 2001), p. 59.

6. Jim Collins, *Good to Great* (New York: HarperBusiness, 2001), pp. 65-89.

plier may indirectly support a sweatshop society somewhere else. They are unlikely to reflect on the fact that their paying several dollars an hour over the minimum wage may still not provide their employees with a living wage. They are neither trained nor rewarded for considering the potentially adverse impact of using more and more sophisticated technology on the social fabric and capital of their local communities. Many people in business conceive of sin as individual, concrete acts of disobedience, dishonesty, or unkindness. As long as one is respectful, kind, and honest in one's interactions with shareholders, employees, customers, and suppliers, one has done enough. Questions of systemic or corporate sin are more or less irrelevant theories best left to the theologians and the academy.

Social cognition theory provides another potential explanation of why Christians in business may tend to see so few fundamental conflicts. Dissonance theory has been discussed since the late 1950s: it posits that an inconsistency between one's behavior and one's beliefs causes an uncomfortable "arousal" that individuals will seek to reduce. As a result, people will tend to avoid "cognitions" that are inconsistent with their behavior.

> Consistency theorists in general have had much to say about selective perception as a function of consistency with prior attitudes. They posit that people seek out, notice, and interpret data in ways that reinforce their attitudes. Dissonance theory in particular predicts that people will avoid information that increases dissonance; that is, that people favor information consistent with their attitudes and behavior. . . . Thus, from the outset people are biased . . . to gather data that reinforce their beliefs.[7]

Christians in business regularly align their behavior with market forces. They are trained to do so, they are rewarded for doing it well, and they are severely punished when they fail to do so. Given that this is deeply entrenched behavior, it is not surprising that Christians in business should find it difficult to accept that this behavior may in some sense be violating their deeply held religious beliefs. Dissonance theory accurately predicts that they will tend to explain away any apparent inconsistencies (e.g., "while sometimes costly in the short term, virtuous behavior will always pay off in the long run").

7. Susan Fiske and Shelley Taylor, *Social Cognition* (New York: McGraw-Hill, 1991), pp. 468-71.

Finally, the ever-increasing speed of business itself could be contributing to this insensitivity. It is beyond dispute that, driven by the need for ever-greater efficiency in the face of global competition and enabled by increasingly sophisticated technology, the pace of business is rapidly accelerating. Voice mail, e-mail, pagers, cell phones, wireless PDA's, and countless other gadgets ensure that workers are constantly on call, blur the line between work and home, and create a demand for greater and greater emotional attentiveness to productivity. Mark Cuban, owner of the Dallas Mavericks professional basketball team, described his earlier business life in these terms: "You try to do as much as you can for as long as you can stay awake. What price do you have to pay to win? That price is the 'sprint.' You have to build your business faster than anyone else. The 'sprint' doesn't have a finish line. There's never a point where you can say, 'We've made it.'"[8] One of the consequences of all this speed is that, as more and more productivity is being crammed into each minute, some things are being pushed out — most notably, the opportunity for reflection.

> The lack of time is an unfortunate characteristic of today's Americans, and volumes have been written about how it is hurting our children and our families, but it is hurting our morality just as much. For if we decide that we do not have time to stop and think about right and wrong, then we do not have time to figure out right from wrong, which means that we do not have time to live according to our model of right and wrong, which means, simply put, that we do not have time for lives of integrity.[9]

Overlapping Values

In short, there are a number of reasons to suspect that more conflicts exist between the call of the gospel and the demands of the market than most Christians in business will recognize. Still, this is unlikely to be the whole story. We need to consider two other possible explanations of why Christians perceive so few conflicts between what it takes to be good in business and what it takes to be a good disciple. First, it is possible that in the con-

8. Robert Reich, *The Future of Success* (New York: Vintage Books, 2002), p. 123.
9. Stephen L. Carter, *(integrity)* (New York: Basic Books, 1996), p. 29.

text of economics and the marketplace, the gospel is not so countercultural after all; second, it is possible that the market is not quite as rigid and unforgiving as the foregoing discussion might suggest.

When asked about conflicting values, many businesspeople retreat to the "good ethics is good business" mantra. While this is clearly overstated as a universal rule — not all ethical decisions redound to financial success — it would not be recited so regularly if there were not many pieces of anecdotal evidence to support the general proposition. For example, honesty to customers does tend to build brand loyalty, which in turn helps build sales. A service orientation can positively differentiate one company from its competitors. Attention to the needs of one's employees does increase worker loyalty and reduce costly turnover. Adopting a corporate mission that points the business to some purpose beyond simply making more money for shareholders is more likely to capture the imagination of employees, excite their own personal sense of vocation, and thereby bring forth better ideas and better effort. Sensitivity to community values regularly does result in enhanced goodwill and political support for new ventures. In short, doing business "God's way" often seems to be not only ethically right but also strategically prudent.

Theologically, the existence of such overlapping values is probably best described by referring to the doctrine of common grace. The biblical creation accounts describe how God created a good earth and richly provided for it. Human beings were invited to participate with God in the stewardship of this created order. In particular, men and women were called to cultivate and guard the Garden, to work it in a manner that would cause it to be fruitful and flourish. Before the Fall, this work was to be easy, creative, and a joyous expression of at least a portion of humanity's identity. Set in the context of God's shalom, there was a complete alignment between the worship of God, care for the environment, and the cultivation of loving relationships on the one hand, and the fruitful multiplication of God's rich provisions on the other.

However, this harmonious arrangement was disrupted by the unwillingness of humans to accept limits and their choice to become gods unto themselves, which was expressed (at least mythically) through a single act of disobedience. The third chapter of Genesis records the results: the relationship between human beings and God is disrupted; the relationship between men and women is disrupted; the relationship between human beings and the environment is disrupted; and, most importantly for our present purposes, the experience of work is distorted. Rather than a joyous expression of God-given creativity, work becomes, in the words of Dorothy Sayers, "irksome."[10]

> Cursed is the ground because of you; in toil you shall eat of it all the days of your life; thorns and thistles it shall bring forth to you; and you shall eat the plants of the field. In the sweat of your face you shall eat bread. . . . (Gen. 3:17-19, RSV)

In effect, then, conflicts between the market forces that drive today's global production of goods and services and God's kingdom values can be traced back to this rupture in God's original harmonious design. But the extent of the disruption is an ongoing subject of theological debate. Some argue that the *imago dei* in which men and women were first created was severely distorted. This group ("Radical Fall") holds that human beings are nearly incapable of discerning God's true design in the created order (at least apart from Scripture and the work of the Spirit). For others, however, the Fall produced a somewhat less radical result. While they concede that the *imago dei* has been marred, they emphasize that much of God's original design remains apparent both within and around us and can be discovered through a reflective use of our rational faculties. For them, God's harmonious principles for the production of goods coincident with human flourishing as initially established in the Garden of Eden were not essentially undone by the Fall; rather, they were "merely" distorted.

For our purposes, it is sufficient to suggest that there is at least a possibility that some aspects of God's initially intended perfect design remain embedded in the fabric of the world we live in today. According to Scripture, full redemption is found only in Jesus Christ.

> Outside of redemption, however, the devastating effects of sin in creation are also restrained and counteracted. God does not allow man's disobedience to turn his creation into utter chaos. Instead, he maintains his creation in the face of all the forces of destruction. . . .
>
> The theological tradition offers another way of understanding the restraint of creation. Some theologians have called the curbing of sin and its effects God's "Common Grace." Through God's goodness to all

10. Dorothy Sayers, "Why Work?" in *Creed or Chaos?* (New York: Harcourt, Brace, 1949).

men and women, believers and unbelievers alike, God's faithfulness to creation still bears fruit in humankind's personal, societal and cultural lives. ["Common Grace" is valuable in that it reflects] a recognition that God never lets go of his creatures, even in the face of apostasy, unbelief, and perversion.[11]

In short, the doctrine of common grace suggests that in some way the fabric of God's initial design — a design that provided for the production of goods in harmony with right relationships — remains embedded in our world and finds expression, albeit imperfect and distorted, in the marketplace. Such a theological conclusion would neatly explain why righteous behavior will frequently yield financially positive results, but why it does not universally and uniformly do so. Therefore, good ethics is good business — at least much of the time.

Hiding in Market Imperfections

Traditional economic theory teaches that in a purely competitive market, with perfect information, all inefficiencies will be punished. A company with a higher cost of goods (and with no offsetting higher value of product) will quickly go out of business. This should be bad news for the Christian in instances where ethical behavior is more expensive than the alternative.

By and large, however, actual markets are far from perfect. Spillover effects (sometimes referred to as "externalities") are not adequately captured, and inadequate information (with the corresponding effect of higher transaction costs) regularly distorts market signals. The fact that businesses often deviate from their assigned roles as financial self-maximizers also leaves pure market assumptions in the realm of the theoretical. In short, in the real market, as opposed to a theoretical one, there appears to be a modest amount of "slop" in the system, and this slop may help dampen perceived kingdom/market conflicts. Specifically, a third reason why Christians may not experience greater tension between the values of the gospel and the tenets of capitalism is that, at the margins, the added

11. Albert M. Wolters, *Creation Regained: Biblical Basics for a Reformational Worldview* (Grand Rapids: Eerdmans, 1985), pp. 49, 50.

costs of behaving ethically or "Christianly" can be absorbed and hidden in market imperfections.

Consider, for example, this hypothetical situation: your company is licensed to make baseball caps branded with your local team's logo. Only one other manufacturer is licensed to produce baseball caps with the same logo. Both you and your competitor have concluded that it will be most efficient to manufacture the caps in one of the *maquiladoras* in Mexico, and you set up your factories next door to each other. Independently, you each calculate that the going market rate for the employees you need to operate your plant is five dollars a day; but you also determine that, in order to provide your employees with a sustainable, livable wage, you would need to pay a daily salary of twice that amount — ten dollars a day. Your competitor hires a workforce and pays market wages. However, because you are motivated by your Christian faith and a conviction that to pay less than a living wage is not to respect the dignity of workers, who are made in the image of God, you choose to pay ten dollars a day. What happens?

First, the "good ethics is good business" function kicks in. As word gets out, the demand for jobs in your company is so high that you can hire the best workers in the area. Moreover, once they are hired, your employees show remarkable loyalty: very low rates of absenteeism and turnover. Because you have a superior workforce, your per-employee productivity is significantly better than your competitor's is.

Of course, you can't ignore the salary differential. Without adjusting for the effects of your enhanced productivity, the salary differential is $5 per employee per day. After adjusting for your higher level of production, the salary differential is reduced to $2 per employee per day. This is a marked improvement, but your ethical behavior has still not paid for itself. In the short term and in the long term, your decision to pay your employees a living wage will still be a net drag on the cost of your goods. For purposes of this hypothetical situation, assume that this net cost translates into a $.50-per-cap added expense.

Now suppose that you and your competitor need to maintain about a 50 percent profit margin on each cap you sell in order to maintain a "return on investment" that is satisfactory to your investors. Consequently, your cap must carry a retail price that is one dollar higher than the identical cap your competitor is selling. Classic economic theory suggests that you are done for. The rational consumer will hasten to buy the $13 cap rather than the $14 cap, and you, with your high-minded ethics, will be out of business.

But what really happens? It turns out that your caps are for sale at a sporting goods store on the east side of town, and your competitor's caps are sold in a retail store on the west side. Customers seeing your caps at the east-side store don't know that they cost a dollar less across town; even if they did know it, most of them would decide that the transaction costs (i.e., additional gas and travel time) would dwarf the one-dollar savings and make the trip not worth the effort. Consumer demand for branded baseball caps at price points under $15 tends to be fairly price-inelastic, so you don't lose many sales to customers who simply choose to go without the cap. In short, you sell almost as many caps as you would have had your caps been priced at $13. The very modest difference is reflected in a nearly imperceptible reduction in rates of returns to your shareholders. Under these assumptions, then, it appears that what economic theory suggests will be a train wreck between an unforgiving marketplace and the faithful disciple turns out to be not much more than a small bump in the road.

Of course, not all ethical choices come so neatly packaged.[12] Most markets are not artificially constrained by license agreements. Many products have a high degree of price elasticity, and often the costs of making an ethical choice will have a much higher net impact on the cost of goods. Still, what this example suggests is that at least in some cases — most notably when the costs of behaving ethically are not too much higher than the costs of other alternatives — imperfect market information and transaction costs can insulate ethical decisions from adverse market reactions. Moreover, the "free-market" model assumes that all firms are rational and motivated solely by financial gain. It posits a set of competitors who will act to maximize their financial returns subject only to an established set of

---

12. Obviously, this example is a greatly simplified picture of how the market forces might actually work. In this hypothetical situation, there are only two competitors. This creates an oligopoly in which both sellers might collect some level of monopoly pricing. If the company paying only market wages elects to take advantage of monopoly pricing, the ethical competitor may not be forced out of business but may only be required to relinquish some or all of the enhanced prices attributable to the oligopoly. As noted in the text, this example ignores the elasticity of prices; it also ignores the fact that the retail outlets that are distributing the caps may be much more price-conscious purchasers than the ultimate consumers. Still, for the purposes of our example, none of these refinements would undercut the general thrust of the argument.

rules (typically, the law). In fact, however, many businesses elect to act in a way that is not in their best financial interests simply because they perceive it to be "right to do so."

In 1990, Amar Bhide and Howard Stevenson published the results of what they characterized as extensive interviews aimed at proving that "honesty is the best policy."[13] By their own admission, they came up short: "Treachery, we found, can pay. There is no compelling economic reason to tell the truth or keep one's word — punishment for the treacherous in the real world is neither swift nor sure" (p. 121). Bhide and Stevenson specifically looked at the traditional arguments advanced by economists and game theorists to the effect that trust will be enforced in the marketplace "through retaliation and reputation." In fact, they found very few cases where they could demonstrate actual adverse consequences for business-people who abused trust, either in the short term or the long term. Conversely, they found many examples where deceitful behavior was unquestionably rewarded. Power in the marketplace, they found, can be an effective substitute for a trustworthy reputation. Moreover, most breaches of trust are shrouded in ambiguity and complexity, and it is simply too difficult to sort out and assign responsibility for past behavior. "Business people learn . . . that it is really not worth getting hung up about other people's pasts" (p. 125). Retaliation is likewise inefficient: it costs too much in time and money to get even. Nor can one make a solid economic case for honoring what prove to be unprofitable commitments: "The net present values, at any reasonable discount rate, must work against honoring obligations" (p. 127).

> Given all this, we might expect breaches of trust to be rampant. In fact . . . most business people . . . do try to keep their own word most of the time. . . . The importance of moral and social motives in business cannot be overemphasized. A selective memory, and careful screening of the facts may help sustain the fiction of profitable virtue, but the fundamental basis of trust is moral. We keep promises because we believe it is right to do so, not because it is good business. (pp. 127-28)

While the Bhide and Stevenson article focuses on trust-breaching behavior, the same principle can be found at work along other ethical dimen-

---

13. Amar Bhide and Howard Stevenson, "Why Be Honest If Honesty Doesn't Pay?" *Harvard Business Review* 68 (Sept.-Oct. 1990): 121-29.

sions. When a company elects not to fire a longtime loyal employee who is closing in on retirement age even though she is slowing down and could be replaced by a new hire who would be more effective and command a lower wage, the company is choosing to retain the older employee because "it is right to do so, not because it is good business." When a company elects to pay for a more expensive mode of waste disposal because it is safer for the surrounding community than a cheaper but legal alternative, it is making this choice because "it is right to do so, not because it is good business." And when a company agrees not to squeeze the last drop from a captive supplier's prices even though it has the market power to command a cheaper price, it is again doing so because "it is right to do so, not because it is good business." In short, businesspeople are not purely economically rational actors; they are also moral beings. And this works to the advantage of others who seek to make moral choices in business settings. A Christian's choice of a kingdom-value approach will not prove to be a competitive disadvantage if it turns out that his or her competitors are making comparable choices.

Future Trends

To summarize up to this point: market slop, common grace, and a diminished capacity to recognize existing tensions may all be factors contributing to what seem like infrequent conflicts between God's desires and the demands of the marketplace. However, there is reason to suspect that this may be changing and that the frequency of perceived market-kingdom conflicts may be on the rise.

Of course, to the extent that such conflicts are real, recognizing them more frequently is a good thing. In the past two decades there has been an explosion in popular attention to the integration of faith with work and business. For example, *The Marketplace Annotated Bibliography* of 2002 identified more than 700 books that addressed issues dealing with the intersection of Christian faith and issues of work, business, and vocation.[14] The vast majority of the books referred to have been published since 1985. The new books that continue to be produced range from scholarly re-

14. Pete Hammond, R. Paul Stevens, and Todd Svanoe, *The Marketplace Annotated Bibliography* (Downers Grove, IL: InterVarsity Press, 2002).

search projects to popular inspirational works. This outpouring of books is being supplemented by CDs, videos, periodicals, websites, and other materials, all of which focus on the call to live out one's faith in the marketplace.[15] In short, it is increasingly unlikely that a sincere Christian will intentionally segregate his Christian life from his work in business. But as he attempts to integrate the two, it is also less and less likely that he will fail to see the inherent tensions between his faith and his economics. Again, heightened awareness is a good thing. It may, however, substantially increase the dissonance a Christian in business experiences as he seeks to navigate between competing demands.

But the increase in perceived conflicts will likely be attributable to more than just heightened awareness. The number of actual conflicts, perceived or not, is likely to increase as markets become more and more rigorous. Various factors, such as the increase in available information, the increase in the speed of delivering such information, and the increased mobility of global capital, are likely to shrink the range of market imperfections and make "hiding in the slop" more difficult. Furthermore, as markets become increasingly global, a decline in the shared moral code that guides business behavior is likely. Thus an ethical Christian may find herself in competition with others in business who truly play by a set of rules that leave the Christian at a disadvantage.

To highlight these changes, let's return for a moment to the manufacture and sale of the baseball caps. In that hypothetical situation, the two manufacturers sold their apparel in sports stores located on opposite sides of town. Diminished information and the transaction costs associated with traveling across town made it unlikely that consumers would choose the $13 cap over the $14 cap based solely on the price differential. But suppose that we now change the case somewhat. Consider what happens if, instead of selling at separate stores, both manufacturers sell their caps through the team's online store. When a consumer electronically enters the store, she sees two caps listed: they are in all physical respects identical, but one is listed at $14 and the other at $13. Now the choice is obvious to the consumer, and the manufacturer who declined to pay living wages to its employees drives the more ethically minded company out of business, virtually overnight.

15. Pete Hammond, "Some Wonderful North American Stirrings," urbana.org, Summer 2002, http://www.ivmdl.org/reflections.cfm?study=79 (accessed June 17, 2005).

The obvious difference between the two cases relates to the availability of information and the elimination of transaction costs. Since the internet makes pricing information readily available and reduces the transaction costs associated with preferring one cap over the other, the actual market conditions of the case approach more closely the theoretical conditions assumed by classical economics. The result is that any remaining market imperfections in the system are not large enough to hide the higher costs of doing business in an ethical fashion, and the "Christian choice" becomes an anticompetitive one.

Of course, not all retail business is moving from stores to online platforms. But the general trend is clearly in the direction of more and more consumer information available in a shorter and shorter time frame. As the availability of this information increases, the consumers' ability to sort out and find the least expensive option will likewise continue to increase and put pressure on the higher-cost producer; this will be true whether the higher costs are attributable to simple production inefficiencies or to the higher costs of ethical behavior.

Heightened availability of information and reduced transaction costs will play out not only at the level of the ultimate consumer but up and down the supply chain, and at different levels within the company itself. For example, given the ease of moving capital, one should expect a growing intolerance for less than optimal returns on investment. Since there is an increase in available information and a declining amount of "stickiness" in capital transactions, even small dips in returns can unleash what Thomas Friedman has referred to as the "electronic herd."

> The wheels today have been so thoroughly greased that huge amounts of what economist David Hale calls "gypsy capital" can move around the world to exploit buying and selling opportunities anywhere, with transaction costs that are virtually zero, transmission costs that are virtually zero and speeds that are virtually instantaneous.[16]

As I have observed above, in addition to less than perfect information and the existence of transaction costs, one of the factors that so far has dampened the market/kingdom conflicts has been the presence of many actors in the business community who share a common cultural under-

16. Thomas Friedman, *The Lexus and the Olive Tree* (New York: Anchor Books, 2000), pp. 129-30.

standing of "right and wrong." This common heritage causes Christians and non-Christians alike to behave, at least some of the time, in a "moral" way rather than a purely rational, economic, and self-interested way. In other words, regardless of whether any individual businessman in the United States claims to be a Christian, until recently he would nonetheless have grown up in a relatively homogenous culture with Judaeo-Christian roots and would likely share a reasonably uniform understanding of ethical behavior.

Homogeneity, however, is in decline. While the United States has always been a nation of immigrants, the character of the immigrant population is changing. For example, in 1940 more than 85 percent of people who had come to the United States as immigrants were of European descent. By 1995, 75 percent were from non-European countries, principally Latin America and Asia.[17] During the 1990s, roughly 45 percent of all net additions to the labor force were expected to be nonwhite; and, of this group, half were expected to be first-generation immigrants.[18] Between 1990 and 2005, the Labor Department estimates that only about one-sixth of the new workers coming into the workforce were Euro-American men.[19] Since males of European descent have traditionally dominated the higher ranks of business managers, such a significant switch portends potentially huge cultural changes in the ways that businesses will operate in the future.

There is also a parallel (and potentially related) change in the religious identification of U.S. citizens:

> The United States appears to be going through an unprecedented change in religious practices. Large numbers of American adults are disaffiliating themselves from Christianity and from other organized religions. . . . Identification with Christianity has suffered a loss of 9.7 percentage points in 11 years . . . 14.1% do not follow any organized religion. This is an unusually rapid increase — almost a doubling — from only 8% in 1990. . . . From 1972 to 1993, the *General Social Survey* of the *National Opinion Research Center* found that Protestants constituted about 63% of the population. This declined to 52% in 2002.

17. Norma Carr-Ruffino, *Managing Diversity: People Skills for a Multicultural Workplace* (Needham Heights, MA: Simon and Schuster, 1998), pp. 1-4.

18. Taylor Cox, *Cultural Diversity in Organizations: Theory, Research, and Practice* (San Francisco: Berrett-Koehler, 1994), p. 3.

19. Carr-Ruffino, *Managing Diversity*, pp. 1-4.

Protestants are expected to slip to a minority position between 2004 and 2006.[20]

Moreover, this only focuses on the changing demographics and beliefs of the United States. An even more pervasive trend is the increasing globalization of business. Even if the United States were to remain as homogenous as ever, U.S. businesses would increasingly be competing with businesses housed and staffed by managers growing up in different countries and different cultures. In short, there is less and less reason to expect that Christians will be able to find refuge in a common cultural heritage that they share with their competitors.

One should not make too much of these trends. Changing demographics at the front end of the workforce are likely to only slowly transform the upper ranks of management. Significant acculturation of the new employees will likely occur along the way. And even though there appears to be a shift away from Christianity, polling data in 2001 still reflects that over three-fourths of Americans identify themselves as Christians.[21] More significantly, there is no reason to believe that the Judaeo-Christian heritage has a particular monopoly on values such as integrity and kindness. Indeed, the infusion of cultural influences from more communal societies could actually work to create a marketplace that is more accepting of the Christian community orientation than the traditional individualistic orientation of American business.

Still, as the ethical orientation of others in the workplace grows more and more diverse, it seems likely that Christians in business will experience more, rather than fewer, occasions when at least some of their competitors are willing to act in a way that maximizes market returns at the cost of ethical values that Christians would ascribe to. Thus, the growing diversity of the marketplace, for all of its strengths, suggests that Christians in business will likely experience an increasing number of times when pursuit of kingdom values will put them at odds with the demands of the market.

---

20. "Religious Identification in the U.S." http://www.religioustolerance.org/chr _prac2.htm (accessed June 17, 2005), citing *American Religious Identification Survey (2001)* (Graduate Center of the City University of New York and the General Social Survey of the National Opinion Research Center).

21. Ibid.

Mitigating Strategies

In short, there is reason to believe that Christians in business are likely to become increasingly aware of instances where a choice for the kingdom is a choice to be less competitive — partly because Christians will become more sensitive to these tensions, and partly because the market will become more rigorous and create more tensions. What, then, should a Christian do? What strategies might a Christian adopt either to help reduce the number of instances where the conflicts will occur or to best respond when one confronts such conflicts?

One possible response might be to attempt to enlist the market in service of kingdom values. Specifically, Christians might consider three possible market-constraining strategies that could help reduce the number and extent of kingdom/market conflicts. Two involve government action, and the third involves a branding exercise.

The first strategy should be the easiest for Christians to support because it is designed to render markets more, rather than less, efficient. Christians in business could support regulations that seek to capture the cost of externalities and properly force their inclusion in the related cost of goods. Returning to our baseball cap example, suppose that the manufacturing process used in dying the caps results in toxic waste that needs to be disposed of. Further, suppose that the environmental laws of Mexico allow for the disposal of the toxic waste by dumping it directly into nearby waterways, even though it is well known that this will cause adverse health effects for residents of nearby communities. As an ethical manufacturer, you decline to dispose of your waste in this way; instead, you use an expensive waste-disposal process that removes the harmful chemicals before the liquid is discharged. Because your unethical competitor does not do this, and because you are in a highly competitive market, you end up at a severe business disadvantage.

However, most economists would argue that your competitor's cost of goods is artificially low because one of the costs of production has not been adequately captured. This lower cost distorts the market response. In effect, more people will buy caps of this kind than would otherwise make the purchase if the true manufacturing costs (including externalities) had been captured. This will, in turn, distort the flow of capital by providing an artificially enhanced return on investment for capital used in the manufacture of these caps. Under classic economic theory, the failure to capture the externalities renders the market less, rather than more, efficient: "[A]lthough efficiency requires that all benefits and costs be weighed regardless of where they fall, market participants weigh only their own."[22] In other words, market participants will only weigh those costs that they are required to bear.

Thus Christians can, in some instances, argue for policies that simultaneously improve the efficiency of the market and reduce the number of times that competitive choices conflict with kingdom values. Since a Christian ethic will be concerned with all humans, any approach that fairly incorporates the costs imposed on all such persons is likely to bring the market into closer alignment with the kingdom.

The traditional approach for capturing externalities is through government regulation. Such regulations can take a variety of forms, ranging from a flat prohibition of activities that impose external costs to the establishment of some form of credit system (e.g., pollution credits) that would allow market participants to weigh the costs and make their own decisions about whether it is more efficient to pay the added price or correct for the adverse behavior. (Of course, pointing out that there are multiple approaches does not suggest that all such approaches are equally ethical; but it is sufficient for the purposes of this chapter to note that the adoption of any such approach would tend to move the markets toward an outcome more compatible with Christian ethics.)

A second strategy worthy of consideration (again involving government regulation) is to simply regulate to the ethical standard. In the example we have been using, if Mexico had established a minimum wage commensurate with a living wage in that country, then the law would in effect have leveled the playing field between you and your competing manufacturer of baseball caps. In competitive terms, your decision to pay an ethical wage would no longer put you at a business disadvantage because all of your competitors would be required to do so as well.

Of course, to argue for the implementation of either of these first two strategies, Christians in business would need to shed their traditional antipathy toward government involvement in business. Business rhetoric often casts government regulation as an inappropriate interference with the market, an interference that limits economic growth, reduces individual choice, and interferes with market efficiency. And Christians in busi-

22. Lindblom, *The Market System,* p. 147.

ness are often just as strident as non-Christians are in defense of those market values. Of course, Christians should also be willing to affirm that market values are not the only social values worthy of consideration. As Rebecca Blank has noted:

> For Christians, government programs may serve as an instrument to help support the values and responsibilities taught by their faith. The important role that the Christian faith ascribes to community suggests that Christians within a democratic society should be particularly interested in helping to define the "common good" pursued by government. Government legislation that limits the scope of markets may support values that are consistent with Christian teaching, particularly when it protects individuals from choices that might bring harm to them and others. Government programs that redistribute income and respond to economic need may directly satisfy the Christian responsibility to exhibit particular concern for the poor.[23]

Inviting additional government regulation, however, is not a panacea. The traditional business hostility to regulation is not without some basis in fact. Invariably, government regulations introduce inefficiencies that advance neither market values nor other social values. The paperwork and related filings required to show compliance with regulations and the costs of enforcement can often add inefficiencies that threaten to overwhelm the social values being promoted by the regulation in the first place. In addition, it is very difficult to tailor regulations with sufficient precision to appropriately address each specific situation. Therefore, virtually all regulations end up being both over- and under-inclusive. Moreover, equating ethics with legal compliance also tends to foster a minimalist approach that asks, "How much do I have to do?" and "Is there any way around this?" rather than "What should I do?"

Another difficulty associated with the government regulatory strategies relates to the increasingly global nature of business. Because businesses often have the capacity to relocate, capital tends to flow downhill to the lowest-cost environments. For example, if one government chooses to "artificially" raise wages by imposing a minimum-wage statute, capital is likely to go in search of a less labor-friendly setting.

---

23. Rebecca Blank and William McGurn, *Is the Market Moral?* (Washington, DC: Brookings Institute, 2004), p. 49. See also Blank's chapter 10 in this volume.

> As corporations become increasingly mobile, countries will be forced to compete in order to encourage companies to establish headquarters and plants within their borders. . . . [W]hichever country gives the company the best deal in terms of wages, skills, transportation costs, markets, taxes and direct subsidies is rewarded by corporate presence and the associated benefits. . . . Technology and globalization are rapidly changing the way businesses operate, limiting the ability of governments to restrict — or even control — economic activity.[24]

Hence, "excessive" government regulatory activity imposed by any single jurisdiction could inadvertently result in severe damage to the intended beneficiaries of the regulations in question. Obviously, the less "sticky" the capital, the greater the likelihood of the "race to the bottom" that renders these strategies ineffective.

Notwithstanding these concerns, in some circumstances regulatory approaches may offer the best opportunity to narrow the gap between kingdom choices and inconsistent market signals. A decision about whether any particular regulatory strategy is appropriate will, of course, need to be carefully considered in light of both its potential positive and negative effects. However, Christians in business should, at a minimum, work to set aside their instinctive aversion to any government involvement with business. Rather, they should be willing actively to explore and, where appropriate, work toward implementing strategies that enlist government assistance in minimizing kingdom/market tensions.

A third strategy worthy of consideration is a marketing strategy. In effect, this strategy seeks to allocate market value to an ethical brand or to the emotional value associated with purchasing a product made in a more value-sensitive way. For example, in our hypothetical scenario in which baseball caps are sold side by side in the team's online store, one cap is listed at $14 and the other at $13. As I suggested earlier, all other things being equal, this scenario would result in the manufacturer of the higher-priced caps going out of business rather rapidly. Suppose now, however, that the higher-priced caps also sported a "fair labor" label, administered by a third-party certifying group, that assured the consumer that all employees involved in the manufacture of this cap had been paid fair wages.

---

24. Lester Thurow, "New Rules, the American Economy, and Globalization and the Challenges of a New Century," *Harvard International Review* 20 (Winter 1997/98): 55-56.

In essence, consumers would now be invited to buy a baseball cap for $13 and pay an additional $1 for the ethics brand — and the related good feeling associated with purchasing such a branded product. *If* consumers could readily identify a "fair labor" cap at the point of sale, and *if* the fair labor brand could be adequately marketed so that consumers would understand what it meant, and *if* there was an existing consumer market for ethically branded products (or if advertising could create such a market), then it might be possible for the higher-priced manufacturer with the more ethical operating procedures to stay in business.

That's a lot of *ifs*, however, and while there are some examples of modest levels of success in ethics branding (e.g., fair-trade coffee, SFI and FSC lumber certifications, Patagonia-branded clothing), it is far from clear whether a general consumer market exists (or can be created) for ethically branded goods. One environmentalist has noted a human tendency here: "We quite often act differently when we think of ourselves as consumers than when we think of ourselves as citizens. . . . As consumers, we act more often than not for ourselves; as citizens, we take on a broader vision and do what is in the best interests of the community."[25] For this strategy to be successful, and thereby to allow a Christian in business to operate in an economically rational, self-interested way that is consistent with her values, it requires that consumers stop acting as economically rational, self-interested participants in the market. In effect, it transfers the need to operate contrary to one's economic interests from the business manager to the ultimate purchaser. This has the advantage of not relying on governmental action but it may, in most instances, prove very difficult to bring about.

Concluding Questions

What if these mitigating strategies are unsuccessful? What is a Christian in business to do when she finds herself confronting a kingdom/market conflict? How should she respond? Is the correct answer to blindly pursue the kingdom-value side of the tension and accept the consequences as they unfold? Is this tantamount to encouraging Christians to be in the business

---

25. W. Michael Hoffman, "Business and Environmental Ethics," *Business Ethics Quarterly* 1, no. 2 (1991): 169-84, at 173-74.

of managing failing businesses? Or, given that Christians active in business do so in a fallen world, is a compromise of Christian ethics an inevitable (and thus "acceptable") consequence of the call to be "in the world"? In other words, is the call to live out signs of the coming kingdom bounded by the practical "necessity" of staying in business?

To some extent, the following chapters hint at pragmatic solutions to some of these tensions. As is often the case for theoretical questions, the best answers are often worked out on a case-by-case basis on the ground. And yet these — and many other similar questions — are begging for theologically rich answers spoken in a language that Christians in business will understand. Because there has been such an apparent paucity of market/kingdom conflicts, there has also been a paucity of theological reflection on these questions. As the conflicts increase, however, theologians, pastors, and academicians (in schools of religion, theology, and ethics, as well as in schools of business) will need to begin the difficult work of offering guidance to Christians in business who genuinely desire to please God in their given vocations, but who may be increasingly at a loss for how to do so.

CHAPTER 7

And God Said, Let There Be Many: An Argument for Economic Diversity

Janet Parker

Introduction

In this chapter I seek to contribute to the current debate raging over economic globalization by reflecting on its tendency to reduce and destroy the God-gifted diversity of creation in its socioeconomic, ecological, and cultural dimensions. Amid the arguments of many economists, nation-states, international economic institutions, and multinational corporations that "free-market" economic globalization is both inevitable and desirable, the question that demands reflection is: What is lost by the imposition of a global economic monoculture and the resulting assimilation and destruction of diverse lifeways? In recent years, scientists and environmentalists have succeeded in raising awareness of the importance of biological diversity to human flourishing on Planet Earth. Social scientists and activists from people's movements have begun to generate similar consciousness of the value of preserving human cultural diversity. However, the connections between the diversity of species, the continued survival of many endangered languages and cultures, and *economic* diversity have received far less attention.

In this chapter I assert that the preservation of alternatives to the predominant model of neoliberal capitalism is essential to continued cultural and biological diversity. In other words, I affirm that both biological and cultural diversity are intrinsic goods that we must respect and uphold. The new claim that I make, which is based on emerging work within a variety of academic disciplines, people's movements, and the global ecumenical movement, is that economic diversity is a necessary instrumental good (a means) that makes possible the preservation of the rich diversity of our planet's ecosystems and cultures. As we shall see, we have much to learn from indigenous cultures practicing subsistence livelihoods and from people engaging in communally oriented economic practices that offer life-sustaining and democratically organized alternatives to the reigning model of economic globalization. Theologically speaking, I claim that respect for diversity in all of its forms becomes a foundational moral norm for Christians who seek to be faithful to God's call to promote justice and protect life. This norm is grounded in the biblical witness to a God who creates a world of exuberant diversity, an ecological hothouse of species that God blesses and commands to "be fruitful and multiply."

Finally, my theme in this chapter is rooted in a deep engagement with ecumenical thought. It arises in dialogue with recent efforts of the World Council of Churches and the World Alliance of Reformed Churches to address interlinked dimensions of economic and ecological injustice. It addresses the core conviction of these ecumenical bodies that Christians should resist the temptation to embrace any totalizing economic ideology. Our allegiance is to God and to our neighbor, whom we are called to love as we love ourselves. Christian freedom allows us to recognize and support a diversity of exchange systems when such diversity best serves human and planetary well-being. The biblical imagination, interpreted afresh by biblical scholars and ecumenical theologians, points the way toward a more sane understanding of an economy that serves, rather than exploits, human and other-than-human life.

The Wild Facts

The proverbial writing is in red ink all over the wall, and the warning bells are ringing. The 24th General Council of the World Alliance of Reformed Churches, while meeting in 2004 in Accra, Ghana, declared:

> We are challenged by the cries of the people who suffer and by the woundedness of creation itself. We see a dramatic convergence between the suffering of the people and the damage done to the rest of creation. The signs of the times have become more alarming and must be interpreted.[1]

1. World Alliance of Reformed Churches, *Covenanting for Justice in the Economy and*

The Millennium Ecosystem Assessment (MEA) was launched by United Nations Secretary-General Kofi Annan in 2001 with the objective of assessing the consequences of ecosystem change for human well-being. Produced by more than 1,300 scientists from ninety-five countries, it does not mince words in speaking of planetary distress. The MEA found that "nearly two-thirds of the services provided by nature to humankind are found to be in decline worldwide. In effect, the benefits reaped from our engineering of the planet have been achieved by running down natural capital assets."[2] Here are some of the facts:

- At least one-quarter of marine fish stocks are overharvested, and in many sea areas the total weight of fish available to be caught is less than one-tenth of what it was before modern industrial fishing practices were introduced (p. 10).
- Since 1935, approximately 35 percent of mangroves (tidal basin forests) and 20 percent of the world's coral reefs have been destroyed. Mangroves and coral reefs are not only important wildlife habitat but also protect coastal communities from storms, erosion, and even tidal waves. Areas with less damage to the natural coastline fared better in the Indian Ocean tsunami than areas that had lost their coastal ecosystems (pp. 5, 9-10, 12). Destruction of coastal ecosystems in Louisiana and Mississippi also contributed to the severe impact of Hurricane Katrina in 2005.
- The explosion in the use of fossil fuels for energy in this century has increased the amount of carbon dioxide gas in the air by about one-third, contributing to global climate change as now widely recognized by scientists (p. 13).
- The MEA finds that 12 percent of birds, 25 percent of mammals, and at least 32 percent of amphibians are threatened with extinction in the next century. Other scientists have estimated that, if current trends continue, we could *lose up to two-thirds of the biological diversity* of the planet in the twenty-first century.[3] The MEA estimates

---

the Earth, Document GC 23-English, 24th General Council meeting in Accra, Ghana, July 30-Aug. 13, 2004, par. 5-6.

2. The Board of the Millennium Ecosystem Assessment, "Living Beyond Our Means: Natural Assets and Human Well-Being," March 2005, p. 5. Available at http://www.millenniumassessment.org/en/Products.BoardStatement.aspx.

3. Peter H. Raven and Jeffrey A. McNeely, "Biological Extinction: Its Scope and Mean-

that humans have increased the rate of global extinctions a thousandfold over the "natural" rate typical of earth's long-term history.[4]

The board of the Millennium Ecosystem Assessment boils these statistics down to the bottom line: "At the heart of this assessment is a stark warning. Human activity is putting such a strain on the natural functions of Earth that the ability of the planet's ecosystems to sustain future generations can no longer be taken for granted" (p. 5).

On October 16, 2004, World Food Day, the UN Deputy Secretary-General Louise Frechette announced that an unprecedented loss of biodiversity was threatening the world's 900 million rural poor by reducing their food supplies. She explained that biodiversity is the key to healthy ecosystems that support the subsistence livelihoods of the poor. Economies that are geared to produce for local survival needs rather than for selling at a profit on the market are called "subsistence economies." The loss of biodiversity affects people living in subsistence economies directly and immediately, because they farm the land, raise animals, hunt, harvest the forests, and fish the seas primarily to provide food for their own families, not to produce a surplus to sell on the market.

Even the urban poor and farm workers who labor on large commercial farms often supplement their diets with food grown in small garden plots or fish caught in local rivers and lakes. As fish and animal species become extinct, and topsoil and plant species are lost, more of the poor go hungry. Freshette emphasized that the loss of biodiversity is not only a problem for the world's poor, but that "[g]iven the growing interdependence among countries and expanding trade in agricultural goods and services, maintaining biodiversity for food security is as much a global priority as a local one."[5]

In addition to providing the base for the world's food supply, biological diversity is the source of almost limitless other goods and services that humans need. Scientists are only beginning to discover all the medicinal benefits of the world's plant biodiversity, and plants remain the primary source of medicine for 60 percent of the world's people. Biological organisms create soil, protect watersheds, absorb pollution, regulate climate, and

---

ing for Us," in *Protection of Global Biodiversity: Converging Strategies,* ed. Lakshman D. Guruswamy and Jeffrey A. McNeely (Durham, NC: Duke University Press, 1998), p. 20.

4. MEA, "Living Beyond Our Means," p. 15.

5. UN News Service, "Biodiversity losses threaten world's 900 million rural poor, UN says," 18 Oct. 2004.

even produce the very oxygen necessary for life on earth. Biodiversity experts Peter Raven and Jeffrey McNeely have given this warning: "Clearly, much of the quality of ecosystem services will be lost if the present episode of extinction is allowed to run unbridled for much longer."[6]

Many expected the twentieth century to be the century of progress, the century in which humankind would stride into a future of universal prosperity rooted in the expansion of industrial capitalism and the global market economy. A significant minority of the world's population has enjoyed rising incomes and wealth; yet billions have been excluded from the benefits of development and new technologies. An estimated *fourteen to thirty thousand people die every day* from poverty-related diseases such as malaria, AIDS, tuberculosis, diarrhea, and respiratory disease, their bodies weakened by chronic hunger, lack of clean water, and unsanitary living conditions.[7] Over 1 billion people (18 percent of the world's population) lack access to clean water, and 2.6 billion (40 percent of the world's population) lack access to proper sanitation.[8] Furthermore, inequality within and between countries has increased significantly since the early 1980s, meaning that while the poor (and poor countries) have gotten poorer, the rich (and rich countries) have gotten richer.[9] Globalization of the capitalist market economy, the rising tide that was supposed to lift all boats, has not delivered on its promise. Some have risen into the world's middle and upper classes, but many have fallen farther behind.[10] The UN Human De-

6. Raven and McNeely, "Biological Extinction," pp. 27-28.

7. From Peter Gleick, "The Human Right to Water," *Water Policy* 1, no. 5 (1999): 487-503.

8. Statement by Zephirin Diabre, Associate Administrator of the United Nations Development Programme at the High-Level Segment of the Thirteenth Session of the Commission on Sustainable Development, 21 Apr. 2005.

9. The United Nations *Human Development Report* for 1999 says: "Inequality has been rising in many countries since the early 1980s. . . . Inequality between countries has also increased. The income gap between the fifth of the world's population living in the richest countries and the fifth in the poorest was 74 to 1 in 1997, up from 60 to 1 in 1990 and 30 to 1 in 1960" (United Nations Development Programme, *Summary: Human Development Report 1999* [New York: United Nations Development Programme, 1999]).

10. Economist Jeffrey Sachs notes that, while the numbers of the extreme poor (income of less than $1 a day) have fallen in East and South Asia since 1981, they have increased in sub-Saharan Africa and Eastern Europe, while the extreme poverty rate in Latin America has remained stuck at around 10 percent (Sachs, *The End of Poverty: Economic Possibilities for Our Time* [New York: Penguin Books, 2005], p. 21).

velopment Report for 2005 notes: "In human development terms the space between countries is marked by deep, and in some cases, widening inequalities in income and life chances."[11]

Creation's Integrity

Advocates for the environment and advocates for the poor do not always grasp the connections between the two concerns, but awareness is growing that the crises of poverty and the environment are interlinked. A group of leading theologians convened by the National Council of Churches issued a report in 2005 that places concern for human beings within the framework of concern for the earth, recognizing that a healthy planet is a prerequisite for human flourishing. In "God's Earth Is Sacred," the authors make a plea: "This is *not* a competing 'program alternative,' one 'issue' among many. In this most critical moment in Earth's history, we are convinced that *the central moral imperative* of our time is the care for Earth as God's creation."[12]

Is this an overstatement of the case? For those of us who are used to thinking of "the environment" as a separate sphere apart from "society" and "economy" and "religion," these statements may indeed seem overblown. But what if we were to look with new eyes at Life as a whole fabric, not as a disparate collection of colorful threads, and what if we were to begin to see how all the threads are woven together to form a garment that protects us from elements that are inhospitable to human life? What if we were to retrain our eyes to see nature not as one separate issue we might be concerned about among others, but as the very foundation of every element of human life on earth, including our economies, our social relationships, our cultural forms, and the health of our very bodies?

The World Council of Churches has coined a phrase that elegantly expresses the fundamental unity of life on earth: the "integrity of cre-

11. United Nations Development Programme, *Human Development Report 2005*, p. 3. Furthermore, the report notes that in 2003 "18 countries with a combined population of 460 million people registered lower scores in the human development index (HDI) than in 1990 — an unprecedented reversal."

12. National Council of Churches News Service, "God's Earth Is Sacred: An Open Letter to Church and Society in the United States," released Feb. 14, 2005, available at http://www.ncccusa.org/news/14.02.05theologicalstatement.html.

ation." Emerging awareness of the threats to Planet Earth in the 1980s caused the WCC to add "the integrity of creation" to long-standing concerns for justice and peace. Increasingly, people realized that the human goods of justice and peace were tied inexorably to the health of the planetary systems sustaining human society. Scientists and theologians alike have come to recognize that the earth is a one-time natural endowment, and that humankind and otherkind are relatives on this green oasis of life in the vast stretches of space.[13]

Ecofeminists contribute the image of the "web of life" to the discussion of creation's interrelatedness.[14] Rejecting a mechanistic, Western worldview that views the universe as a collection of replaceable, autonomous parts, ecofeminists see a universe that is alive with spirit, infused with the sacred, and fundamentally interconnected.[15] Nothing that exists is self-contained or essentially independent; as a result, ecofeminists speak of the "primacy of relationship." Beverly Harrison puts it this way: "Our life is part of a vast cosmic web, and no moral theology that fails to envisage reality in this way will be able to make sense of our lives or actions today."[16]

The Biblical Call to Protect Creation

Surprising as it may seem, a number of biblical scholars are now arguing that this view of human societies as embedded within the entire web of life is consistent with the biblical understanding of creation in the book of Genesis. For Christians and Jews, the biblical view of creation provides a *theological* rationale for valuing the diversity of life on earth, in addition to

---

13. Larry Rasmussen, *Earth Community, Earth Ethics* (Maryknoll, NY: Orbis Books, 1996), pp. 98-103.

14. Ecofeminists address the connections between the oppression of women and the domination of nature as they critique the "logic of domination" that underlies all hierarchies of gender, race, class, and species.

15. Janet Parker, "For All Our Relations: Ecofeminist and Indigenous Challenges to Sustainable Development" (PhD diss., Union Theological Seminary in New York, 2001), pp. 208-09.

16. The phrase "primacy of relationship" is Beverly Harrison's, from her widely read essay "The Power of Anger in the Work of Love," in *Making the Connections*, ed. Carol S. Robb (Boston: Beacon Press, 1985), p. 16.

the economic and scientific reasons mentioned above. Not only is biological diversity essential to the survival of life on earth; it is also *God-given* and *God-mandated*. That is, Christians are called to value, protect, and celebrate the astonishing complexity and diversity of earthly life because God created it and because God mandates our care and preservation of the entirety of creation, not just the bits we enjoy, find aesthetically pleasing or economically profitable.

On page one of the Bible, the first verse of Genesis, we read, "In the beginning . . . God created the heavens and the earth. . . ." What did God create? Multiplicity! Diversity! Swarming skies, teeming waters, and fecund soils and plants. It is entirely possible to read Genesis 1 as a paean to the staggering complexity and diversity of life on earth. Everything that God creates comes in multiples: waters (vv. 2, 6-7, 9-10), day and night (v. 4), plants (vv. 11-12), light and darkness (vv. 14-18), aquatic creatures (vv. 20-22), birds (vv. 20-22), mammals, reptiles, and insects (vv. 24-25), and humans as male and female (vv. 26-28). Nothing that God creates is unitary or uniform. As if to drive the point home, the priestly author of Genesis uses the phrase "of every kind" for all of the living creatures that God creates. God also ensures that life on earth will continue through the blessing of procreation: vegetative life reproduces through seed (v. 12), but birds, fish, and humans receive a direct command from God to "be fruitful and multiply" (vv. 22, 28).[17] The command to multiply is not limited to human creatures, and in fact the first creatures to be blessed and addressed directly by God are birds and fish![18]

Biologists teach us that most species reproduce through the mixing of genetic material, which increases the diversity of life on earth and the survivability of each species. Theologically speaking, God's provision for procreation indicates that the profusion of biological diversity on Planet Earth is God's intention for creation (thus, as I suggested in the introduction, biological diversity is an intrinsic good). In addition, Christians and Jews perceive a special role for humankind in preserving God's gift of creation, though not all agree on how to understand that role.

17. Oddly and inexplicably, while birds, fish, and human beings receive the direct command to "be fruitful and multiply," nonhuman animal life does not. Perhaps the command to animals is assumed.

18. Mark Brett, "Earthing the Human in Genesis 1–3," in *The Earth Story in Genesis*, ed. Norman C. Habel and Shirley Wurst (Sheffield, UK: Sheffield Academic Press, 2000), p. 77.

The most prominent debate in this regard is between proponents of "dominion" and proponents of "stewardship." Dominion advocates emphasize Genesis 1:28, where God commands human beings to "subdue" the earth and "have dominion" over it. Stewardship advocates prefer to draw on the second chapter of Genesis, pointing to God's instruction to the earth creature (Hebrew: *adam*) to "till and keep" the earth (Hebrew: *adamah*). The contrast between the commands to the human creatures in Genesis 1 and 2 is not insignificant. The Hebrew words for "subdue" and "dominion" connote human mastery and sovereignty over the earth; the Hebrew words for "till and keep" denote serving and conserving the earth.[19] Fundamentally, the question pivots on the proper role of humans in their relationships to otherkind: are we meant to be "lords" of the earth, as befitting those created in the "image of God," or are we better understood as "plain member and citizen" of the larger earth community, to borrow Aldo Leopold's phrase.

In an era when human power has the capacity to destroy the earth, the question is: Which understanding better serves the cause of life, reinforcing human exploitation of the planet or modeling human service to creation? Old Testament scholar Ted Hiebert recommends that Genesis 1:28 should relinquish its dominance over the Christian imagination in favor of the message of Genesis 2:15.[20] The clear trajectory within contemporary biblical and theological studies is to move from interpretations of Scripture that sanction domination of nature to those that exhort stewardship of the earth on behalf of present and future generations.

This excursus on Genesis illustrates a cardinal theological principle in relationship to the natural world: "Creator-based value." For Christians, the value of nonhuman life and the gifts of the earth derive not from their usefulness to human beings but directly from their relationship to the Creator. Noting that God repeatedly declares all of God's creations "good"

---

19. See Norman Habel, "Geophany: The Earth Story in Genesis 1," pp. 45-47, and Carol Newsom, "Common Ground: An Ecological Reading of Genesis 2–3," pp. 62-65, in *The Earth Story in Genesis*. It is noteworthy, however, that many scholars say that the overall thrust of the priestly creation story, which climaxes not in the command to humans to have dominion but in the Sabbath vision of harmony and rest (Gen. 2:1-3), implies clear limits to human control over nature. See the essays by Howard Wallace and Mark Brett in *The Earth Story in Genesis*. See also Larry Rasmussen, *Earth Community*, pp. 230-32.

20. Theodore Hiebert, "The Human Vocation," in *Christianity and Ecology*, ed. Dieter T. Hessel and Rosemary Radford Ruether (Cambridge, MA: Harvard University Press, 2000), pp. 135-54.

(Gen. 1:4, 10, 12, 18, 21, 25, 31), Calvin DeWitt says that human beings must learn to respect the intrinsic God-given value of all creation. Musing on the biblical creature "Behemoth," known to moderns as the hippopotamus, DeWitt wryly observes:

> In this view, a human being does not first ask, concerning the hippo: Can I eat it? How can I shoot it? How can I market it? How can I get it out of my way? Instead the questions are: What does the Creator think of this creature? How in my relationship to it should I honor its Owner? How might I learn to live with it? How does it fit into the larger system of which it is part?[21]

As I have noted above, religious leaders and theologians are paying attention to the destructive impact human beings are having on God's good Creation and are mounting a prophetic critique of what some call a "false gospel." The authors of "God's Earth Is Sacred" call for us to repent for the human crimes against nature:

> We have become un-Creators. Earth is in jeopardy at our hands. . . . We have listened to a false gospel that we continue to live out in our daily habits — a gospel that proclaims that God cares for the salvation of humans only and that our human calling is to exploit Earth for our own ends alone. This false gospel still finds its proud preachers and continues to capture its adherents among emboldened political leaders and policy makers. . . . The secular counterpart of this gospel rests in the conviction that humans can master the Earth. . . . However, the sobering truth is that we hardly have knowledge of, much less control over, the deep and long-term consequences of our human impacts upon the Earth.[22]

If we are in fact becoming "un-Creators," we must face up to the cultural roots of the current interlinked crises of poverty and the environment. As theologian Larry Rasmussen says, "The crisis is not one of nature . . . as nature is commonly conceived. . . . Earth's distress is a crisis of culture."[23]

---

21. Calvin B. DeWitt, "Behemoth and Batrachians in the Eye of God: Responsibility to Otherkind in Christian Ethics," in *Christianity and Ecology,* ed. Dieter T. Hessel and Rosemary Radford Ruether (Cambridge, MA: Harvard University Press, 2000), pp. 298, 300.

22. NCC News Service, "God's Earth Is Sacred."

23. Rasmussen, *Earth Community,* pp. 7-8.

The crisis of culture threatening to suffocate life on earth is complex, but one taproot is the particular economic system dominating the current drive toward economic globalization and "free trade."

Neoliberalism and "Free-Market" Economics

Supporters and critics alike agree that the dominant economic system of our time is a capitalist market system rooted in a philosophy that believes free trade and free markets are the best way to organize human economic life. This philosophy achieved ascendancy in the West in the 1980s, during the Reagan/Thatcher eras in the United States and Britain, and was epitomized by Margaret Thatcher's famous declaration that "there is no alternative" to the global free-market system. Since the fall of the Soviet bloc, the capitalist market economy has truly gone global, and supranational institutions have been created to facilitate the expansion of a genuinely global economy through the mechanisms of free trade and free investment. The International Monetary Fund (IMF) and the World Bank, created after World War II, have been pressed into service to promote economic globalization, and new institutions, such as the World Trade Organization (WTO), have been created to facilitate the process of globalization. Regional trade agreements like the North American Free Trade Agreement (NAFTA) have been signed between countries in a particular region in order to lower barriers to the flow of capital, goods, and services and to achieve greater economic integration in the region. Policies that lower trade barriers and open up domestic markets to foreign goods and services are known as "trade liberalization" policies. The philosophy underlying this globalizing capitalist economic system has been dubbed "neoliberalism," because it builds on the ideas of classical liberal philosophers such as Adam Smith and David Ricardo, who laid the foundations of capitalist economic theory.[24]

Few would dispute that neoliberalism is now the dominant economic ideology operative in the world today, shaping the agendas of nations around the world and driving the economic practices of corporations large and small. Yet, despite the hegemony of this ideology in today's

---

24. Cynthia Moe-Lobeda, *Healing a Broken World: Globalization and God* (Minneapolis: Fortress, 2002), pp. 63-65.

world, protesting voices are coming from many quarters to protest the failure of neoliberal capitalist economics to account for human and environmental values and needs. Concerns about human well-being, the common good, care for the poor, the demands of justice, love of neighbor, and environmental impacts are literally "externalities" to modern economic theory: they are not factored into the calculations that drive much economic policy-making.[25]

The critique of neoliberalism is not limited to "left-leaning" critics who are disenchanted with the project of capitalist globalization. Grassroots opposition to neoliberalism has arisen within churches around the globe, and that opposition has found its voice within the World Alliance of Reformed Churches. At the aforementioned meeting of the General Council in Accra, Ghana, delegates described core tenets underlying neoliberal globalization that they find problematic. These include the beliefs that:

- Unrestrained competition, consumerism, unlimited economic growth and accumulation of wealth is *[sic]* the best for the whole world;
- Ownership of private property has no social obligation;
- Capital speculation, liberalization and deregulation of the market, privatization of public utilities and national resources, unrestricted access for foreign investments and imports, lower taxes, and the unrestricted movement of capital will achieve wealth for all;
- Social obligations, protection of the poor and weak, trade unions, and relationships between people are subordinate to the processes of economic growth and capital accumulation.[26]

Or, as sociologist William Robinson warns:

Greased by neoliberalism, global capitalism tears down all nonmarket structures that have in the past placed limits on, or acted as a protective

25. See Charles Lindblom, *The Market System: What It Is, How It Works, and What to Make of It* (New Haven: Yale University Press, 2001), an excellent description of the market system, including his lucid assessment of what markets do well and what they fail to do. Lindblom's point — and the point of this chapter — is not to abolish markets, but to resist reigning notions of "market fundamentalism," which presume that markets can accomplish social goods that lie outside their scope and that demand human political choices and a managerial state to establish and maintain democracy and social welfare.

26. World Alliance of Reformed Churches, *Covenanting for Justice*, par. 9.

layer against, the accumulation of capital. Nonmarket spheres of human activity — public spheres managed by states and private spheres linked to community and family — are broken up, commodified, and transferred to capital.[27]

Supporters of economic globalization and trade liberalization believe that it is the best system available for creating economic growth. Proponents argue that economic growth will alleviate poverty and hunger, provide the resources necessary to (eventually) protect the environment, and create prosperity for more and more people on the planet.[28] However, a United Nations report assessing the impacts of globalization on human development issued a warning in 1999, noting that more progress has been made in opening and protecting global markets than in protecting people and their rights and that "competitive markets may be the best guarantee of efficiency, but not necessarily of equity."[29]

The World Council of Churches (WCC) has also expressed grave concern over the direction and consequences of neoliberal economic globalization, asking the questions "Wealth for Whom? At what price?" In its report on the UN World Summit on Sustainable Development, held in Johannesburg in 2002, the WCC declared:

> [T]he underlying development paradigm, with its strong emphasis on economic growth and market expansion, has served first and foremost the interests of powerful economic players. It has further marginalized the poor sectors of society, simultaneously undermining their basic security in terms of access to land, water, food, employment . . . and a healthy environment.[30]

27. William I. Robinson, *A Theory of Global Capitalism: Production, Class, and State in a Transnational World* (Baltimore: The Johns Hopkins University Press, 2004), p. 81.

28. An interesting example of a progrowth argument is the report that launched the "sustainable development" movement in the international community, entitled *Our Common Future*, but known colloquially as the "Brundltand Report," which, while acknowledging that there are "biophysical limits" to growth, nevertheless called for increased economic growth as crucial for developing countries to achieve poverty reduction and environmental protection. See World Commission on Environment and Development, *Our Common Future* (Oxford: Oxford University Press, 1987), pp. 43-44, 51.

29. United Nations Development Programme, *Summary — Human Development Report 1999* (New York: UNDP, 1999), p. 1.

30. Pamela K. Brubaker, "The International Concept of Wealth Creation and Social

Concern is growing among Christians worldwide about the impacts of the global market economy on people and the earth. The WCC believes that there is another way to achieve the goals of human development and prosperity that we all seek. The report from the Eighth Assembly of the WCC, held in 1998 in Harare, Zimbabwe, declares that the ecumenical community seeks "an alternative way of life of community in diversity," a way of life that affirms God's gift of life to *all* of creation.[31]

What will this "alternative way of life of community in diversity" look like? Certainly, it will contain some new elements that emerge out of the creativity of movements by people around the planet who are resisting the destructive impacts of neoliberal economic globalization. We are, after all, seeking a way forward, not a magician's trick of turning back time to a romanticized earlier era. On the other hand, our "way forward" must find a way to honor and preserve the deep collected wisdom of peoples who over millennia have found sustainable ways of living in harmony with the earth. In particular, we must honor the aspirations of millions who *choose* to preserve cultural forms, economic practices, and traditional knowledge and ways of life that still serve them well. Cultural diversity is itself an intrinsic good for humanity, and it deserves our protection. If we are a people who truly value freedom, as most Christians and also most Americans claim to, then we must protect the freedom of people who wish to reject elements of the global economic system that they find to be destructive of their families, communities, or cultures. It is this freedom to preserve meaningful and valuable ways of life — the right to practice self-determination — that is at the heart of many of the struggles against globalization that are taking place today. Among those who are fighting for "economic democracy" and resisting destructive elements of the global market economy, indigenous communities are particularly noteworthy because of their unique contributions to cultural and biological diversity on the planet. Their story deserves particular attention as we unpack the linkages between economic, cultural, and biological diversity.[32]

Justice: A WCC Perspective," presented at the WCC-World Bank-IMF Encounter, Geneva, Feb. 13-14, 2003, p. 5.

31. World Council of Churches, "Together on the Way," Report from the Eighth Assembly, Harare Assembly, December 1998, available at www.wcc-coe.org.

32. According to one UN definition, indigenous peoples are "the descendants of those who inhabited a country or a geographical region at the time when people of different cultures or ethnic origins arrived, the new arrivals becoming dominant through conquest, oc-

Luchando para defendernos
("Fighting to Defend Ourselves")[33]

The indigenous peoples of Mexico (there are 54 main indigenous peoples speaking 240 languages and dialects other than Spanish) have a message for the world: they are not extinct. Nor are the Mayans, Zapotecs, Nahuas, Mixtecs, Totonacs, Huastecs, and all of the other indigenous peoples of Mexico relics to be studied in museums; rather, they are living cultures that would very much like to remain that way.[34] This message was explosively delivered to the world by the infamous Zapatista Mayan rebellion in the southern state of Chiapas in 1994. The movement was intentionally launched two hours after the North American Free Trade Agreement (NAFTA) went into effect.[35] The Zapatistas called for "an end to 500 years of oppression and 40 years of development." They ushered onto the world stage a kind of revolt that is very different from typical guerilla movements, for they are seeking not to seize the reins of state power but to win the democratic right to govern their own communities according to their cultural traditions.[36]

The Zapatistas are only the visible tip of a massive indigenous movement in Mexico that is rising up and demanding attention. The untold story is that "[p]aralleling the Zapatista revolt, an explosive but pacific social movement of ecological inspiration has been growing during the last decade in practically each main indigenous region of rural Mexico." Indigenous communities are fighting to defend a way of life based on sustainable use of the natural environment and equitable access to land and resources.[37]

---

cupation, settlement or other means." Indigenous peoples are believed to be the original, or native, inhabitants of a particular territory. See United Nations High Commissioner for Human Rights, *Fact Sheet No. 9 (Rev. 1): The Rights of Indigenous Peoples* (Geneva: United Nations, 1997), pp. 1-2.

33. The Spanish phrase comes from the Campeche Mayans of the Mexican Peninsula as reported by anthropologist Betty Faust, in Betty Bernice Faust, *The Plumed Serpent: Technology and Maya Cosmology in the Tropical Forest of Campeche, Mexico* (Westport, CT: Bergin and Garvey, 1998), p. xxv.

34. Victor M. Toledo, "Biocultural Diversity and Local Power in Mexico: Challenging Globalization," in *On Biocultural Diversity*, ed. Luisa Maffi (Washington, DC: Smithsonian Institution Press, 2001), pp. 474, 483.

35. NAFTA is a trade and investment treaty concluded between the United States, Canada, and Mexico that went into effect in 1994.

36. Rasmussen, *Earth Community*, pp. 128, 130.

37. Toledo, "Biocultural Diversity," p. 482.

In fact, there are many ways of life that are endangered in contemporary Mexico, corresponding to the many different cultural and economic forms represented by Mexico's indigenous groups. There are fisherfolk, forest-dwellers, small farmers, and small-scale cattle ranchers, among others. What is striking about the indigenous peoples of Mexico is the diversity of livelihoods that they practice — and the *logic* behind this variety. That logic is common to indigenous cultures throughout the world: it is based on the recognition that economic practices should be in harmony with the natural environment of a given locale. In other words, economic activities should conserve and protect the local environment rather than deplete or assault it. Ecologist Victor Toledo notes that indigenous peasants in Mexico generally practice a nonspecialized form of agricultural production that cultivates diverse species utilizing a wide variety of landscapes: *milpa* fields, forests, home gardens, wetlands, and small areas for raising livestock. This has the ecologically beneficial result of preserving much more biodiversity in agricultural areas than we find in the huge plantation-style, single-crop farms favored by industrial agriculture (pp. 476-79).[38]

The result of this exquisite sensitivity to local environments and the effort to harmonize economic strategies with environmental conditions is a remarkable correspondence of areas of high biological diversity with resident indigenous populations. Toledo notes that the main biosphere reserves (protected areas) in Mexico are surrounded by or belong to indigenous communities, who often actively participate in managing these areas (pp. 474-75).

In fact, Mexico can be seen as a microcosm of a worldwide phenomenon that scientists are beginning to recognize; that there is a verifiable link between cultural and biological diversity on the planet. The twelve countries in the world with the highest degree of biodiversity (Mexico ranks third) are almost all countries with large indigenous populations. These indigenous populations have what has come to be called "traditional ecological knowledge" (TEK), which has enabled them to live in harmony with their environments over millennia.[39] TEK arises out of the

38. A *milpa* is a traditional Mesoamerican field containing 20-25 species of plants and trees, forming a "polyculture" rather than a monoculture of one crop characteristic of industrial agriculture.

39. Two excellent books dealing with TEK are Virginia D. Nazarea, ed., *Ethnoecology: Situated Knowledge/Located Lives* (Tuscon, AZ: The University of Arizona Press, 1999), and

specific relationships indigenous peoples have developed with their traditional territories: these are *place-based* cultures.[40]

Indigenous cultures in Mexico and their ecologically sustainable economic practices are under severe pressure today by global market forces and the political ideology of neoliberalism, neither of which values small-scale producers or cultural diversity. In Mexico, sweeping changes accompanied the implementation of NAFTA beginning in 1994. As Maria Castillo points out in her book *Land Privatization in Mexico,* the Mexican government, in order to pave the way for NAFTA, amended the Mexican Constitution in 1992 to allow for the privatization of *ejidos,* lands that are communally held by peasants (rather than privately owned).[41] Prior to the 1992 amendment, they were inalienable: they could not be sold (pp. 30-32, 85). For millions of Mexican peasants, *ejidos* had offered access to land and self-sufficiency. As a result of the *ejido* system and government support for *ejido* farmers, Mexico had achieved self-sufficiency in corn production by the end of the 1950s (p. 39).[42]

However, in the minds of international lenders, multinationals, and economic elites in Mexico — the proponents of free trade and investment — *ejidos* became an obstacle that prevented the "development" of the Mexican economy. The amendment to the Constitution in 1992 removed this obstacle. *Ejidos* may now be bought by individual *ejidatarios* (*ejido* dwellers), sold into other private hands, mortgaged, and used as collateral for loans. *Ejido* land is now a commodity on the market like any other commodity.[43] The loss of these communally held lands, which are the lifeblood of many indigenous populations, has greatly accelerated because of the privatization of the *ejidos.*

Fikret Berkes, *Sacred Ecology: Traditional Ecological Knowledge and Resource Management* (Philadelphia: Taylor and Francis, 1999).

40. The Global Biodiversity Strategy declares: "Cultural diversity is closely linked to biodiversity. Humanity's collective knowledge of biodiversity and its use and management rests in cultural diversity; conversely, conserving biodiversity often helps strengthen cultural integrity and values." World Resources Institute, World Conservation Union, and UN Environment Programme, *Global Biodiversity Strategy: Policy-makers' Guide* (Baltimore: WRI Publications, 1992), p. 21.

41. Maria Teresa Vazquez Castillo, *Land Privatization in Mexico: Urbanization, Formation of Regions, and Globalization in* Ejidos (New York: Routledge, 2004), pp. 1-3.

42. See also David Barkin, *Distorted Development: Mexico in the World Economy* (Boulder: Westview Press, 1990), p. 16.

43. Castillo, *Land Privatization,* pp. 2-6.

What have been some of the effects of NAFTA in Mexico?

- The newly landless Mexicans, those who have lost access to their ancestral *ejido* lands (in some cases forced expropriation by the government on behalf of private investors), have been migrating to the cities in record numbers, which has created a vast urban underclass in Mexico. Some find employment as underpaid workers in Mexican *maquiladoras* (factories owned by multinational and U.S. corporations); others suffer from unemployment; still others migrate to the United States, often illegally, to find work.[44] The nonprofit organization Public Citizen found that 2.7 million farm jobs have been lost since NAFTA came into effect.[45]

- Agricultural production in Mexico is becoming industrialized, following the U.S. model, spelling the end for millions of small producers. "Free trade" ultimately has meant trade between huge multinational corporations on both sides of the border, while small family operations go out of business. Eugenio Guerrero, owner of a small pig farm, was forced out of his family business in 2002 due to his inability to compete with large-scale pork producers in the United States, who now control 40 percent of the Mexican market in pork. Fully one-third of Mexico's swine producers have been put out of business since 1994. As Mr. Guerrero lamented to a reporter, "Mexico will not be a country of producers, it is going to become a country of salesmen."[46]

- In summary, as Victor Toledo documents, changes to the agrarian, forestry, and fishery laws by the Mexican government during 1992 and 1993 forced the Mexican economy to open up to world trade and foreign investment. Toledo says: "These reforms have altered key structural aspects of land tenure and redefined how agriculture, forestry and fisheries fit into the national and international economies.

44. Castillo, *Land Privatization,* pp. 173-77. See also public Citizen's Global Trade Watch, *Down on the Farm: NAFTA's Seven-Years War on Farmers and Ranchers in the U.S., Canada and Mexico* (Washington: Public Citizen, 2001), p. iv.

45. Public Citizen, "You Are What You Eat: Corporate Agriculture vs. Family Farmers in the FTAA," available at: http://www.citizen.org/trade/ftaa/farmers/ (undated; accessed May 5, 2008).

46. Ginger Thompson, "NAFTA to Open Floodgates, Engulfing Rural Mexico," *The New York Times,* International Section, Dec. 19, 2002.

Thus, the North American Free Trade Agreement is leaving without protection both cultural diversity, represented by the peasant small-scale farmers, and biological diversity, embodied in the natural resources of Mexico."[47]

Lessons Learned from Mexico

Mexico is a symbol of the developing nation that is blessed with a rich cultural and ecological heritage and yet is caught in global economic currents that threaten its social and ecological sustainability. Lured onto the conveyor belt of global economic integration through privatization and trade liberalization, Mexico is experiencing a period of great economic restructuring. The dislocations suffered by indigenous peoples and small farmers in Mexico, and the ecological damage associated with industrialized agriculture, are replicated around the world. Andrew Dragun, an economist and director of the International Institute of Development and Environment, published a study on trade liberalization, agriculture, and sustainability that noted the following effects on poor countries (paraphrased):

- Crop specialization has produced fewer types of crops in greater quantities.
- Biodiversity loss has occurred as diverse native plant species are replaced by specialized crops and food products for export to international markets. Large-scale agriculture also has resulted in extensive deforestation.
- There has been disruption of local diets and increased health problems as traditional foods are replaced by less healthy Western food products.
- Dislocation of communities has occurred as land is privatized and removed from common use, resulting in conflict and inequity.
- There has been an increase in political corruption and military conflicts.
- Environmental "non-management" has taken place because people have lost traditional ecological knowledge and discarded traditional ways of stewarding biodiversity.

47. Toledo, "Biocultural Diversity," p. 486.

In essence, Dragun found that the agricultural trading system benefits richer countries and harms poorer countries, indicating that the global market system is skewed in favor of the developed nations. Dragun concludes:

> [T]here are grounds to believe that the processes of trade liberalization will not be uniform. . . . [T]here is a pressing need for serious analysis and policy initiative in a wide range of settings, particularly where the risk of environmental deterioration and social dislocation in the poorer counties of the world is clearly very high. Fundamentally, it could be the case that poorly conceived trade liberalization certainly threatens the sustainability of many individual countries. . . .[48]

The fact that most of the world's cultural and biological diversity resides in poorer nations means that the negative impact of the global trading system on these countries is more than a matter of economic equity; it is also a blow to the cultural and ecological patrimony of the whole world. As species are extinguished through misguided agricultural and trade policies, and as languages and whole cultures are lost through the displacement of indigenous peoples off their lands and separation from their traditional livelihoods, we all lose.

Custodians of Biodiversity

As I discussed above, researchers have demonstrated a verifiable link between the areas of highest biological diversity on the planet and the presence of indigenous peoples.[49] The recognition that indigenous peoples are often the best custodians of the earth's biodiversity has been called the "Rule of Indigenous Environments": "Where there are indigenous peoples

48. Andrew K. Dragun, "Trade Liberalisation, Agriculture, and Sustainability," in *Sustainable Agriculture and Environment,* ed. Andrew K. Dragun and Clem Tisdell (Cheltenham, UK: Edward Elgar Publishing Limited, 1999), pp. 17-19.

49. One measure of cultural diversity is the existence of distinct language groups. By this measure, indigenous peoples account for the vast majority of the cultural diversity on the planet, since most of the 6,000 languages still spoken on the planet are indigenous languages. See Luisa Maffi, "On the Interdependence of Biological and Cultural Diversity," in *On Biocultural Diversity,* p. 4.

with a homeland there are still biologically-rich environments."[50] Anthropologist Andrew Gray explains:

> One reason for this [correlation between biological and cultural diversity] is that the species-diverse environments in which indigenous peoples live are deeply embedded in their production activities and spiritual relations. . . . Indeed, as several contributions to this volume demonstrate, indigenous peoples themselves conserve and create biodiversity.[51]

Gray indicates that the connection between the presence of indigenous peoples and biodiversity is explained both by their "production" activities, or their economic practices, and by their "spiritual relations." Furthermore, the "Rule of Indigenous Environments" indicates that the existence of a "homeland" is a crucial aspect of the link between indigenous peoples and a species-rich environment. For indigenous peoples, this means political self-determination and some measure of sovereignty over their traditional territories. One indigenous activist at the United Nations said: "Without self-determination and the recognition of the inherent rights over territory and land and natural resources of indigenous peoples, there will never be any so-called sustainable development."[52]

What this tells us is that the preservation of our rich human cultural and biological heritage requires solutions that integrate political, economic, and religious elements. The "integrity of creation" demands no less.

Another World Is Possible

The last decade has witnessed an extraordinary rise in people's movements around the globe that are committed to the belief that "another world is

---

50. B. Q. Nietschmann, "The Interdependence of Biological and Cultural Diversity," Occasional Paper no. 21 (Center for World Indigenous Studies, Dec. 1992), p. 3 (cited in Luisa Maffi, ed., *On Biocultural Diversity*, p. 11).

51. Andrew Gray, "Indigenous Peoples, Their Environments and Territories," in *Cultural and Spiritual Values of Biodiversity*, ed. Darrell Addison Posey (Nairobi, Kenya: United Nations Environment Programme, 1999), pp. 61-62.

52. Carol Kalafatic, personal interview, New York City, August 24, 2000. At the time of the interview, Kalafatic was the liaison for the International Indian Treaty Council to the United Nations.

possible." Coalitions of farmers, indigenous peoples, grassroots women's organizations, environmental organizations, human rights activists, youth, and others have converged to mount fierce resistance to the hegemony of free trade and free markets. This diverse movement rejects any system that prioritizes profits over people and the earth, or favors capital accumulation over communities.

Even more remarkable is the recent emergence of Christian voices joining this cry for "another world." The WCC's Ninth Assembly, meeting in 2006 in Porto Alegre, Brazil, endorsed the AGAPE call — a call for "Alternative Globalization Addressing People and Earth." The call describes a seven-year process of study and dialogue leading up to the Assembly, and concludes the following:

> This process has examined the project of economic globalization that is led by the ideology of unfettered market forces and serves the dominant political and economic interests. . . . Meeting in Porto Alegre, Brazil, the home of the World Social Forum (WSF), we are encouraged by the constructive and positive message of the movements gathering in the WSF that alternatives are possible. We affirm that we can and must make a difference by becoming transformative communities caring for people and the earth.[53]

Meeting a year and a half earlier in Accra, Ghana, the 24th General Council of the World Alliance of Reformed Churches launched a similar challenge to the project of neoliberal economic globalization. Drawing on a Reformed tradition invoked only during times of serious crisis, the General Council called member churches to enter into a *processus confessionis,* a "process of recognition, education, and confession," which was intended to result in a faith commitment to global economic justice as "essential to the integrity of our faith in God and our discipleship as Christians."[54] In Accra, the representatives of the world's Reformed churches recognized that saying "yes" to global economic justice (and ecological sanity) also required saying "no" to a prevailing economic system that is becoming total-

---

53. World Council of Churches, "Alternative Globalization Addressing People and Earth — AGAPE: A Call to Love and Action," in *Programme Book, Ninth Assembly, Porto Alegre, February 2006* (Geneva: World Council of Churches, 2006), pp. 111-15.

54. World Alliance of Reformed Churches, *Covenanting for Justice in the Economy and the Earth,* pars. 1, 16.

itarian in nature through its relentless squeezing out of all alternatives and the drive to incorporate the entire world into its globalizing market logic. Remarkably, both the World Council of Churches and the World Alliance of Reformed Churches are using the language of "empire" to describe the totalitarian tendencies of neoliberal capitalism. This is the statement of the 24th General Council:

> As we look at the negative consequences of globalization for the most vulnerable and for the earth community as a whole, we have begun to rediscover the evangelical significance of the biblical teaching about Empire. . . . Today, we define Empire as the convergence of economic, political, cultural, and military interests that constitute a system of domination in which benefits are forced to flow from the weak to the powerful.[55]

Modeling their statement after the famous Barmen Declaration,[56] the 24th General Council proceeded to enumerate a series of confessional statements spelling out what Christians are called to affirm and reject. At the heart of the statement is the following confession:

> We believe in God, Creator and Sustainer of all life, who calls us as partners in the creation and redemption of the world. . . . We believe that God is sovereign over all creation. "The earth is the Lord's and the fullness thereof" (Psalm 24:1).
>
> Therefore, we reject the current world economic order imposed by global neoliberal capitalism and any other economic system, including absolute planned economies, which defy God's covenant by excluding the poor, the vulnerable and the whole of creation from the fullness of life. We reject any claim of economic, political, and military empire which subverts God's sovereignty over life and acts contrary to God's just rule.[57]

---

55. World Alliance of Reformed Churches, "Mission Section Plenary Report," 24th General Council meeting in Accra, Ghana, July 30-Aug. 13, 2004, par. 1.1.

56. The Theological Declaration of Barmen was issued in 1934 by the Confessional Synod of the German Evangelical Church, which was drawn together for the purpose of challenging Nazi imperialism.

57. World Alliance of Reformed Churches, *Covenanting for Justice in the Economy and the Earth*, pars. 17-19.

To Christians in industrialized nations, the language of "empire" may seem inflammatory or overblown. Many of us do not perceive ourselves to be living in an empire. Yet we would be wise to listen to the voices of Christians in other parts of the world who are speaking out about the impact of the global economy on their communities. These Christians are not seeking to condemn us but to enlist our solidarity and our aid. They are crying out for us to wake up to the pain that the neoliberal economic system is causing billions of people and countless other species on our planet. In order to wake up, however, we must reject the Thatcherist myth that "there is no alternative." For as Proverbs warns us, "where there is no vision, the people perish" (Prov. 29:18). Creating room for a wider diversity of economic policies and practices will allow us to protect the God-given cultural and biological diversity of our planet for future generations.

Six Steps to an Economy of Life for People and the Earth

1. Redefine the Economy

In Alice Walker's novel *The Color Purple,* Shug tries to help Celie overcome her overly narrow understanding of God, which according to the religious scripts of her time had taught her that God was an "old white man." But God, envisioned as an old and white male, no longer had the power to save Celie from the forces that enslaved her. So Shug urges Celie to expand her perception of God, explaining that "you have to git man off your eyeball." If we are going to nurture an economy of life for people and the earth, we have to get *homo economicus* off our eyeball. *Homo economicus* is the view of human beings that underlies and drives neoclassical economic theory. *Homo economicus* is the human being stripped down to an isolated, rationalistic, profit-maximizing, self-interested, competitive individual. The economic theory behind neoliberal capitalism does not factor in human beings as persons embedded in communities, capable of cooperation, motivated by love and compassion, and spiritual in nature as opposed to purely materialistic.[58] As a result, whole dimensions of human economic and social life are left out of contemporary economic theory.

58. See Cynthia Moe-Lobeda, *Healing a Broken World,* p. 59.

For example, as feminist economists have demonstrated, the work of *social reproduction* (i.e., all the activities that flow from the unpaid labor of caring for children and the elderly, volunteering in socially useful causes, and maintaining a home and family) are literally not counted in standard economic indicators such as the gross domestic product (GDP). If a productive caring activity does not involve the exchange of money, it doesn't count as economic activity. As economist Athena Peralta observes, however, the economy is bigger than markets. The economy includes caring labor that takes place outside the marketplace as well as the production of goods and services that are sold in markets. Subsistence activities such as the production of food for one's family rather than for selling on the market are another aspect of the economy that are left out of standard economic figures. And it is precisely these broader aspects of economic life that fall outside the market that correspond to the dimensions of human nature missing from *homo economicus,* that is, the caring, other-directed, spiritual dimensions of human life. Peralta and others urge that we recognize these other dimensions of economic life and stop making hierarchical distinctions between the subsistence, or caring, economy and the market economy.[59] Ultimately, we must recognize that the entire human economy is embedded in the "Great Economy," the economy of nature that provides all the resources and energy that make human life possible.[60]

2. Recognize Existing Economic Diversity

Once we get *homo economicus* off our eyeball and redefine the economy, we discover that human economic life is actually much more diverse and varied in scope than most people realize. In fact, while the share of the world economy that participates in the global market system is large and increasing, a significant segment of the economy globally is still dedicated largely to subsistence production. For example, traditional multicropping

59. Economist Athena Peralta, citing UN sources, notes that women's unpaid work globally is valued at US$ 11 trillion per year, a third of the global GDP of US$ 33 trillion! See Athena K. Peralta, *A Caring Economy: A Feminist Contribution to Alternatives to Globalisation Addressing People and the Earth (AGAPE)* (Geneva: World Council of Churches — Justice, Peace and Creation Team, 2005), pp. 20, 43-44.

60. The phrase "Great Economy" was originated by Wendell Berry; cited in Rasmussen, *Earth Community, Earth Ethics,* p. 111.

farming systems oriented toward subsistence needs rather than the export economy still produce approximately 20 percent of the world's food supply.[61] As I suggested above, subsistence farming based on multicropping conserves much more biological diversity than export-oriented, large-scale agriculture based on monocropping. While subsistence economies and other systems, such as bartering economies, exist largely outside the market, there are other alternatives to the dominant economic paradigm that make use of markets in more human- and eco-friendly ways. For example, local cooperatives, in which an enterprise such as a factory or a farm is owned and managed by the workers themselves, are more accountable to local communities and thus to human and environmental health. These cooperatives are popping up around the globe, and while some sell their products on the global market, many are more oriented toward local production and consumption.

Anthropologist Eugene Hunn offers a compelling vision of these existing alternatives to the global market economy:

> [T]he present global market system, like that of the monolithic edifice of feudalism before it, is cracked and creviced. The "interstices" of the system may shelter alternative modes of production. The stubborn persistence of contemporary subsistence-based communities — like weeds that push up through cracks in the pavement — sustains that belief. Such communities . . . hold the world market and the national governments that serve it at bay. We should lend them our support, as their survival serves us all by preserving in the practice of their daily lives examples that alternatives exist to the present world order.[62]

3. Make Diversity an Organizing Principle in Our Economic Theory and Practice, Reversing the Trend Toward Homogenization and Uniformity

It is important at this juncture to clarify that I am not against markets per se, nor against international trade in goods and services as a segment of a

61. Miguel A. Altieri, "The agroecological dimension of biodiversity in traditional farming systems," in Posey, ed., *Cultural and Spiritual Values of Biodiversity*, p. 291.

62. Eugene S. Hunn, "The Value of Subsistence for the Future of the World," in *Ethnoecology*, pp. 33-34.

healthy human economy. Markets play an essential role in coordinating the provision of goods and services, and few of us would want to go back to a world in which we could never buy or sell products across national borders. What I wish to reject is *market fundamentalism*. Market fundamentalism argues that, in virtually all cases, the "invisible hand" of the market can be trusted to produce the best outcome and that regulation of the market should be severely limited. Furthermore, it assumes that subsistence economies that operate outside the free market economy are "backward" and should be hastened toward extinction. Finally, market fundamentalism enthrones private property rights as a sacred cow of modern culture, and it seeks to abolish a diversity of other forms of property ownership, such as "common property," collective property rights, or state ownership of property. What we need here is the *recognition and protection* of diverse economic systems, forms of property ownership, and economic practices simply *because of* the intrinsic relationship between economic diversity and other forms of diversity that humans value, namely cultural diversity and biological diversity.

Eugene Hunn makes the provocative claim that subsistence economies, which encode and use the "traditional ecological knowledge" of generations of humans living in a particular place, are critical to the evolutionary future of our species. Why? Because the ecological knowledge embedded in these traditional cultures and subsistence economic practices functions like a blueprint for a way of life that has been successful, sometimes for millennia, in sustaining human life within a particular ecosystem. Making space for these traditional communities to continue to exist as an alternative alongside the global market economy provides us with choices for our future as a species and preserves critical knowledge of diverse ecosystems.[63]

4. Protect Collective/Communal Property Rights and Access to Common Lands

Economic diversity requires that an exclusive focus on private property rights give way to the legal and political recognition of a diversity of forms of property rights. The very concept of "private property," particularly with

---

63. Hunn, "The Value of Subsistence," pp. 26-27.

respect to the ownership of land or natural resources, is alien to many indigenous cultures. Rather than the *right to possess,* indigenous peoples see
themselves as having *the responsibility to care* for their land and the creatures that inhabit it. Most indigenous cultures practice communal forms of
land use. Because they often do not own legal title to individual parcels of
land, indigenous peoples are frequently dispossessed by unscrupulous governments or corporations who come in and grab their land under the per-
nicious *terra nullius* fiction, the Western colonial concept that land inhabited by indigenous peoples is "empty." Legal regimes, including *sui generis*
systems that recognize and protect the communal nature of much property
ownership and knowledge in indigenous and traditional communities, are
long overdue.[64] Different possibilities have been suggested, such as "Community Intellectual Rights (CIRs)" and "Traditional Resource Rights
(TRRs)."[65] Property-rights regimes that protect community-based knowledge and biological resources should be combined with land-tenure regimes that acknowledge communal rights to land, including the "use
rights" of local communities to continue using their traditional common
lands for subsistence purposes.

With regard to our case study of the effects of NAFTA in Mexico,
making room for diverse forms of property ownership should slow the
rush to privatize *ejidos* and preserve space within the Mexican economy
for collectively owned and managed *ejidos* to exist as valid alternatives to

64. *Sui generis* refers to the development of new legal systems or the adaptation of
traditional legal systems to serve a particular purpose, such as the protection of the intellectual property rights of communities rather than individuals. Indigenous peoples are lobby-
ing the international community, at the WTO and the UN level, for the creation and recognition of *sui generis* systems. See Darrell Posey, "Introduction: Culture and Nature — The
Inextricable Link," in *Cultural and Spiritual Values of Biodiversity,* p. 11; see also Dutfield,
"Rights, Resources and Responses," in Posey, ed., *Cultural and Spiritual Values of Biodiversity,* pp. 508-11.

65. The idea of a collective intellectual-property-rights regime was suggested by the
Third World Network, a prominent activist organization working on behalf of the rights of
Two-Thirds World peoples. See G. S. Nijar, *Towards a Legal Framework for Protecting Biological Diversity and Community Intellectual Rights — a Third World Perspective* (Penang: Third
World Network, 1994). "Traditional Resource Rights" were proposed by Darrell Posey as an
alternative to conventional intellectual property rights, which protect only individuals and
corporations; see D. A. Posey, "Traditional Resource Rights: de facto self-determination for
indigenous peoples," in *Voices of the Earth: Indigenous Peoples, New Partners and the Right to
Self-determination in Practice,* ed. Leo van der Vlist (Utrecht, The Netherlands: International
Books, 1994).

the privatization of these lands. We need policies that encourage the preservation of those *ejidos,* which still serve the social, ecological, and economic well-being of local people.

5. Incorporate Values and Reorient Priorities

Economics is not a value-free enterprise! Our economic theories and practices reflect core values and assumptions about human nature, the kind of society we want to live in, and the things that we prioritize. Do we prize competition over cooperation? Do we value compassion as an organizing principle for human societies, or do we enshrine individual liberty above all else? Are we willing to make any sacrifices so that others' basic needs may be met, or is the accumulation of wealth our highest goal? Do we see ourselves as lords of creation or as stewards of a planet that essentially belongs to God? These and other questions are answered every day when we make decisions about how we participate in — and shape — our global economy. The WCC has clarified the values dimension of economic life and has called for an *agape* economy that honors God and serves life:

> *Agape* relationships reflect that all life has its common root in God's free grace and life-giving love. Grace is God's power to sustain and renew creation, and to turn us from death to life. Discrimination, exclusion, and an unequal distribution of wealth and power deny the values of the *agape* community and violate the commandment to love God and neighbor.[66]

Ulrich Duchrow and Franz Hinkelammert, an economist and theologian respectively, suggest a nonnegotiable ethical criterion for judging economic systems. They make this statement: "Action has to prioritize the creation of conditions enabling the life of all people and the earth. Only on this basis can individual means to reach individual ends be judged and put into practice. In old-fashioned terms, this ethic of life is called the ethic of the common good." In biblical terms, it is the requirement to love our neighbor. Duchrow and Hinkelammert elaborate that "basic human needs

---

66. World Council of Churches, *Alternative Globalization Addressing Peoples and Earth (AGAPE): A Background Document* (Geneva: World Council of Churches Justice, Peace and Creation Team, 2005), p. 14.

are absolute criteria."[67] Modern industrial society has not yet shown itself willing to meet these basic ethical criteria, choosing instead to allow *homo economicus* to determine economic policies. The question that looms is: "Whom shall you serve?" Do we serve an economic theory based in problematic and flawed assumptions, oriented toward ensuring the welfare of the few at the expense of the many? Or do we serve the God who gave us this good green earth, who calls us to sacrificial love for one another, and who charged us with the responsibility to care for God's creation?

6. Reorient International Institutions to Ensure the Above Five Steps

In order to implement the steps enumerated above, we must put a dual strategy into place. Sustainable local and regional economic policies must be nurtured while macroeconomic policies at the global level are instituted to support the above five goals. At the heart of this dual strategy is the principle of economic democracy and self-determination. Local communities need to have more control over their own resources, and this democratization of economic power must be recognized by global economic institutions such as the World Bank, the IMF, and the WTO. Communities and nations should have the right to say no to harmful structural adjustment policies, to get out from under unpayable foreign debt, to support domestic agricultural production for local food needs, and to veto development projects that harm local communities. Indigenous communities should have the right to control their traditional territories and to reject the incursions of multinational corporations that are seeking, for example, to exploit their mineral resources.

International treaties, such as the Convention on Biological Diversity, and international trade agreements offer an opportunity to enshrine these rights. However, as currently structured, most international economic institutions and trade agreements serve the interests of investors and absentee owners over the interests of farmers, workers, and local communities. Duchrow and Hinkelammert say that "all levels, from the local to the global, are to be reorganized. The question is only: from what angle

67. Ulrich Duchrow and Franz Hinkelammert, *Property for People, Not for Profit: Alternatives to the Global Tyranny of Capital* (Geneva: WCC Publications, 2004), pp. 161-62.

and in whose interest? We say from the perspective of the local people and their interest."[68] More formal recognition at the international level of economic democracy and the principle of self-determination will serve to increase economic diversity.

Conclusion

If one conviction could sum up all of the course changes proposed above, it is that (many) human beings must regain our understanding of "the big picture." Those of us who participate in and benefit from current arrangements have allowed one dimension of human life, the economic, to subsume every other dimension until *homo economicus* has threatened to devour all other meaningful aspects of being human. The "free-market economy" has become our god, and profit-making, efficiency, and competition our creed as we have lost sight of the earth economy on which we all depend. Most tragically, we have lost our place in the community of life, thrusting ourselves in a Promethean gesture into a position of presumed solitary pre-eminence, from which we peer down upon the litter of disposable species that we believe have been created for our convenience.

What we desperately need to learn from indigenous peoples, eco-feminists, and many in the global ecumenical community is that human beings are but one strand in the vast web of life, and that we are utterly and terrifyingly dependent on our other earthly relationships. Listening to these voices, we learn that we are kin to all life — in effect, all living beings are the "neighbor" that Christ calls us to love. If human beings are to survive and thrive together with other life forms on this beautiful planet, we must eschew all totalitarian tendencies, economic or otherwise. Christian freedom demands no less. After God completed the work of creation, "God saw everything that he had made, and indeed, it was very good" (Gen. 1:31). Is it not our calling as human beings, and as people created in God's image, to cherish and preserve that goodness?

68. Duchrow and Hinkelammert, *Property for People,* p. 168.

PART III

Labor and Vocation
in the Global Market

CHAPTER 8

Knowledge Work, Craft Work, and Calling

Robert D. Austin and Lee Devin

If I were to put you in front of a dock and I pulled up a skid in front of you with fifty hundred-pound sacks of potatoes and there are fifty more skids just like it, and this is what you're gonna do all day, what would you think about — potatoes?[1]

I been sewin' the same stitch for the last nineteen years. Last week they put me on a new one. I think I'm gonna like this one a lot better.[2]

The worker . . . bore evidence of [diseases] . . . the joints in his fingers might be eaten by the acid . . . you could scarcely find a person who had the use of his thumb . . . the base of it had been slashed, till it was a mere lump of flesh against which the man pressed the knife to hold it . . . their knuckles were so swollen that their fingers spread out like a fan . . . pluckers had to pull off [acid-painted] wool with their bare hands till the acid had eaten their fingers off. . . .[3]

1. Comments by a manual laborer in an interview recorded in Studs Terkel, *Working* (New York: Pantheon Books, 1972), p. xxxiv.
2. Comments of a textile worker recorded by Professor Jan Hammond, Harvard Business School, while writing a case on a garment factory in the American South. Personal communication with Jan Hammond.
3. Description of an early twentieth-century meat-packing plant, in ch. 9 of Upton

Some parts of this chapter are adapted, by permission of Pearson Education Inc., from ch. 5 of Rob Austin and Lee Devin, *Artful Making: What Managers Need to Know About How Artists Work* (Upper Saddle River, NJ: Financial Times Prentice Hall, 2003).

For the Greeks, the grim realities of physical work, its bodily nature and transitory effects, compared unfavorably with the life of the mind, which brought humans closer to the gods.[4] According to Plato, the body "enslaved" humans; its need for sustenance demanded work that made people "too busy to practice philosophy" and prevented them from "seeing truth."[5] Medieval Christians continued in these beliefs. Aquinas argued "that the active life impedes the contemplative, because it is impossible for anyone to be involved in external works and at the same time give himself to divine contemplation."[6] This view underlay the monastic tradition, which required the devout to separate themselves from earthly concerns and to engage in contemplation that earned credit toward salvation.[7] Physical labor, the province of animals and varlets, made life in the monastery possible, but labor and work held different places in God's plan. More favorable interpretations portrayed work as a means of purification,[8] a way to avoid the idleness that leads to unholy desires,[9] or, at best, a "secondary piety" with a distinctly lower place in any divine hierarchy.[10]

Renaissance thinkers broke with this tradition. Enthusiasm for creative work prompted an interpretation of the divine that centered less on

---

Sinclair, *The Jungle* (New York: New American Library, 1906). According to an oft-repeated story, reading this book over breakfast prompted President Theodore Roosevelt to rush to the White House window and vomit. There is an on-line searchable version of the book at http://www.online-literature.com/upton_sinclair/jungle/.

4. For a cogent summary of these beliefs and how they evolved over time, see Lee Hardy, *The Fabric of the World: Inquiries into Calling, Career Choice, and the Design of Human Work* (Grand Rapids: Eerdmans, 1990), pp. 6-16. Hardy quotes Hannah Arendt, who notes that, for the Greeks, a "capacity for immortal deed," an "ability to leave imperishable traces behind" marks the best of people as truly human, separated from animals (Arendt, *The Human Condition* [Chicago: University of Chicago Press, 1958], p. 19).

5. Plato, *Phaedo*, trans. David Gallop (Oxford: Clarendon Press, 1975), 66b-d.

6. Aquinas, *Summa Theologica*, II, 2nd, Q. 182, quoted in Hardy, *The Fabric*, p. 18. Hardy also quotes the sixth-century pope Gregory the Great: "The contemplative life is greater in merit than the active, which labors in the exercise of present work, while the other already tastes with inward savor the rest that is to come."

7. C. H. Lawrence, *Medieval Monasticism* (London: Longman, 1984).

8. Adriano Tilgher, *Work: What It Has Meant to Men Through the Ages* (New York: Arno Press, 1977), p. 41, quoted in Hardy, *The Fabric*, p. 23.

9. *The Rule of St. Benedict*, trans. Anthony C. Meisel and M. L. del Mastro (Garden City, NY: Doubleday, 1975), p. 10.

10. Eusebius of Caesarea, *Demonstratio Evangelica*, trans. W. J. Ferrar (London: SPCK, 1920), bk. I, chap. 8.

God removed from human activity and more on God's active role as Creator of the universe. Humans, made in God's image, also have creative powers: they are not bound, as are animals, to rote instinctive behaviors; they can learn and by learning can improve their processes and outcomes. The individual craftsman who lovingly shaped materials into a unique object for a particular purpose approached divinity by "imitat[ing] God the artisan of nature."[11]

Martin Luther moved the theology of work further in this direction. According to Luther, the duties that attach to our earthly *stations* are "fruits of the Spirit." *Vocation* is the call to love one's neighbor that comes to each person through execution of these duties.[12] In this sense of vocation, or *calling*, work gains religious significance. The activities of work are holy because they are assigned by God, part of God's grand design, nothing less than a way of carrying the cross, sharing in Christ's suffering. Calvin also argued for a divine interpretation of work:

> [W]e know that men were created for the express purpose of being employed in labour of various kinds, and that no sacrifice is more pleasing to God than when every man applies diligently to his own calling, and endeavors to live in such a manner as to contribute to the general advantage.[13]

In this expansive conception, so long as the work is not aimed at base consumption or vain accumulation, the divine can be found in almost anything a person might do.

Although the Christian idea of vocation persists today, it has retreated under the challenge of the Industrial Revolution. As principles of mass production and scientific management took hold, they made a mockery of Luther's stations and divinely ordained duties. The most perfunctory look at eighteenth- and nineteenth-century mines, mills, and factories reveals stations designed, not by God for the general advantage, but by humans for worldly enrichment. Workers had less and less control over

11. Marsilio Ficino, *Platonica Theologica*, XIII, 3 vols., ed. Raymond Marcel (Paris: n.p., 1964-1970), p. 3, cited in Hardy, *The Fabric*, p. 28.

12. Hardy, *The Fabric*, pp. 46-47. Luther quotation is from *Luther's Works*, vol. 26 (St. Louis: Concordia, 1958), p. 217.

13. John Calvin, *A Commentary on the Harmony of the Evangelists*, vol. 2, trans. William Pringle (Grand Rapids: Eerdmans, 1949), p. 143, quoted in Hardy, *The Fabric*, p. 56.

their work, which they undertook in unsafe and dehumanizing conditions. It was difficult to square these experiences with the idea of work as vocation. This kind of work, critics suggested, drew people back toward animal-like rote repetition and deprived them of any sense of likeness with God.[14]

As mass production displaced craft, theological philosophy gave way to economic practicality. Focus on efficiency and economies of scale moved attention from the "meaning" of work to its worldly "purpose": to create economic value. The technologies and practices that evolved throughout the eighteenth, nineteenth, and twentieth centuries reshaped the contours of costs that lay beneath work. Given these new contours, managers reshaped work to maximize business value. Workers became mere cogs in the resulting systems, leading many to regret "the lost sense of work as divine calling."[15]

But history never stands still, and arrangements of work continue to change. The work of a website designer or biotech researcher in the twenty-first century differs extravagantly from that of a factory or slaughterhouse worker one hundred — or even twenty — years ago. Technological transformations now underway create the potential for new work structures. Our aim in this chapter is to show that there is reason to think that a good deal of future work will have a worker-centered structure resembling that of preindustrial craft. If so, "knowledge workers" of the future will be less oppressed than factory workers have been, and work may, for many, reclaim its status as a form of God-like creativity.[16] We base this hopeful view on simple pragmatism: in an economy based on knowledge and innovation, exploitation will not create value.

14. The secular version of this argument is mounted most famously by Karl Marx. See, e.g., "Alienated Labor," in *Karl Marx: The Essential Writings,* ed. Frederic L. Bender (Boulder, CO: Westview Press, 1972).

15. Emil Brunner, *Christianity and Civilization,* part 2 (New York: Scribner's Sons, 1949), p. 69.

16. It is possible, of course, to identify benefits to workers that resulted from the Industrial Revolution. Many workers, for example, improved their overall wealth and standard of living as their jobs industrialized. Some critics disagree (strenuously) that working conditions have, on the whole, been degraded by the changes that followed the Industrial Revolution. Others who acknowledge degradation in some cases may not agree that it is a direct and necessary consequence of industrialization. In this chapter we will not debate the adequacy of the various critiques of industrial working conditions. Our subject is the changes currently underway and their likely effects.

In the space available here, we will not be able adequately to address important questions raised by our argument. Most notable among these are: Will all people be able to do this new kind of work? What will become of those who cannot? In the medieval world a learned class assumed a privileged position; the world of knowledge work could produce a similarly exalted caste. We also will not fully address questions about the fundamental fairness of a world shaped by these new processes. We merely observe that evolving structures that give workers greater control in creating value also give them greater opportunities to be wholly involved in their jobs and thus to create and capture value for themselves. This *seems* more in keeping with an idea of work as vocation. But questions about fairness will remain.

Work that transforms knowledge into economic value promises to be vocationally rich. This promise contains potential for movement toward productive relationships among work, workers, and God. But nothing about it prevents work that both Protestant Reformers and medieval theologians would have considered a vain, even sinful, accumulation of personal wealth, for example. Future work will return important choices to workers, and it will locate responsibility for right living solidly within each individual.

At the heart of our argument about the shifting character of work, we analyze the determinants that shape work processes. This somewhat technical analysis has implications for the realization of the Christian idea of vocation, and, more broadly, for a theological view of work.

Preindustrial Making

Try to envision the preindustrial world. Imagine having no idea of interchangeable parts, of economies of scale, of the possibilities of electrically powered machinery, of optimally efficient work processes. In order to help you cast your thoughts back to such a time, we have invented a description of medieval manufacturing that conforms to that world's facts of life as scholars have discovered them.[17] We use this narrative to develop

---

17. Examination of the history of daily life in ancient times is a recent development in scholarship. For obvious reasons (common workers did not write about themselves, and no one else wrote about them either), it is difficult to find out about ordinary people. We have

our description of work in preindustrial, industrial, and postindustrial settings.

An Armory on the River Severn

Hugh of Llangeth, operator of the armory in the village of Upton on the River Severn, has worked ever since he can remember. He believes that to be human is to work, that in work lies his best chance for salvation and a return to God's grace. His parents sold him at age nine to Garth the miller. He showed promise as a fabricator in wood and metal, especially at carving the oaken gears through which the water wheel drives the millstones. These gears wear out quickly, so a good carver is always in demand.

After the miracle of his escape from drowning in the millrace, Garth gave his mill to the monks and passed Hugh on to the childless Philip the armorer. Hugh worked for Philip, as an apprentice, as a journeyman, and

relied on the following in constructing our tale: Patricia Basing, *Trades and Crafts in Medieval Manuscripts* (New York: New Amsterdam Books, 1990); Morris Bishop, *The Middle Ages* (Boston: Houghton Mifflin, 1987); Jane Watkins, ed., *Studies in European Arms and Armor* (Philadelphia: Philadelphia Museum of Art, 1992), contributions by Claude Blair, Lionello G. Boccia, Evertt Fahy, Helmut Nickel, A. V. B. Norman, Stuart W. Pyhrr, and Donald J. La Rocca (in the C. Otto von Kienbusch Collection of the Philadelphia Museum of Art); John Cherry, *Medieval Craftsmen: Goldsmiths* (Toronto: University of Toronto Press, 1992); Marshall Claggett, *The Science of Mechanics in the Middle Ages* (Madison: University of Wisconsin Press, 1959); Clifford Davidson, *Technology, Guilds, and Early English Drama*, Western Michigan University Early Drama, Art, and Music Monograph Series, 23 (Kalamazoo, MI: Medieval Institute Publications, 1996); *A History of Technology and Invention: Progress Through the Ages*, 2 vols., ed. Maurice Dumas, trans. Eileen Hennessey (New York: Crown Publishers, 1969); *Medieval England as Viewed by Contemporaries*, ed. W. O. Hassall (New York: Harper and Row [Harper Torchbooks], 1965); Jacques Le Goff, *Medieval Civilization, 400-1500*, trans. Julia Barrow (London: Basil Blackwell Ltd., 1988); Edward Miller and John Hatcher, *Medieval England: Rural Society and Economic Change, 1086-1348* (London: Longman, 1978); George Ovitt, Jr., *The Restoration of Perfection: Labor and Technology in Medieval Culture* (New Brunswick, NJ: Rutgers University Press, 1986); Matthias Pfaffenbichler, *Medieval Craftsmen: Armourers* (Toronto: University of Toronto Press, 1992); Norman John Greville Pounds, *An Economic History of Medieval Europe* (London, New York: Longman, 1974); *The Didascalicon of Hugh of St. Victor: A Medieval Guide to the Arts*, trans., with introduction and notes, by Jerome Taylor (New York: Columbia University Press, 1961); Albert Payson Usher, *A History of Mechanical Inventions*, rev. ed. (Cambridge, MA: Harvard University Press, 1962); Lynn White, Jr., *Medieval Technology and Social Change* (London: Oxford University Press, 1962).

finally as a master and partner — and almost as a son. Upon Philip's death (the great wheel took his arm), Hugh, who was nineteen, married Philip's widow, who was thirty-nine, and began the manufactory's specialization in armor. He became an important member of the guild, the Armorer's Company, and by the time we catch up with him, he is recognized as the area's leading fabricator of armor.

The manufactory has expanded and now includes, in accordance with strict company rules, two journeymen and four apprentices. Hugh has added, with a dispensation from the company, half a dozen other skilled workers, under the pressure of his contract with the king for munition armor. The company has been adamant about restricting Hugh to one shop and one forge; this limitation has forced him to send out (for others to make) some parts of the armor. The king's contract has exacerbated Hugh's difficulties in securing supplies of wood, charcoal, and iron. The forest retreats before the woodcutters, and flooding in the mines renders them unworkable.

Hugh cannot approve of the expansions made necessary by large orders for munition armor. He doesn't mind someone other than himself, maybe a journeyman or even a gifted apprentice, working on rings, interlocking and riveting them into a cloth of mail. He tolerates the millman because the latter is very good at this dangerous work of polishing the finished plates — and because this was the job that killed Philip. He accepts the hammer men, because that is mere toil, not real work. But lately, Johan, a youngster with an uncanny gift for tempering, has been pestering him to make a series of anvils, each formed to a stage in the shaping of the armor, and to put a man to work on each anvil: in this way a piece of armor would be handed down a long bench from one man to the next, and would arrive fully shaped at the end, ready for tempering, polishing, and assembly.

These methods worry Hugh. A beautiful and effective (for Hugh, they are the same) harness fits like skin, and it grows like skin as Hugh shapes every part into interdependent harmony with every other. A harness of armor is part of the man who made it, and the man who made it is a part of the harness. To divide up the manufacture of it in the way Johan is proposing removes something. Hugh doesn't know what to call that something, but he feels the loss keenly. To make only one small piece of the harness — is that worker a true guildsman? Is that work part of the mystery? Or is it fit only for unskilled, interchangeable varlets repeating unskilled, interchangeable gestures?

In his conversations over a tankard of ale at the Pig and Pie with Brother Jerome, whose monastery took over Garth's mill and now has the best collection of river-driven machinery in the valley, Hugh has begun to wonder about something Jerome calls "progress." Brother Jerome has a broad mind for ideas, and thus he is not always in favor with his abbot. "There should be no limit to our desire to serve well," says Jerome, "for if we have virtue, surely it's the gift of our Blessed Lord, and to fail our gifts is to fail Him." Hugh doesn't buy this, but what can he do? How can he personally fabricate and test 1,200 harnesses in the time allowed? He can't. It's that simple. How can he refuse such an honor from the king, perhaps letting that idiot over in Camberwell get the commission? He can't. It's that simple.

Sometimes Hugh longs for the days when he worked at the forge with only an apprentice to look after the fire. He hammered the plates out of billets he carried from the nearby mine. He shaped them into pieces, each of proper thickness, annealing them to keep them malleable under his hammer. He assembled, took apart, and reassembled a harness to be sure every piece worked flawlessly with every other, closing gaps and easing frictions. He baked the parts with charcoal to turn them into steel, then tempered each to the right combination of hardness and flexibility. He polished each black and rough-edged piece, sitting at the great wheel, watching the scale shed off to reveal the gentle colors of the temper, seeing the heart of the metal shine through. Then the final assembly: filing, riveting, buffing, and fitting. Once he had made a parade armor out of gilt copper: a gorgeous living thing that fit its man like metal skin, dazzling with its elaborate engravery, red velvet picadills edged in gold, and lobster-tail *chapel de fer.*

None of that now, alas.

When he has filled this commission, perhaps he'll go back to his true craft and ignore Johan's troubling suggestions. The more he ponders, the more this munition armor worries Hugh. He makes these hundreds of harnesses, not to measure for each man, but to measurements-in-general. They'll be handed out at random, which is neither aesthetically nor ethically right. The company knows it's not right; Hugh knows it's not right. But who can resist the king?

Armor should be fitted to individual men, and it should fit. Hugh hates to think of soldiers chafing in ill-fitting breastplates and helmets, cursing him for their pain and trouble. These current methods of working don't permit the control Hugh needs to guarantee his product; the city inspectors can't keep up with production; and the armor goes out with only rudimentary examination, no individual testing.

What, after all, are the uses and virtues of armor? First, it must protect the wearer. Armor of proof must be tested against bolt and blow, and that cannot be done for the number units that must be finished in the time allotted. And everyone knows the variable quality of materials. Second, armor must allow the wearer to move freely on horseback and on foot. But these qualities are in tension, because the more protection armor affords, the heavier it is and the more difficult to wear. Two squires can put a knight on his feet if he's unhorsed, but Hugh has designed engines for lifting him onto his charger. That parade armor that he made out of copper moved like silk. The baron he made it for could dance in it — and he did — though his woman dented it with her fist when he stepped on her foot. One of the craft's chief mysteries consists of bringing these contrasting virtues of strength and flexibility together. In response to the commission, Hugh's armory needs to churn out munition armor so fast that Hugh doesn't feel he owns it at all. But he knows who will be blamed if a bolt pierces a cuirass or a morning star crushes a helmet.

Twelve hundred complete harnesses, at 16 shillings apiece! And more to come if these are manufactured well. Which they will be — because Hugh can't help himself there. He will make them to the best of his ability, and his best is *the* best. But what can he do with so many shillings? As Brother Jerome reminds him, God gave him the gift of his skill so that he can keep his family and support his soul, not so that he can pile up the world's goods in this vain way. The worldly reasons for working are as clear in Hugh's mind as the spiritual: work provides the necessities of life for his body, which in turn supports his soul and provides some cushion against the vagaries of climate and conditions. Work prevents idleness, the source of so many evils; it restrains concupiscence by mortifying the flesh; and it allows him to give alms to the poor, to participate vicariously in the monks' fervent contemplation, which in turn earns salvation for his entire community.

But twelve hundred harnesses — that's a lot of alms! It makes Hugh's head hurt. Brother Jerome puts into words three main questions:

- How can the Armorer's Company maintain its standards in the face of the new demand for quantity?
- To what degree must munition armor be of the same quality as a custom harness?

- At what point does a harness cease to be an expression of Hugh's calling and become instead an impersonal object, not part of God's purpose? At what point has work degraded to toil, and thus does not contribute to God's glory or Hugh's salvation?

The Costs and Benefits of Preindustrial Making

About making goods for sale, Hugh had sensibilities different from ours. The preindustrial fabricator made unique things one at a time. While the form and purpose of a given product might remain constant (what started out to be a wheel ended up a wheel), this early fabricator understood that everything in that wheel, including his work, depended on everything else.

A wheelwright performed operations on materials (wood, metal, animal fat) and arranged them in a form, for a purpose. A wheel had two forms: the ideal, which was perfectly round, and the actual, which was as round as possible. Each wheel had many purposes, depending on the viewpoint of the use. A pair of wheels could carry a cart, and that was a major purpose. At the same time, making and selling them provided a living for the wheelwright. For the farmer who hauled his produce to market, wheels also provided a living.

To our modern eyes, the problem with Hugh's way of working was the cost. In Hugh's armory the costs of production were high, and he incurred them every time he made anything. Preindustrial making generated three kinds of cost: (1) the effort and resources required to arrange and rearrange equipment and materials, or the *reconfiguration* cost;[18] (2) the effort and resources lost when something tried didn't work, or the *exploration* cost; and (3) the effort and resources consumed in making each part of the final product, or the *variable* cost. Hugh needs to adjust his fire to account for differences in the iron content of a new batch of ore, and thus he incurs reconfiguration cost; recycling an incorrectly tempered blade that broke under testing incurs exploration cost; the work and materials used to make a helmet, independent of reconfiguration and exploration, combine as a variable cost. The sum of these three costs we call *iteration* cost.

Note that we can separate the components of iteration cost (recon-

18. Charles M. Keller and Janet Dixon Keller, *Cognition and Tool Use: The Blacksmith at Work* (Cambridge, UK: Cambridge University Press, 1996).

figuration, exploration, variable) only in our postindustrial imagination. For Hugh, they were intermingled: reconfiguration and exploration happened every time he made a helmet. Customer preferences, material properties, his own variable performance — management of variation in all of these constituted his expertise. No matter how many helmets he made, no matter how similar some might be to others, he incurred all three costs every time. Even if he made a set of similar helmets, differences in materials and the accumulation of differences in the outcomes of uncertain processes required constant process adjustments (reconfiguration and exploration). His expectations about the cost of making a helmet would remain roughly constant, no matter how many he made.[19]

Most of Hugh's materials resisted reconfiguration. To change ore into steel, and to shape steel into parts of a harness of armor, was difficult and time-consuming. Because he worked with expensive, often rare materials, Hugh expected to incur high exploration costs every time he tried something new, which he did every time he made anything. Of course, Hugh did not think in these terms. He aimed to make a thing that would fit its purpose. He had no alternative to reconfiguration and exploration costs. Changing to fit the purpose and exploring the best ways to do that were fundamental to his mystery, the most important part of what he was doing. Because these activities had high costs, he charged a high price. Ordinary men could not afford Hugh's armor, so it was no wonder that his main customer was the king. Therefore, few transactions could occur, which created limited economic value. Replicated across the society, such limited-value creation supported a dismal standard of living. In Calvin's terms, this costly work only modestly furthered the "general advantage." But the carefully guarded secrets of the craftsman did give him leverage to keep a good part of the value for himself rather than giving most of it up to the customer or, as would become true with industrialization, to the owner of the making system.

Figure 1 illustrates the nature of transactions in Hugh's armory.[20] Because Hugh incurs the high costs associated with reconfiguration and exploration nearly every time he makes something, it does not matter much, in terms of average cost, how many he makes. His process is customized to

19. This assumes that the blacksmith is already a master, that he has already mastered the skills of his craft.

20. For the complete mathematical derivation of this figure, see Robert D. Austin and Lee Devin, "Determinants of Work Process Structure: Understanding Methodology Debates in Software Development," Harvard Business School working paper, July 15, 2005.

Figure 1: The benefits and costs of preindustrial making

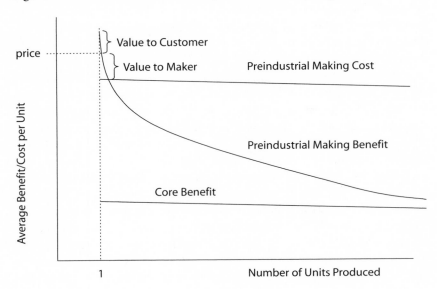

its purpose: making requires roughly the same magnitude of expenditure each time. We see this in the nearly flat "Preindustrial Making Cost" line (no economies of scale here).

Benefit to the customer is a different story. Hugh makes everything one at a time, and they are one of a kind: or, in modern terms, he customizes his product. It provides good value to the buyer, but not as much to someone else. The benefit from Hugh's way of working is therefore much greater for the first unit he makes than for subsequent units of the same thing. Actually, Hugh would not ordinarily think of making a second unit exactly like the first (unless that same customer ordered it). In Figure 1, we see that benefit falls off dramatically after the first unit, reflecting the fact that a second unit is not nearly as valuable to someone for whom it is not customized. The second unit of armor, made for a tall nobleman, typically won't fit the short nobleman who walks into Hugh's shop next. The falling benefit line approaches a level of "core benefit": the modest protection the armor provides even if it doesn't fit.

We also see from Figure 1 that customizing (usually) yields one transaction for one unit. The customer pays a price somewhere between benefit and cost. Each party captures value: Hugh gets paid more than it costs him to make the armor, and the customer gets a benefit worth more than the price he paid. Even if Hugh were inclined to make another just like this one, he would have to sell it at a loss. The customized item is not valuable enough to someone other than the first buyer that it commands a price higher than the cost of making it.[21] It is this reality that limits the number of transactions and the potential for general advantage to the community.

Toward Industrial Making

Some version of Hugh's manufactory could have been running in England or on the continent during the seven centuries from 900 to 1600. The earlier we imagine it, the more heartfelt the connection between Hugh and his product. His idea that the harness would grow under his making, its many parts fitting each to the other, persisted throughout this time, but gradually the interdependence among the maker, materials, form, and purpose wore away. The degree of divinity Hugh would have claimed for his work would have first grown through this time, with Renaissance elaboration of the theology of work, then subsided before growing pressures to industrialize.

As the world grew commercial, the armor's purpose evolved from fulfilling the vocation of the maker (to do God's work) and a function for the buyer (to protect him) to include economic value for people in the middle who had nothing to do with the making of armor or the wearing of it. As earlier purposes became part of new commercial ones, relationships among maker, materials, and form gradually changed from interdependent to independent and preplanned. The mystery moved from the *making* itself to *figuring out how to make*. The sensibility of a maker evolved from that of Master Hugh to that of young Johan, and eventually to that of Eli Whitney, Henry Ford, and Frederick Taylor.[22]

---

21. There might be a buyer somewhere in this world to whom a second, identical unit could be sold at a profit. But limited systems of distribution made it exceedingly unlikely that the buyer could be matched with the seller so that another transaction could occur. This eventuality would not be something Hugh could count on.

22. Many others cultivated industrial thinking at more or less the same time as Whitney, Ford, and Taylor did. In Europe, musket-makers, Jacquard loom operators, and many others were working with similar ideas; in the United States, it was especially the bicycle industry. We use Whitney, Ford, and Taylor as illustrations because they are so widely known that they have

Industrial Making

Eli Whitney never profited much from his most memorable invention, the cotton gin. Patent disputes and outright theft tied it up in litigation for most of his life. However, he did achieve a national reputation as a maker of machines, and it was in this persona that he offered the U.S. Secretary of the Treasury a proposition that "announced the advent of America's industrial future."[23] Whitney undertook "to Manufacture ten or Fifteen Thousand Stand of Arms."[24] That he had only recently seen a musket up close for the first time offered no impediment to his boldness. He chose to make muskets because only the national government had the resources he needed to implement his ideas. He asked himself what the government needed that he could make with his as-yet-untried "interchangeable system." The government needed muskets, so Whitney chose muskets. He thought in a way our medieval Hugh could not think: about how to structure his new factory *before* he decided what to make in it.

As a child, Henry Ford just knew that he could "build a good serviceable watch for around thirty cents." He calculated his breakeven point at two thousand watches per day. "Even then," he said, "I wanted to make something in quantity."[25] A little over thirty-five years later, he'd be thinking about Model Ts, about lowering the price to a point where his workers could buy one.

Ford's way of organizing work became known as "mass production." Ideas of mass production filled the air of the new century. Most elements of Ford's Highland Park factory were already in use somewhere or other; Ford's men borrowed and invented as they reduced the time it took to make a car. At most other automobile factories, men carried a chassis from station to station until it got wheels. Then they pushed it. Under Ford's direction, a group of engineers and shop foremen created a *moving system* of conveyors, assembly lines that brought together parts and the accumulating chassis.

Ford's moving lines began with a setup for building magnetos and spread throughout the factory. Engines came next, then transmissions,

---

become archetypes. For a more nuanced treatment, see Michael J. Piore and Charles F. Sabel, *The Second Industrial Divide: Possibilities for Prosperity* (New York: Basic Books, 1984).

23. Jeannette Mirsky and Allan Nevins, *The World of Eli Whitney* (New York: Macmillan, 1952), p. 137.

24. Mirsky and Nevins, *Eli Whitney,* p. 138.

25. Henry Ford, *My Life and Work* (Garden City, NY: Doubleday, 1922), p. 24.

then the whole car. In August 1913, it took 12.5 man-hours to assemble a chassis. The first moving line cut that to 5 hours, 50 minutes; on December 1, 1913, the time had dropped to 2 hours, 38 minutes; and by January 1914, the time to assemble an automobile had fallen to an average of 1 hour, 33 minutes.[26] In less than a year Ford had reduced assembly time by a factor of eight. The number of cars produced increased amazingly: in 1911-12, Ford made 78,440 Model Ts; in 1912-13, the company made 168,304; 248,307 in 1913-14; and in 1916-17, an astonishing 730,041.[27]

Taylor applied the ideas of Whitney and Ford to workers. What, he asked, could a tool, a machine, and a worker accomplish in a day if they worked together at peak efficiency?[28] Before Taylor, the answer lay in the accumulated shop wisdom of the workers. Hugh and his fellow armorers banded together in a guild to protect their mysteries, which had evolved over centuries and had been handed down from masters to apprentices. Taylor had a mission: to pry open those mysteries, to expose them to the light of "science," and thus to make life better for everyone.[29]

Desiring to improve not only the owner's profits but the worker's situation, Taylor made sure that, when he set the rates and quotas for a day's work, he had based his numbers on quantities "scientifically" measured. To establish such values, he broke jobs down into their smallest gestures. Hovering at the machinist's shoulder, he timed every move over and over, suggesting improvements in arrangements and even individual gestures, until he could present his rate, method, and quota as the one best way to do the job. Taylor applied Whitney's idea of interchangeable parts to the workers: interchangeable units of labor.

Taylor and metallurgist Maunsel White also measured the speeds at which various tools cut steel. They heated some tools well beyond temperatures "known" to ruin tool steel. To everyone's astonishment, the "ruined"

---

26. Allan Nevins, *Ford: The Times, the Man, the Company,* with the collaboration of Frank Ernest Hill (New York: Charles Scribner and Sons, 1954), pp. 471ff.

27. Nevins, *Ford,* p. 475.

28. Sources for this section include Frederick Winslow Taylor, *The Principles of Scientific Management* (New York: Norton, 1967; first published in 1911 by Frederick W. Taylor); and Robert Kanigel, *The One Best Way: Frederick Taylor and the Enigma of Efficiency* (New York: Viking Penguin, 1997).

29. One of the chief sources of worker opposition to Taylor's methods was his insistence on scheduled rest periods. The men could not believe that he wasn't trying to slow them down so as to pay them less.

tools cut faster and wore longer than any of the traditionally tempered tools, by a factor of four or five. Taylor and White took out patents, and Bethlehem Steel mounted an exhibit at the Paris Exposition during the summer of 1900. Although its exhibition area was placed far from the center of the Exposition, the Bethlehem lathe stole the show, cutting steel at unheard-of speeds, churning out blue-hot chips that could light cigarettes.

But the long-term consequences of Taylor-White steel were not visible at the 1900 Paris Exposition. The new cutting tools rendered shop and craft mysteries, the worker's advantage, obsolete. None of the craft wisdom applied to these new steels. Taylor had a free hand to apply his systems everywhere in the shop.

Just as Whitney broke his musket down into parts, Taylor analyzed each step of a job into gestures. The same gestures could be organized for each new job, and this organizing could be done, not by the machinist according to hard-won ancient wisdom, but by a new worker, Taylor's creation, the *rate clerk*. With clean hands and a white collar, in an office far from the dirt and clamor of the shop, a rate clerk could list the gestures required for any job, sum up the time they should take, and deliver instructions to the machinist (carefully wrapped to protect them from the worker's dirty hands) telling a worker how to do the job and how much time to take at it. Control of the shop, of the manufacturing itself, passed from the machinist to the clerk. The firm could now hire workers who were less skilled, less experienced, less expensive, and less uppity.[30]

Sequential Processes Emerge

As manufacturers improved shop methods, work took on a new shape. In order to achieve interchangeability and to create the productivity of Highland Park, the company had to specify every part of every product in advance. Taylor's rate clerks similarly prespecified every aspect of the making. Design separated from production. Industrial makers drove down unit costs and drove up the number of transactions. Workers bought

---

30. In the decades since his contributions to management, Taylor has often been demonized as the intellectual force behind the industrial dehumanization of work. While there is truth to this charge, there is evidence that Taylor did not intend to render work less rewarding, and it is important to realize that he worked in a different time, in different conditions, and without the benefit of our hindsight into unintended consequences.

things that formerly only the rich could afford. Henry Ford said: "[T]he question was not, 'How much can we get for this car?' but 'How low can we sell it and still make a small margin on each one?'"[31]

The brilliance of Whitney, Ford, and Taylor lay in a crystallizing insight: if high costs of reconfiguration and exploration limit transactions, *let's stop incurring those costs.* How? Stop adjusting each thing to its unique purpose. Let the customer adjust.

This great idea is simple and obvious in hindsight, but radically subversive in its time. Industrial methods don't avoid the costs of reconfiguration and exploration. They extract them from the making of the product, place them at the front of the process, and relabel them "product development" and "process engineering." The costs associated with reconfiguration and exploration can then be spread equally across all manufactured units. The application of technology and improvements in process design can also reduce variable costs, often dramatically. All this makes it possible to lower the unit price. The great leap in thinking was: If we can lower the price enough, customers won't mind that the product no longer perfectly suits them. If the price is right, many customers will buy a knife that, although not fitted to them, cuts pretty well. They will trade perfect for cheap and functional.

Lower price also means many more transactions. People with one knife can afford several. This creates economic value for the seller in the form of additional profit from many more transactions (even if each transaction provides a smaller profit), and functional value for the buyer in the form of useful (not perfect) knives. Each additional transaction created additional wealth and improved living conditions. Descendents of Whitney, Ford, and Taylor continued to refine production systems, and the world benefited from more and more transactions. The great economic engine of the developed world roared to life, and the potential for increases to the common advantage expanded.

Figure 2 displays the arrangement of benefits and costs in industrial practice. The sequential structure, which spreads reconfiguration and exploration costs across many units, yields economies of scale. In Figure 2, the "Industrial Making Costs" curve dips sharply. That's a good thing, because when we make products for average users rather than customizing for individuals, they provide lower benefits. In Figure 2, the "Industrial Making Benefit" curve has become flat: users get only core benefit from a

---

31. *Cycle and Automobile Trade Journal,* X (Jan. 1, 1906), quoted in Nevins, *Ford,* p. 282.

Figure 2: The benefits and costs of industrial making

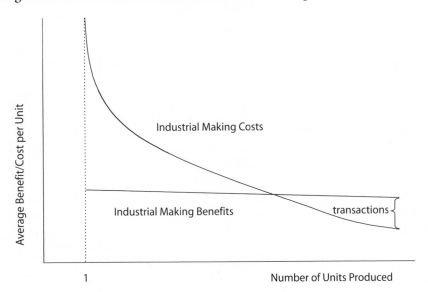

generic product. But when the cost curve dips far enough, we get many more transactions. Getting the cost curve to dip far enough is the purpose of Highland Park. The "transactions" region in Figure 2 is the heart of the increased standard of living in industrialized economies. It presents the potential for tremendous increase in the amount of general advantage derived from work.

But there remains the matter of how the advantage gets shared. At their worst, industrial approaches left workers with little leverage, less control, and a grim work-life that made a joke of efforts to imagine work as vocation. However, as we shall see, when we move beyond industrial work, there is hope for change in this characteristic.

Toward Postindustrial Making

As "Taylorism" spread through American and European industry, it created an increasingly invidious distinction between knowing and doing, thinking and making, and between classes of workers: white-collar workers and blue-collar workers. The new class, the white collars, made possible what Taylor called "scientific management." Taylor believed that implementing his principles improved the lot of working men and women. But that modifier, "working," tells the story. By distinguishing between "working" and something else, the division of the "blue collars" from the "white collars" dehumanized the blue collars, just as the medieval distinction between toil and work had dehumanized varlets. Scientific managers increasingly conceived of "workers" as material on which to perform money-saving, profit-increasing operations and experiments. And in thinking in this way, they lost access to the worker's skill, experience, and resourcefulness.

We cannot sustain this division between thinking and doing as we move toward postindustrial work. This new kind of work creates value from innovation, from doing things differently than they were done before. Methods that follow preset instructions do not (intentionally) deliver differences from past practice (when they do, we call that a "quality problem"). Industrial work creates its values from effectiveness in delivering *consistency*. Postindustrial work produces valuable *inconsistency*. This requires a different worker doing a different kind of work.

Postindustrial Making

Cost reduction plays an important role in the transition to postindustrial making, just as it did in the transition from preindustrial to industrial making. But postindustrial making, which is often knowledge-based, results mainly from *reconfiguration* and *exploration* cost reduction, not *variable* cost reduction. Computing industry pioneer J. C. R. Licklider described in 1960 how technology could play a role in reducing reconfiguration and exploration cost:

> Present-day computers are designed primarily to solve preformulated problems or to process data according to predetermined procedures. The course of the computation may be conditional upon results obtained during the computation, but all the alternatives must be foreseen in advance. . . . However, many problems that can be thought through in advance are very difficult to think through in advance. They would be easier to solve, and they could be solved faster, through an intuitively guided trial-and-error procedure in which the computer

cooperated, turning up flaws in the reasoning or revealing unexpected turns in the solution.[32]

This logic applies to making things as well as to solving problems. The great benefits of the Industrial Revolution came when "predetermined procedures" built "preformulated" products. Industrial systems could make various products, but "the alternatives [had to be] foreseen in advance." However, innovative work, which seeks novel rather than predetermined outcomes, would be easier and would go faster if, as Licklider says, it used a "trial-and-error procedure in which the computer cooperated, turning up flaws in the reasoning or revealing unexpected turns."

The application of technology described by Licklider makes the guided trial-and-error process cheap by reducing reconfiguration and exploration costs. As a result, new value-creation possibilities appear, along with new ways of organizing work. Knowledge work arranges and performs operations on ideas, symbols, and other "thoughtstuff"; therefore, it can have lower iteration cost than physical work to begin with, because it is easier to rearrange thoughtstuff than metal. But it is the evolution of technologies that most powerfully transforms the cost contours that shape work. Stefan Thomke has documented the many ways that technology can reduce iteration costs.[33] Simulation software crash-tests virtual cars far more cheaply than crashing real cars does; robotic experimentation equipment tests drug-development compounds with inhuman speed; version-control systems permit rolling back from "mistakes" in software development; and prototype-generation technologies and methods allow rapid building and testing of new ideas.

Figure 3 shows how postindustrial making, characterized by cheap and rapid iteration, enters the story of making. Cheap iteration, a feature of low reconfiguration and exploration costs, amounts to a low cost of making the first unique unit. The average cost line in this figure resembles the one in Figure 1, but is much lower. Therefore, the potential for industrialization is small. You could arrange work processes in a sequential, industrial manner, but you wouldn't gain much. The rationale for sequential, industrial arrangement of work has weakened.

32. J. C. R. Licklider, "Man-Computer Symbiosis," *IRE Transactions on Human Factors in Electronics,* HFE-1 (March 1960): 4-11.

33. See Stefan H. Thomke, *Experimentation Matters: Unlocking the Potential of New Technologies for Innovation* (Cambridge, MA: Harvard Business School Press, 2003).

Figure 3: The benefits and costs of postindustrial making

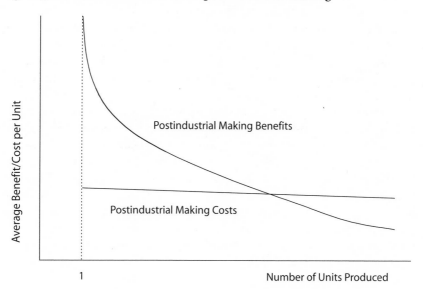

Because industrialization offers less potential benefit here, the work no longer needs to be directed toward the needs of an average user. We can move back toward customizing, toward making what a particular customer wants, toward the shape of preindustrial making. It is no coincidence that the shapes of benefit and cost curves in this figure are similar to the ones that described Hugh's work (even if average costs are much lower). Hugh would be happy to see that we can again craft a product to its purpose. A customer needn't put up with the knowledge work equivalent of munition armor. A software program, a strategy, a play production, even a new shirt — these can be made in endless and subtle variations. Structured *iteratively,* in cycles of doing and doing again, a making process can produce outcomes for any occasion.

Mass production developed out of the need to diffuse high reconfiguration and exploration costs across a large number of units. When those costs are not very high to begin with, or when technology can lower them, we don't need mass production. We can claim larger profit margins from individualized transactions, harvesting market niches inaccessible to a standardized product; and we can execute such transactions again and again.

We replace large numbers of cheap and rapid *repetitive* transactions with large numbers of cheap and rapid *iterative* transactions. Instead of a large number of similar units, as in industrial settings, we can make an ongoing (theoretically unending) series of units different from each other, each one benefiting from unique and value-adding innovations. We can reconceive the process outcome each time, achieving a large number of unique transactions. This way of working moves beyond industrial methods.[34]

Henry Ford's reductions in the time it took to assemble a chassis predate by decades computer simulation and related technologies. Both applications of technology produced startling shifts (one of which is still underway) in the way we arrange work. Architect William J. Mitchell notes that "digital technology allows architects to reduce reliance on standardization and repetition and to produce designs that respond more sensitively to varied conditions and needs." He offers the example of the Stata Center at MIT, a building of a complexity that could not have been achieved in an earlier time.[35] It is a creation of advantage that could not have resulted from older methods of making.

---

34. Creating value through customization doesn't simply mean giving every individual exactly what he or she wants or infinite proliferation of product choices for individual consumers. A growing body of research in psychology and marketing indicates that more and more choice for individual consumers doesn't mean increasing consumer satisfaction. See, for example, Barry Schwartz, *The Paradox of Choice: Why More Is Less* (New York: Ecco, 2004). The biggest source of value from customization is the ability to target products to market niches where there are relatively small (but economically significant) numbers of customers who aren't interested in standard products. Customization capability coupled with widely used low-cost distribution (e.g., via the internet), creates potential for what some have called "hyperdifferentiation." See, for example, Eric K. Clemons, Rick Spitler, Ben Gu, and Panos Markopoulis, "Broadband and Hyperdifferentiation: Creating Value by Being Really Different," in *The Broadband Explosion: Leading Thinkers of the Promise of a Truly Interactive World,* ed. Robert D. Austin and Stephen P. Bradley (Boston: Harvard Business School Press, 2005). In simple terms, from the producer's perspective, it means that you can make and profitably sell something with special features that you would not have been able to make and sell before.

It is also important to distinguish between the customization we are describing here and what has sometimes been called "mass customization." Often, mass customization systems are systems that can produce a very large number of nonetheless *prespecified* outcomes. The postindustrial processes we describe can produce outcomes that are not prespecified; this is not a capability that most mass customization systems share.

35. William J. Mitchell, "Constructing Complexity in the Digital Age," *Science* 303 (Mar. 5, 2004): 1472-74.

The Characteristics of Postindustrial Work

We can view many late-twentieth-century advances in making practices as the result of looking simultaneously back toward preindustrial making and forward toward postindustrial making. Management gurus Peter Drucker and W. Edwards Deming, among others, realized in the 1950s and 1960s that workers themselves can best understand the complexities of evolving systems of making.[36] They saw that in a rapidly changing world the value of customization and innovation will increase, that making aimed at numerous niche markets can compete with mass production for mass markets,[37] and that technology would drive down the costs of reconfiguring plants and equipment. Increasingly, today, the game shifts from efficiency to improvement, from replication to innovation, from minimizing cost to maximizing the customer's willingness to pay. In the future, rate clerks and their modern equivalents won't be the primary source of improvement, innovation, or high-profit margins. To improve the product or service, workers themselves must take the initiative to manage and monitor systems under their control. Workers must once again become people, with individual skills and flaws, not interchangeable units of labor. Thinking about workers as people will inexorably lead management to consider how to make profitable use of all their human powers, not a mere straitened repertoire of Taylorized gestures.

The balance of power has already shifted in many settings. Consider as evidence the changed relationship between an organization's quantifiable assets and its market success. Unlike materials or equipment, the innovative competencies of people cannot be readily inventoried or listed on balance sheets; nor can the ability of employees to adapt and improvise, or the synergy of teams. One result of this is that, in some business sectors, factors that contribute substantially to a firm's market success elude financial measurement. Such "intangible assets" complicate valuation of firms and signal the return of the workplace to pre-Taylorist dependence on skill, knowledge, and lore.[38]

36. Peter Drucker, *The Age of Discontinuity: Guidelines to Our Changing Society* (Burlington, MA: Butterworth-Heinemann, 1968); W. Edwards Deming, *Out of the Crisis* (Boston: MIT Press, 1982).

37. This argument has recently received much attention in the popular press in discussions of "the long tail." See Chris Anderson, *The Long Tail: Why the Future of Business Is Selling Less of More* (New York: Hyperion, 2006).

38. Google, which at this writing (spring 2006) remains a dangerous mystery to its

In a knowledge economy, the unique characteristics of individual employees pose challenges for managers. Lucinda Duncalfe Holt, a software company CEO, has observed:

> [Technical workers are] very difficult to control. . . . They're your most precious commodity and your worst nightmare. You have no idea what they're doing. They literally sit there with 42 little windows open on their 17-inch monitor. When [your business shifts] you'll often find the seeds for the shift in that group because they're not really paying attention to you all along anyway. They were worried about some way-out-there trend. They'll see it and there will be something there. [The key to managing] change is in that group of folks you don't have a lot of control over.[39]

Managers rarely know what these employees know, cannot do what they do, and have no information about work progress except what employees willingly report. The work tends to be multidimensional, idiosyncratic, and oriented toward problem-solving (even in factory settings).[40] To those who are not experts, it appears strange and formless; and it is difficult to observe, measure, and evaluate. Collaboration, which is common in such work, masks individual contributions. Problems of observation, measurement, and evaluation become problems of control. Ivan Sutherland, the manager of some of the researchers who created the internet, says of those workers: "You can maybe convince them that something's of interest and importance, but you cannot tell them what to do."[41] There is no way that the Taylorist rate clerks can run this race.

The abilities that managers cannot directly observe nevertheless manifest themselves. A highly able employee may have several useful skills, and that complicates staffing. You can't build a team by the numbers, or by reading résumés. People match up differently, and chemistry counts. "Cast

---

competitors, epitomizes this aspect of the knowledge economy. The firm encourages its employees to spend up to 20 percent of their time on personal projects, and it eschews conventional strategic planning. No one knows what they'll do next, including them.

39. Robert D. Austin and Patrick D. Larkey, "Performance Based Incentives in Knowledge Work: Are Agency Models Relevant?" *International Journal of Business Performance Management* 2, nos. 1/2/3 (2000): 57.

40. The Toyota Production Systems provides a factory-based example of this.

41. Michael A. Hiltzik, *Dealers of Lightning: Xerox PARC and the Dawn of the Computer Age* (New York: HarperCollins, 1999), pp. 145-46.

of characters" becomes a better metaphor than does "team." Processes designed on the industrial assumption of interchangeable units of labor function poorly when applied to those folks who are looking at 42 windows on their 17-inch screens.

Such knowledge artisans often enjoy their work. Unlike many alienated industrial workers, who work only for their paycheck, knowledge workers may see their job as an end in itself. For some — perhaps many — monetary compensation is not the primary source of gratification in work. These workers have a relationship with their work that Hugh of Llangeth would recognize and approve of.

When skilled workers are motivated and innovation is needed, questions arise about the degree to which they *should* be asked to comply with imposed structure. Plans and the systems that require people to comply with plans may keep workers doing what they are doing even when they ought to be doing something else. Holt clearly suggests exactly this: "[The key to managing] change is in that group of folks you don't have a lot of control over. . . ." Computer industry maven Tom DeMarco,[42] speaking about software-development projects, makes a similar point: "The best thing you can do . . . is get on top of an absolutely out-of-control team . . . you can't steer it, you can't make it go faster or slower, but it is making tremendous progress."[43]

Outcomes emerge in this kind of work, and managers are not the first to see the direction that the business should take. Mintzberg and McHugh have noted the importance of business activities that are not fully planned, of outcomes not fully predicted, in fast-moving organizations they call "ad-hocracies":

> Sometimes it is more important to let pattern emerge than to force an artificial consistency. . . . Sometimes an individual actor . . . creates his or her own pattern . . . ; other times, the external environment imposes a pattern . . . ; in some cases, many different actors converge around a theme, perhaps gradually, perhaps spontaneously; or sometimes senior managers fumble into strategies. . . . To manage this process is not to preconceive strategies, but to recognize their emergence and inter-

42. Among other distinctions, Tom DeMarco has received the Warnier prize for "lifetime contributions to the field of computing."

43. Tom DeMarco, as quoted in Robert D. Austin, *Measuring and Managing Performance in Organization* (New York: Dorset House, 1996), p. 113.

vene when appropriate. . . . To manage in this context is to create the climate within which a wide variety of strategies can grow . . . to watch what does in fact come up and not be too quick to cut off the unexpected. . . .[44]

In this management game, value creation slips through the fingers of micro-managers: they must depend (not altogether comfortably) on workers' cooperation.

Within knowledge work, the idea of work as vocation gains new life and new potential. Even by the standards of the Greeks, work that unites the active life with the life of the mind earns some claim to divinity. With its basis in innovation, knowledge work approaches the Renaissance ideal of emulating God the craftsman. Because it shifts power back to workers, knowledge work allays at least some of the concerns of social critics about worker exploitation. Because it shifts work choices from planners to workers, knowledge work supports the ideal of work as a calling; it succeeds particularly in what Jeff Van Duzer and his colleagues at Seattle Pacific University propose as a way business can contribute to right living and a right relationship with God: by "provid[ing] opportunities for vocationally rich work through which people develop and exercise their creativity and their gifts, thus contributing to their communities."[45] However, it leaves each individual with a choice about the ends to which the work will be directed. Thus objectives inconsistent with Christian vocation, such as vain accumulation, remain possible.

Caveats, Open Questions, and Conclusions

> [In this job] you get a feeling you're okay, you get smarter, and that's nice, I like to be smarter. You get the satisfaction of "Ah, I understand

---

44. Henry Mintzberg and Alexandra McHugh, "Strategy Formation in an Adhocracy," *Administrative Science Quarterly* 30, no. 2 (June 1985): 160-97.

45. Jeff Van Duzer, Randal S. Franz, Gary L. Karns, Tim Dearborn, Denise Daniels, and Kenman L. Wong, "Toward a Statement on the Biblical Purposes of Business," in *Business as a Calling: Interdisciplinary Essays on the Meaning of Business from the Catholic Social Tradition,* ed. Michael Naughton and Stephanie Rumpza (St. Paul: University of St. Thomas, 2004. Available at http://www.stthomas.edu/cathstudies/cst/mgmt/publications/businessasa calling.html.

this." You get the ah-ha feeling and you get happy, see more opportunities. I like to learn new stuff, because if I don't — ugh.[46]

This [job] is a place where I've found a lot of hope. At a personal level, it is a place that spoke to all of me in ways that other places didn't. There's so much honor and regard given the soul, and the emotional life, and the life of the imagination. And it's not pie-in-the-sky; it's not a kind of idealist vision that has no substance or reality to it. It doesn't feel simply indulgent and luxurious and irrelevant. It feels essential. It feels, to me, like something that brings me back and can bring other people back to what counts.[47]

As postindustrial work becomes more important to economic value creation, the structure of work departs from industrial models. It follows that postindustrial principles of management will differ from those of the industrial era. These principles are not fully in place yet; they will take time to invent, learn, and develop. We have barely hinted at their nature, though we have written about it at length elsewhere.[48] Here we've only briefly suggested that these new principles will result in more worker-centered value creation.

Who can do this kind of work? To make unpredictable products out of intangible materials requires education, expertise, and experience. Because of this, we face a significant risk that postindustrial societies may shake down into rigid caste systems. Imagine a knowledge economy elite supported by a large class of service jobs that do not produce much of economic value and do not support a decent standard of living for workers. It is far from self-evident that everyone will have postindustrial opportuni-

---

46. A graphic designer explaining why he likes his job; from interviews for the Artful Making project, Robert Austin and Lee Devin, principal investigators, 2005.

47. Quote from Nancy Shaw, a staff member at People's Light and Theatre in Malvern, PA. As we have argued elsewhere, the way this theater runs is emblematic of the coming, and in places already arrived, world of knowledge work. Robert D. Austin, "The People's Light and Theatre Company" (Boston: Harvard Business School Publishing, 2000), Harvard Business School case number 600-055.

48. For example, see Robert D. Austin and Lee Devin, *Artful Making: What Managers Need to Know about How Artists Work* (New Saddle River, NJ: Financial Times Prentice Hall, 2003); see also Robert D. Austin and Richard L. Nolan, "Stewards vs. Creators: Disputes and Disconnects on the Front Lines of Business Innovation," Harvard Business School working paper, 2005.

ties and material comfort. Juan Enriquez has suggested a life-sciences-intensive scenario in which a huge portion of the world's ability to create economic value might lie within a few miles radius of MIT.[49] If this or something like it happens, our society may become medieval in ways that offset any divine potential within knowledge work.[50]

What does a society owe to people who cannot participate in its economy? As a matter of policy, we can choose to trade efficiency in an economic system for additional fairness. We do this already, often at points where economic activity intersects with morality: we outlaw prostitution or the sale of human organs, even though transactions in these areas would create economic value, strictly speaking. But we'll have to decide collectively how much of this we will do to care for less able neighbors. Such questions are hardly unique to postindustrial societies, but the transition to a knowledge-based economy prompts us to revisit them and provides new opportunities for getting answers more nearly correct. But it also poses new challenges. In our increasingly globalized world, jobs flow across national boundaries far more easily than people do. Education will be important, but our schools do not as yet prepare the next generation for knowledge work jobs. Meanwhile, emphasis on standardized courses and test scores prepares workers for the economy we're leaving, not the one we're entering. These issues present us with our latest opportunity to define ourselves before history, each other, and our gods.

The hopeful state of the work we describe should materialize, but there are reasons it might not. One possible obstacle: the market malfunction known as *monopoly*. In postindustrial work, the need to innovate transfers initiative and control from managers to workers. But by colluding to control the flow of new products to consumers, successful monopolies can reduce their need for innovation. All other things being equal, businesses will move in this direction as conditions allow. Even free markets need rules to avoid malfunctions that serve private interests at the expense of general advantage. This issue is separate from questions of trading efficiency for fairness. Markets become both unfair and inefficient without co-

---

49. Personal communication with Juan Enriquez.

50. We might also worry that some people do not have the innate inclination or capacity for self-directed work. This may not be entirely a matter of education, and it may generate difficulties, especially for workers with established patterns of behavior. If work has always meant just following instructions, you may have a hard time switching to self-directed work.

herent and enforceable rules about conditions of ownership, legitimate uses of market information, and allowable forms of collusive behavior.

We might also worry about the ownership claims in the knowledge economy. As we have seen, value creation depends less and less on aspects of the business that can be counted and inventoried, more and more on intangible materials and assets. The sources of economic value have never been so difficult to define. This has led companies to seek broader ownership of new sources of value. At the beginning of the twenty-first century, an intellectual property free-for-all is underway. Patents edge ever closer to assigning ownership of ideas. A major chemical company seeks to patent common pig-breeding techniques.[51] Other companies apply for ownership rights in the genetic material of common food crops. As long as rules remain unclear concerning which of the new sources of value can be owned, companies can't afford to let competitors gain an upper hand in the free-for-all; therefore, ownership claims will grow ever more expansive. Broad interpretations of ownership rights in the new sources of value could certainly interfere with creative work. Arrangements that slow innovation and shift power away from workers remain a lively possibility.

If we can avoid these dangers, however, future work might be something Hugh of Llangeth could understand and approve of. If he were suddenly to appear in a research lab or on a software development team in the year 2020, he would notice arrangements that look very much like the master/apprentice relationship he enjoyed with Philip. He might see daily application of mysteries unavailable to managers. He might see a level of care and interest in work reminiscent of the time he spent making that gilt copper parade harness. If we can avoid the perils of malfunctioning business and market systems, future work will be kinder than the work of the industrial past, and it will be a better fit with the Christian ideal of work as vocation.

---

51. See http://www.organicconsumers.org/monsanto/pigs.cfm.

CHAPTER 9

Christian Manufacturers at the Crossroads

Shirley J. Roels

Introduction

On Saturday the manufacturer read of Bono's plea and the Gates Foundation's attack on "stupid" world-wide poverty.[1] On Sunday this wealthy person was moved by a sermon on the global nature of Christian neighborliness. Now it's Monday in the everyday life of this Christian leader who is living at the crossroads of global need, imperfect market systems, and changing occupational structures. To some degree, lesser or greater, this businessperson knows that Christian beliefs and free-market systems are not perfect overlaps. Furthermore, the personal sense of one's neighbor is more palpable among those in the same economic circle than for those living in grinding poverty thousands of miles away. On the one hand, this is an era in which growth, hope, poverty, and pain are all more closely intertwined; on the other, the more depersonalized global economy detaches us from any neighbor's economic experiences. At times some of these collisions are more obvious than others. Still, market activity is the time-bound means available through which this manufacturing leader can express Christian neighborliness. If we make progress in framing this bellwether crossroads, it can guide us in other choices still ahead. We can remain hopeful that what we learn can provide light for our path as we move into a new and different economic era.

So now the question: How do Christian manufacturing leaders, given their particular positions in the greater economic constellation, live and

---

1. "Persons of the Year: The Good Samaritans," *Time*, Dec. 26, 2005, pp. 38-88.

choose on Monday? The world is re-sorting the places and the processes through which goods are produced and distributed. To great wonder and delight, the civic, familial, political, and religious cultures that encourage economic productivity are being discovered in many global pockets. Benefits are beginning to flow for diverse global groups that have rights and access to raw resources, productive technology, financial capital, and pools of able employees. Yet all this change causes struggle in balancing economic opportunity, costs of production, and existing commitments to real people in real communities. In this era of great economic transformation, what is the Christian calling of the manufacturer for that part of the economy on the current cusp of economic change and globalization?

Change in the U.S. manufacturing environment is a real and pressing economic problem. According to Al Frink, U.S. assistant secretary of commerce for manufacturing and services, manufacturing makes up 15.8 percent of the U.S. economy's annual output; but when one considers its ripple effects, it represents 50 percent of the gross domestic product (GDP).[2] Further evidence arose during the January 2005 hearings for the new U.S. secretary of commerce, Carlos Guttierez, when members of congressional committees noted that in the four prior years, U.S. manufacturing companies had shed 2.7 million jobs.[3] As a case in point, between June 2000 and August 2005, the number of manufacturing jobs in the state of Michigan alone declined by 26 percent, a loss of 234,300 positions.[4] These are losses with substantial effects.

The evidence of this economic change also cuts across many industries. In Lynn, Massachusetts, a city of 80,000 people, three of every five workers were once employed in shoe manufacturing. But the last of the Lynn shoe factories closed over five years ago; since then, the sale of Massachusetts-based Reebok shoes to Adidas (a German-based company) is triggering more questions about potential shifts in the remaining shoe design and marketing jobs from New England to India.[5] In Michigan the

2. "Czar wants respect for manufacturing," *Grand Rapids Press*, Oct. 6, 2004.

3. "About trade deficit . . . Senators pepper former Kellogg chief with questions about unfair competition," *Grand Rapids Press*, Jan. 6, 2005, C3.

4. "Economy struggles to pick up steam," *Grand Rapids Press*, Aug. 22, 2005, B4. This article notes that, while that shift is dramatic, the national decline in manufacturing jobs during the same period was 18 percent, not far behind in terms of percentages.

5. "Reebok-Adidas deal another blow to New England," *Grand Rapids Press*, Aug. 10, 2005, C6.

plants that produce automotive parts, bowling balls, and refrigerators are being replaced by Mexican operations. These Mexican plants welcome that manufacturing work because it fills the abandoned capacity that is left when others of their businesses shift operations to mainland China. For North Carolina-based manufacturers of home furnishings, raw woods are now containerized, shipped east, tooled by Chinese woodcarvers, and returned to the United States as finished furniture products.[6] While furniture prices are declining, so is the manufacturing value that those in North Carolina can add. Change in production strategies is pervasive.

Meanwhile, we live in this tumbling turbulence that mixes emerging markets with mature ones, new manufacturing strategies with older plants, and new communities of need with older communities of commitment. Perhaps it is an era in which Charles Dickens's famous opening line of *A Tale of Two Cities,* "It was the best of times, it was the worst of times," applies once again. But given this muddle, what is the claim of Christian social justice on the vocation of the manufacturer? In light of the Christian witness, what is required of those who are the leaders, employees, and shareholders in U.S.-based manufacturing? How do we frame our Christian calling as economic participants so that we can make appropriate decisions in a time of great economic change?

To respond to these concerns, we need to investigate three questions more specifically:

1. What are the underlying dynamics of manufacturing's economic globalization?
2. In light of them, should and can social justice be a primary and direct goal for the individual manufacturing firm?
3. If manufacturing firms can and should make a contribution to social justice, in what ways can they best contribute?

We need knowledge and wisdom in several areas to tackle this topic. First, we must understand more about the globalization of manufacturing. Second, we must consider the meaning of "social justice" as a frame for our decisions. Finally, we must determine practical ways in which the indi-

---

6. Information based on personal interview with Mr. Robert Israel, president of Israel's Designs for Living, a major furniture supplier for West Michigan residents and international hotel chains (Grand Rapids, MI, Spring 2005).

vidual firm can contribute, balancing prior obligations with the press of change. Through this discussion we hope to create a bridge between the call for greater Christian social justice and specific steps that a Christian manufacturing leader may take toward its fulfillment.

The Globalization of Manufacturing

There is an upside associated with this redistribution of productive resources. According to Peter Singer, "[t]he 1997 *Human Development Report* struck a positive note, indicating that poverty has fallen more in the past fifty years than in the previous 500 . . . over a quarter of a century, but taking into account the growth in world population during this period . . . the proportion of people who are undernourished has fallen from 37 percent to 18 percent." Between 1960 and 1993, the Human Development Index (HDI) scores for developing countries have risen consistently, "suggesting that the world's poorer people have become better off overall in terms of income, life-expectancy, and the amount of education they receive."[7] According to the 2005 Human Development Report, "extreme income poverty has been falling. . . . Average per capita income growth in developing countries in the 1990s was 1.5 percent, almost three times the rate in the 1980s. Since 2000, average per capita income growth in developing countries has increased to 3.4 percent — double the average for high-income countries."[8] That 2005 report also notes that when health and education variables are added to this income indicator, "over the last decade the HDI has been rising across all developing regions." While we all desire even more progress in reducing global poverty, real strides are being made during this time of economic change. God's good earth has the needed resources to provide a better life when we use human creativity to make them productive and distribute them well.

Perhaps the correlation between the growth of a global market system and increases in global quality of life is not a tight causal relationship. Yet, in the aggregate, the growing market system and the redistribution of

7. Peter Singer, *One World: The Ethics of Globalization,* 2nd ed. (New Haven, CT: Yale University Press, 2004), pp. 85-87.

8. Human Development Report 2005, 20 and 21, at http://www.hdr.undp.org (accessed Sept. 16, 2005).

manufacturing seem to be powerfully associated with greater global welfare. Global market performance, despite its many limitations and inadequacies, is producing economic well-being at a more rapid rate than was the case in any prior economic era.[9] For many, it is bringing the promise of greater economic power to manage the forces of nature that can leave them hungry and dying. For example, with new sources of production-based employment, current Chinese and East Indian life is much less grim than in the past; and for those in Eastern Europe and Russia, new capital investments are bringing an increase in freedom to determine the course of their own lives.[10] There is a growing global consensus about the broad outlines of preferable economic patterns that support human growth and development. Economist Charles Lindblom says, "A society without any market system at all is not worth considering for our futures."[11] Economist Rebecca Blank observes: "The market has many problems. . . . But there is no viable alternative to the market as an organizing principle for an economic system in a complex society."[12] The global market system and its spread of productive capacity are now deemed necessary to provide economic fruits for those who most need them.

Yet this affirmation of a global market system and all its benefits comes with a price. There is trauma associated with structural economic

9. Singer, *One World*, p. 85. Despite these aggregate global gains, some regions have lost economic ground. Globally, as Singer notes, from 1965 to 1998, while average global well-being increased, sixteen of the world's poorer countries, including twelve in sub-Saharan Africa, had falling per capita income. According to the Human Development Report 2005, 21 (http://www.hdr.undp.org [accessed Sept. 16, 2005]), by 2005 such inequalities were still serious, if not more severe in some cases. The multiple and complex reasons for the most severe inequalities extend far beyond the focus of this chapter. Some would argue that these are failings inherent in a global-market system. Others suggest that these challenges are the results of governmental protection in developed nations that thwart the capacities of free global markets to function, particularly in areas such as agriculture. Still others believe that, on balance, the most severe economic failures are less the fault of a global market system and more the outcomes of ineffective leadership in real situations. All of these possible reasons are compounded by the heavy global debt loads of the very poorest countries, harsh and shifting environmental conditions, and entrenched cultural patterns.

10. Nicholas Wolterstorff, *Until Justice and Peace Embrace* (Grand Rapids: Eerdmans, 1983), pp. 38-39.

11. Charles Lindblom, *The Market System* (New Haven: Yale University Press, 2001), p. 276.

12. Rebecca M. Blank and William McGurn, *Is the Market Moral? A Dialogue on Religion, Economics and Justice* (Washington, DC: Brookings Institution Press, 2004), p. 12.

change. Silicon Valley entrepreneurs experience frantic demand for their next generation of microprocessors and live unbalanced lives. Simultaneously, as the global economy moves from desktops to laptops and from corporate offices to the office-where-you-are, Steelcase Corporation, the leading U.S. producer of office furnishings, sheds 58 percent of its hometown employees.[13]

During such a best-and-worst time, it is difficult to find a frame through which to analyze the dynamics of change. Often we find ourselves in the middle of the maelstrom. We know what is happening, but we may not know why it is occurring or where it will lead. A review of seismic economic shifts in the past two decades will give us better lenses for truly seeing these economic changes. Some aspects of economic change parallel those of prior periods. There have always been competing forces, simultaneously pushing and resisting such shifts. There is nothing new in the early twenty-first century in this regard. Some have always been adopters of new products with new cultural paradigms; others have always thought that emerging change could not alter the markets in which they were embedded. For example, even while consumers were buying their first cars, American buggy-whip manufacturers held onto their production shops, convinced that voluminous demand for their product would continue.[14] They continued to believe that recalcitrant autos couldn't possibly replace reliable animals.

Border-crossing economic change is not new either. For example, the effect of Gutenberg's printing press radiated far beyond Germany to shape the literacy and life of Western people. That press created the possibility of satisfying the mass-market demand for Bibles, biographies, newspapers, and novels in Europe, the Americas, and across colonial empires. Over the next couple hundred years it put producers of traditional manuscripts, no matter where they were located, at a significant economic disadvantage. Economic change has not been bounded by national borders for a long time.

---

13. As of Sept. 1, 2005, Steelcase trimmed employment in the Grand Rapids, Michigan, area from 10,800 to 4,500 employees over the course of the four years between 2001 and 2005. In the process, it has phased out production during the following two years at both of its Grand Rapids plants and a factory in neighboring Kentwood, eliminating 600 more jobs (http://www.freep.com/money/business/steelcase14e_20050414.htm [accessed Sept. 16, 2005]).

14. Theodore Levitt, "Marketing Myopia," *Harvard Business Review* (Sept./Oct. 1975): 26-44, 173-77 (reprint of the Levitt article originally published in 1960).

We should understand such changes as inherent in market systems. Over fifty years ago, in his well-known commentary on capitalism, economist Joseph Schumpeter eloquently expressed this:

> Capitalism, then, is by nature a form or method of economic change and not only never is but never can be stationary. And this evolutionary character of the capitalist process is not merely due to the fact that economic life goes on in a social and natural environment which changes and by its change alters the data of economic action. . . . Nor is this evolutionary character due to a quasi-automatic increase in population and capital or to the vagaries of monetary systems of which exactly the same thing holds true. The fundamental impulse that sets and keeps the capitalist engine in motion comes from the new consumers' goods, the new methods of production or transportation, the new markets, the new forms of industrial organization that capitalist enterprise creates . . . that incessantly revolutionizes the economic structure from *within,* incessantly destroying the old one, incessantly creating a new one. This process of Creative Destruction is the essential fact about capitalism. It is what capitalism consists in and what every capitalist concern has got to live in.[15]

What Schumpeter then called capitalism, we now identify as the market economy; but we still recognize the continuing change he described as part of the market system itself.

The challenge, of course, is that now we humans have built that creative destruction into the inherent structure of an entire *global* economy; and our ready acceptance of such a creative change, almost with a sense of economic determinism, allows room for negative as well as positive aspects of this destruction. Not only can such change be fueled by the healthy creativity of the marketplace, but the resulting flames can also be fanned by greed, shortsightedness, and corruption. Then, because of trade agreements, new technology, and global communications, the time frame in which we allow such changes to occur is a compressed one. We have changed the speed with which underlying economic paradigms and structures are reconfigured; and that change in pace adds a significant new dimension to our human situation. We have made choices over the past few

15. Joseph A. Schumpeter, *Capitalism, Socialism and Democracy,* 3rd ed. (New York: Harper Colophon Books, 1950), pp. 82-83.

decades that place Schumpeter's picture of creative destruction in a much different frame, one that threatens to be more twisted and abstract than Schumpeter ever imagined. It is a picture less bounded by Judaeo-Christian neighborliness, one in which perhaps we presume a global economy that hurtles forward with little human consensus on any common moral frame.

Consider the global economic structure in 1985. The world was still divided into two types of economic systems, the one market-based and the other centrally directed. Cold War empires lined up their politics along that economic divide, competing on a country-by-country basis to provide the paradigms for less developed nations. While the Soviets were determined to influence the Horn of Africa, the United States was just as bullheaded about Central America. In terms of trade, imports and exports were occurring on a more frequent basis than they had in the past; but regional economic treaties, which removed broad tariff and trade barriers, were still limited. Each round of GATT talks led to another, but progress was on a product-by-product basis.[16] "Made in America" was still a label of American pride on clothing, autos, and household equipment. Technologically speaking, the IBM-PC was four years old, and the MAC was not even a toddler. Communication beyond one's home region was by telephone, and fax usage was still being introduced. There were no answering machines and no World Wide Web.[17]

What was the world's economic shape just a decade later? By 1995, Eastern European economies had all collapsed into various states of disrepair. With an economy ravaged by inflation and a highly devalued currency, Russia had retreated from influence on international economic development. The evidence that such state-run economic systems were untenable models for development was substantial. Even China, in a quest to be more self-sufficient, had now developed limited forms of a private market economy among its farmers. Tradewise, the North American Free Trade Agreement (NAFTA) was brand new, having been approved by the U.S. Congress and the legislatures of Canada and Mexico in 1994. It

16. GATT is an acronym for General Agreement on Tariffs and Trade, which was first signed in 1947 to provide an international forum to encourage free trade and reduce tariffs. The World Trade Organization is its successor organization, which was begun in 1995 out of the Uruguay round of GATT negotiations (http://www.ciesin.org/TG/PI/TRADE/gatt.html [accessed Sept. 16, 2005]).

17. Information from http://www.inventors.about.com/library/weekly (accessed Sept. 7, 2005).

smoothed the way for the production and transport of raw materials and finished goods across the continent; economically, though, very little had yet changed. In 1995, the Uruguay round of trade negotiations gave birth to a fledgling, the World Trade Organization (WTO). The personal computer was now widely used, but the answering machine and the internet had just made their public debut.

The landscape in 2005, just another ten years later, looked remarkably different from that of 1995. Sharp divides among nations were replaced by the challenge of fluid but amorphous networks of global terrorists. Simultaneously, over the prior decade (1985-1995), market economies, with some variations by region, had become the norm. China now surpassed the United States to become the country receiving the largest amount of foreign direct investment in the world. In terms of trade, China's eight-year-old automobile company, Chery Automobile, planned to enter the North American auto market in 2007.[18] NAFTA had led to CAFTA-DR (Central American Free Trade Agreement), which made national borders more permeable from Costa Rica to Maine. This was the next step in a strategy that could eventually extend a free trade zone from Canada's Baffin Bay to Argentina's Patagonia.[19] Developing nations, with a few exceptions, were leapfrogging the decades of desktop computers and communication landlines to embrace laptops and cell phones. A robust global information infrastructure allowed facile global identification and communication regarding raw and productive resources on a minute-by-minute basis. Products could be imagined, designed, produced, and marketed in a multitude of world regions, each with its own economic advan-

18. "The New Industrial Revolution: De-verticalization on a Global Scale," *Research on Strategic Change* (New York: Alliance Bernstein, Aug. 2005), p. 4.

19. CAFTA-DR is new trade legislation that was approved by the U.S. Congress in July 2005 and signed by President Bush in August 2005. As of September 15, 2005, it had also been approved by the legislatures of the Dominican Republic, El Salvador, Guatemala, and Honduras, with consideration pending in Costa Rica and Nicaragua. When implemented, this agreement will eliminate 80 percent of tariffs on U.S. exports to participating countries while honoring existing reductions in U.S. import duties for those other countries' goods and improving their U.S. access for textiles and sugar exported from those countries. Remaining tariffs would be phased out over the subsequent ten years. Because of its provisions related to intellectual property rights, antidumping rules, environmental protection, and labor standards, in some circles CAFTA-DR is already beginning to be regarded as a model trade agreement for the future (http://en.wikipedia.org/wiki/CAFTA [accessed Sept. 15, 2005]).

tages. "Outsourcing" and "offshoring" became normal words in the business vocabulary. Perhaps by 2005, as Thomas Friedman observed, this interconnected world was now flat.[20]

The next phase of the market's creative reconstruction is pushing an even bigger wave of structural changes, particularly in manufacturing. In the 1980s and 1990s, U.S. manufacturing firms had already begun to implement better systems for quality assurance, efficient assembly, and healthier supplier relationships. But now they are entering an era when the frame for manufacturing is being even more fundamentally restructured. We are in the process of creating a "devertical" future in which entire industries will be redefined by multiple collaborations among many global partners. The new industrial revolution will be one of networked relationships among trading and producing partners, each of whom provides its special contribution to a product or service. For example, Chery Automobile of China, a new devertical manufacturer,

> has formed a joint venture with U.S. based Visionary Vehicles, a sales and marketing firm. It has also commissioned Italy's Pininfarina and Bertone to design the auto bodies. Lotus Engineering of the UK, Mitsubishi Automotive Engineering of Japan and Austria's AVL are assisting with the engines and drivetrains. A variety of less well-known, mostly Chinese manufacturers will make most of the other auto parts. Chery's main task will be assembling vehicles.[21]

Such a future promises lower barriers to economic entry but the great pain of retooling vertically organized manufacturing firms. As economies of scale in manufacturing shift from a *company* basis to an *industry* basis, what could be further from the integrated manufacturing structures that have dominated the histories of General Motors and the Ford Motor Company?[22] Business leaders in developed economies that are heavily invested in mass vertical manufacturing processes will be required to make hard choices about their business configurations involving plant closings, offshoring, supplier spinoffs, and tight constraints on operational costs. These decisions will affect communities where vast numbers of blue-collar and professional workers have dedicated themselves to particular compa-

---

20. Thomas Friedman, *The World Is Flat* (New York: Farrar, Straus and Giroux, 2005).
21. "The New Industrial Revolution," p. 1.
22. "The New Industrial Revolution," p. 3.

nies. They will alter regional tax bases and the related economic foundations for public goods.

This new phase of the market's creative reconstruction will also be one of significant upheaval in other global labor markets. "Rapidly growing numbers of college graduates hungry for jobs and willing to work long hours at relatively low wages" provides comparative economic advantage for India, China, and Eastern Europe. That will add fuel to the fire of the current offshoring strategies. College graduates in such developing nations are eager to work for about one-tenth the wage of those in developed countries; and those labor markets of college graduates are expanding at a rate of 5 percent per year, as opposed to the 1 percent rate in developed countries.[23] Even those who have felt that their employment futures were less vulnerable will experience new challenges.

All of the economic choices we have recently made and all of these global market dynamics are creating a future in which human winners and losers will be unevenly redistributed across the globe and within a given nation. Global labor markets will now swing so quickly that there will be few advantages on which a given person can count over an adult lifetime. In twenty years, a quarter of a typical North American's lifetime at most, the economic paradigm will change radically. What began as a promising occupation in college may quickly disappear in a given country. For example, in the 1980s, computer programmers were believed to have some of the most secure occupational futures available in the United States; but this country's demand for their labor has shifted because of new software developments and job outsourcing to other countries. Such economic change is no longer limited to generational adjustments, which allow time for children to envision and prepare for a future that is different from that of their parents. The pace of economic change will now require any given person to realize that in one adult lifetime there will likely be significant swings in occupational opportunity, earning power, and household sufficiency, all within a few short years.

All this will bode well for fulfillment among those positioned to take entrepreneurial risk; but it will not help those with less capacity — environmental or personal — for taking such risks.[24] The market will reward those who will be able to take advantage of industrial deverticalization because

23. "The New Industrial Revolution," p. 14.
24. "The New Industrial Revolution," p. 16.

they have the family heritage, educational access, geographic locus, cultural capital, and economic networks to secure those advantages. Perhaps the downward pressure on the wages of some educated young people in developed nations will be offset by the contribution that their advanced education makes to higher productivity. At a minimum, though, these structural changes eliminate promise for those who have only a high school diploma or are at an age where reinvestment in education has few years to provide a job-related return. The plight of manufacturing assembly workers, often males with less education and less stable family backgrounds, is already grim.[25] And for any who lack inherited advantages, the future will be less secure.

The market does not resolve this unevenness in personal attributes or the effects of such labor market changes over time. The restlessness of the global market will reward many, but it will not match the hopes of many others. As in prior economic transitions, along with aggregate economic gain, there will be specific economic pain. But now, given the quickened pace of change, future pain may be swifter, more targeted, and more massive than in the past.

The Manufacturer and Social Justice

In such a time, when change brings aggregate improvements that benefit a great number but more volatility in the unevenness of individual effects, can and should social justice be a manufacturer's responsibility? The answer depends on how we understand social justice.

While Christians affirm the idea of social justice, justice has a variety of definitions that can inform an understanding of manufacturers' responsibilities. Often the difficulty with these frameworks is that they seem to focus on common benefits without taking into account what is economically required to create the possibility of such justice. Neither Catholic nor Protestant definitions of justice seem to consider whether the creation of underlying economic value involves justice issues.[26] David Krueger notes

25. Rebecca M. Blank, *It Takes a Nation: A New Agenda for Fighting Poverty* (New York: Russell Sage Foundation; Princeton, NJ: Princeton University Press, 1997), Section 2.3, pp. 60-61.

26. Karen Lebacqz, *Six Theories of Justice* (Minneapolis: Augsburg, 1986). Lebacqz describes some of these multiple understandings of justice. According to her, the Catholic justice tradition, particularly in the U.S. National Conference of Catholic Bishops' 1985 *Pastoral*

that this is part and parcel of "productive justice," and he argues that expansion of the global economic pie through the creation of global wealth, while not sufficient by itself, is a necessary part of pursuing social justice:

> From a Christian theological perspective, if we are to affirm the enduring legacy and applicability of the common good for a market-based society in a global economy, then we must be able to define and support the respects in which the economic practices of creating wealth, exchanging goods and services in markets, working for business corporations, and making profits are consistent with and practically supportive of a common good of society that stands beyond private goods and interests.[27]

Krueger recognizes that the segregation of economic production from social justice is problematic. For social justice to be possible, economic value must have been created.

Given this divide in such typical Christian constructions, the manufacturer can find a more helpful understanding of social justice embedded in a framework proposed by philosopher Nicholas Wolterstorff in his book *Until Justice and Peace Embrace*. Instead of beginning with the concept of

---

Letter on Catholic Social Teaching and the U.S. Economy, encompasses *commutative justice*, namely, fairness in agreements and exchanges between private parties, *distributive justice*, namely, the allocation of social goods to ensure a minimum level of participation, and *social justice*, namely, the creation of the common good. However, in Lebacqz's view, these Catholic understandings of social justice appear to segregate them from other areas of justice that have more direct links to the creation of wealth. Social justice, understood as the common good, is limited in its particular content related to business firms; and many of its attendant responsibilities are thus assigned to government. Lebacqz then describes the Protestant tradition, as exemplified by the theology of Reinhold Niebuhr, which also endorses the creation of the common good as a goal but tends to emphasize justice as a matter of social claims that compete with each other because of the ubiquity of sin. Attempts to create the common good can always be thwarted by the ill-founded rationality of individuals and institutions, and institutional efforts must be bounded to prevent the imposition of worse conditions on individuals. Similarly, then, in Niebuhr's discussion of justice, Lebacqz is convinced that the links created between the theological vision and economic practice are insufficient. Thus, in Lebacqz's analysis, while social justice involves the creation of the common good in both of these major North American Christian traditions, the responsibility for connecting the required economic growth to that common good is not clearly articulated.

27. David Krueger, *The Business Corporation and Productive Justice* (Nashville: Abingdon, 1997), p. 40.

justice, Wolterstorff begins with the biblical idea of *shalom* as the ultimate goal for God's world. This framework, first described in Hebrew Scripture and more fully developed in the New Testament, describes shalom as "the human being dwelling at peace in all his or her relationships: with God, with self, with fellows, with nature" (p. 69).[28] It is the peace (described in the book of Revelation) in which not only are humans in right relationships, but they are also enjoying those relationships to the fullest. Shalom results in universal flourishing, where a human can hope "to enjoy living before God, to enjoy living in one's physical surroundings, to enjoy living with one's fellows, to enjoy living with oneself" (p. 70).

If shalom is thus understood, then both the proper development and the proper care of the creation, as mandated in Genesis 1 and 2, are needed to create the context in which humanity can flourish and respond to the Creator.[29] Such an understanding provides a framework in which the cultivation of shalom involves *both* the creation of economic value *and* its contribution to the common good.

As Wolterstorff notes, "shalom at its highest is *enjoyment* in one's relationships" that requires not only the love of God but "right harmonious relationships to other *human beings* and delight in human community" (pp. 69, 70). The building of shalom, therefore, requires an ethical community where individuals provide for the rights and needs of others. These are rights of everyone to sustenance, including "food, clothing, and shelter that are adequate for sustaining health and making it possible to contribute to society" (p. 85). They also include individual rights to both freedom of mastery, namely greater control over nature's evil possibilities, and freedom of self-direction, namely a personal voice in determining one's own life course.

In Wolterstorff's framework, then, justice is not separated from human sustenance, rights, and development, which comprise the substance of biblical neighborliness. Instead, it is intertwined as each person enjoys his or her rights in the creation of universal flourishing. Shalom is the governing ideal within which rights are shaped and lead to peace among God,

28. Wolterstorff, *Until Justice and Peace Embrace* (Grand Rapids: Eerdmans, 1983).

29. The original Hebrew text of this passage more clearly conveys simultaneous responsibility for development and care. *Radah* is the Hebrew word translated as "rule" in Gen. 1:28. As part of God's blessing to the earth creature, Adam, the word conveys a ruling that ensures the well-being of the subjects being ruled, stewardship instead of exploitation. In Gen. 2:15, the Hebrew words *abad* and *shamar*, often translated as "work" and "care," also respectively connote the service to and preservation of the created world.

self, fellows, and nature. Shalom is also the bigger house in which social justice is part of the basic frame.

At this juncture in his thinking, Wolterstorff does not explore explicit links between the biblical vision of shalom and economic decisions. But in that regard, his vision still has significant advantages over some other frameworks. If one begins with Wolterstorff's understanding of shalom, there is room under the same biblical umbrella for both the creation of economic value and the just distribution of economic wealth. Both are needed for the universal flourishing that God intends for creatures and the world. For the human being to be at peace, to experience shalom, requires concern for both the creation and distribution of economic wealth. Social justice, as an intricate part of shalom, is woven through *both* activities in order to result in right relationships among all human neighbors.

Wolterstorff's framework has profound implications for manufacturers. Many producers presume that business is principally responsible for the creation of economic wealth, and that government is principally responsible for its just allocation through tax and transfer systems. This framework assumes that one can segregate the concern for social justice from the creation of economic value. Such an understanding separates the achievement of social justice from the core mission of the business and often presumes that the core mission of business is restricted to profitability that creates shareholder value. Such a framework fits the neoclassical economic presumption that shareholders are the principal ones to whom a return on investment is due. For the publicly traded company, it assumes that shareholders control the business directly and that a return on shareholder investment is the foremost and ultimate goal.

However, if one accepts Wolterstorff's framework, that each Christian must strive to develop shalom, and in which universal flourishing and justice are intimately intertwined, then the goals of the business firm take on different shapes. No economic actor, including the manufacturer, is excused from responsibility for social justice in both the creation and distribution of economic benefits. Every economic actor is charged with a dual mandate in creation to both "work it and take care of it" (Gen. 2:15, NIV). No economic actor is excused from responsibility for right relationships, not only with God but also with the whole host of global business stakeholders, including customers, suppliers, employees, local communities, and future generations, as well as shareholders.

This has significant implications for the calling of the manufacturer in a time of turbulent change. Such businesses cannot presume that social justice, as part of achieving shalom, is solely the responsibility of other entities in society. The manufacturer should not say that a shareholder theory of the firm limits the company's obligations to a small group of investors for whom the creation of wealth is the only priority. Instead, "the value created is the sum of the contributions of all . . . stakeholders. In return, each stakeholder deserves a portion of the value created."[30] Stakeholders are not always legal "owners," but that does not prevent them from having legitimate interests and rights related to the activity of a business firm.

Granted, a commitment to multiple stakeholders has different challenges for the publicly traded company than the privately held firm. Legally, because the CEO of a publicly traded firm works for the shareholder-owners, what is possible will be more dependent on the values of those shareholders. Those owners can relieve a CEO of responsibility at any time if they are unhappy with the financial outcomes. They might embrace, tolerate, or rebuff the CEO's attempt to balance multiple stakeholders. In such an environment the CEO must be ready and able to explain, on pragmatic grounds, how honoring various stakeholders contributes to the long-term economic well-being of the firm, perhaps through lower employee turnover, better public image, healthy media relations, less governmental intervention, and greater customer loyalty. By contrast, the private firm, without the public pressures of quarterly performance from ever-observant shareholders, may have more flexibility in balancing diverse stakeholders.

Yet if shalom, the bigger house embedded within social justice, is the foundation for a stakeholder theory of the business firm, then regardless of the legal ownership structure, Christians in manufacturing cannot and should not reasonably separate the goals of economic return from responsibilities for social justice. It is possible that for a given firm there may be disagreement about the relative balance at any given point between economic return and justice in the process. But if a Christian framework for shalom is foundational, every manufacturing leader should have an interest in social justice, because every leader is responsible for nurturing shalom.

Claiming that the manufacturing firm has a social justice *responsibility* does not lead to the conclusion that its social-justice *role* is identical to that of governments. Governments are positioned to level the competitive

---

30. Dennis Bakke, *Joy at Work* (Seattle: PVG, 2005), pp. 157-58.

playing field of business through legislation and regulation. They are instruments for the intergovernmental cooperation that is needed to control tariffs, influence capital flows through fiscal and monetary policy, and create rules for currency exchange. Sometimes, because of their concern for fairness among economic competitors, governments also play a coordinating role that gives CEOs a "cover" to do the right thing. When the interests of some stakeholders are part of public policy, CEOs may have more room to maneuver in the quest for social justice.

In the global economy previously described, however, governments and the intergovernmental regulatory bodies that they have created are insufficient to the tasks of social justice for at least two reasons. First, the power and influence of global regulatory bodies is still underdeveloped. There is only a limited consensus on the authority of entities such as the World Trade Organization, in part because they are young organizations on the global scene. Second, in an era when market effects are direct, decentralized, and varied, those effects will frequently run ahead of or outside the boundary lines that are established through governmental regulation. Governments and their agents are often reactive parties: they cannot be close enough and quick enough in their responses to address market mutations that raise new social-justice questions.

Thus, on a practical level, arguing that government has a specific role related to social responsibility for the global economy does not absolve business of its responsibilities in this regard. The vocation of the Christian in manufacturing remains that of creating greater shalom, that is, greater universal flourishing in the human and natural world. To do so requires active agency for the common good on the part of the manufacturer. Achieving shalom should be embedded in the manufacturing firm's decisions: in its ongoing choices about customers, products, employees, suppliers, shareholders, communities, and the natural environment. The business decision-making frame is no longer limited solely to economic profitability. Instead, it is a frame in which universal flourishing and social justice are deeply intertwined.

What Should the Manufacturer Do?

If one accepts the idea that social justice is inherent in the individual manufacturer's vocation, what should those involved in manufacturing businesses do during a time of great economic change? At the ground level, what decisions should an individual business leader make in ordering this social institution?

On a practical level, it may be difficult, perhaps virtually impossible, for the individual firm to resist the creative destruction that is inherent in the market system. If change is built into a market system and, in the longer run, has the potential to provide aggregate benefits, pursuing social justice may not result in the manufacturer's opposition to structural shifts and changes. Instead of holding on to existing economic paradigms, manufacturers must be more actively involved in managing the pace and process of change. Indeed, effective management of change is a matter of social justice that contributes to the goal of shalom.

The manufacturer may well be required to work, in fact, at the forefront of change to create the breathing space and time to accommodate it with civility. Breathing room is most easily created as businesses grow. When there is business growth, the manufacturer is in the best position to influence both the creation of economic value and the justice that should come in its process. As those who develop new products for new markets are well aware, it is at the forefront of change that employers have the most latitude to do good. Where demographics are growing, needs are shifting and products are changing, and before any of these reach market maturity, the manufacturer is able to work with a higher margin of return. Competitors have not yet narrowed the operating margins through product substitutes or severe price competition. It is at the forefront of new market opportunities that manufacturers are positioned to provide the economic growth needed to increase basic sustenance and more options for millions of people.

What might Christian manufacturing leaders do, then, to invest in managing the forefront of global change? They will need to work smarter and harder at both pace and process as they go the second and the third mile in their vocational responsibilities. Overall, Christian manufacturers must develop a vision that is bigger than national boundaries. They must become producers who see the needs and potential of a whole globe in which universal flourishing is needed. Doing so will require manufacturers, whether they are large or small, to:

1. Research and plan for their businesses more carefully
2. Multiply knowledge of governmental and international policy bodies

3. Reframe customer identity, supplier relations, and production processes
4. Reinvent the covenant between employers and employees
5. Reconsider legal ownership structures for the firm
6. Model Christian virtues and values through everyday business behavior

For manufacturers who attend to these challenges, becoming more global will enhance their ability to contribute to shalom. The first three tasks contribute to human flourishing through more effective economic growth, while the last three more directly address the distribution of economic justice.

A special but essential part of the manufacturer's contribution involves economic productivity in relationship to resources. While God's provision of natural resources and human talent is sufficient to our needs, both need careful cultivation in a complex economy to create the capacities that will help people flourish. Part of the manufacturer's responsibility must attend to the creation of frameworks for human opportunities and connections that foster effective economic exchange. This requires that business research, planning, strategy, and operational refinements be a central part of the manufacturer's calling in a time of change.

Manufacturers will need to pay closer attention to the shifting global economic realities and gain knowledge of the critical influences that are fostering change as they necessarily dig deeper into global business dynamics and determine the implications for their business plans. For example, in the mid 1990s, Unocal, a California-based oil exploration and distribution company, recognized that its future within the U.S. energy economy was limited. Its smaller size and regional location created constraints that larger U.S.-based competitors did not face. Instead of throwing up its hands in despair, Unocal realized that the energy needs of Southeast Asia were significant. There were few firms willing to tackle the transformation required to become the full-service energy producers and distributors that were needed in Thailand, Myanmar, and other Southeast Asian locations. However, because the Unocal leaders did their homework, they knew that the company could provide significant benefits there. They took the risk. In the process, over the next decade, Unocal developed innovative oil-drilling technologies, new networks of trust, and the blessings of leaders from a host of countries. Unocal became a company of global contribution — significant employment and stronger economic return — not a company limited by U.S.-based competitors or one national frame. The firm became an attractive energy production and distribution partner to both U.S. and Chinese companies.[31]

Similarly, Alticor Corporation, a U.S.-based producer and marketer of personal and household care products, recognized that their original face-to-face distribution and promotion strategy was losing appeal in the United States and Western Europe. As it received warning signals of decline, Alticor launched a parallel but global, internet-based sales and marketing company named Quixtar. This web-based strategy could create greater global economic value while penetrating both developed and emerging market economies. Alticor leaders developed this new business structure before eliminating some of their older approaches. Because these leaders actively managed for change, they were able to build more of the future before more of the past was destroyed. Again, good research and careful business planning were essential to human flourishing.

Those who lead in manufacturing will also need to become more knowledgeable about national governments that collaborate on trade conventions as well as the roles of the World Bank, the International Monetary Fund, and the World Trade Organization. These major entities significantly affect the direction and pace of change in the global economy with which the manufacturer intersects. By learning more about their roles and decisions, the manufacturer can discern the direction of economic change, consider its potential pace, and manage the emerging pockets of need and opportunity to which they can best contribute.

There are many places in the world where people would be well served by certain products and have the emerging capacity to purchase them. Based on multiple factors, businesses can still pick which regional and local markets to pursue. But as national and international bodies create new access, firms with valuable products that enhance the quality of life, that contribute to shalom, can find places to serve. For example, when Roger Sant and Dennis Bakke founded AES (Applied Energy Systems) in the early 1980s, they recognized the gradual but global movement by na-

---

31. The Unocal case is discussed in Richard L. Daft and Dorothy Marcic, *Understanding Management*, 4th ed. (Mason, OH: South-western, Thomson Learning, 2004), pp. 107-08. Subsequent to this case write-up, during the summer of 2005, Unocal was purchased by Chevron Corporation for $17.7 billion, as noted in "CNOOC Drops Offer for Unocal, Exposing U.S.-Chinese Tensions," *Wall Street Journal*, Aug. 3, 2005, 1A.

tional governments toward the deregulation of electricity. This provided both need and opportunity, and they believed that they could develop something of economic value, whether people lived in Argentina, Georgia, Pakistan, or Uganda. Together, these two men built a company with a global vision for filling the needs of customers for electrical energy.[32] This example is not meant to suggest that all people can afford the goods and services they need. However, by paying attention to the strategies of national and international organizations, companies can find many customers with demand who are able to fund some variation of their product lines.

Manufacturers must also reconsider their supplier relationships. For example, a manufacturer for whom wood is a raw material needs to spend time learning about the back-and-forth American/Canadian conversations regarding tariffs on softwoods to determine the more logical source of wood in any given year.[33] Producers must learn to plan more carefully about the source of such resources in relationship to their costs. They must structure flexibility into supply chains rather than relying on one channel of raw materials. Creating such flexibility may require outsourcing certain components of the manufacturer's operation as part of the deverticalization of industry.

Greater knowledge about the relationship of plant layout to production costs and the ongoing management of operational costs and newer information-based operational systems that control costs will also be critical. Careful control of inventories in collaboration with suppliers and product distributors is essential, as is the use of robotics for routine tasks. In such decisions, social justice also requires that business leaders recognize short-lived economic phenomena that are generated by fad and fashion, so that plant capacity is not overdeveloped when demand turns lean. Manufacturers must check their sense of hubris about what is bigger and better with a sober perspective on what is sustainable. They must then pay

---

32. Bakke, *Joy at Work,* p. 22.

33. The softwood import tariff is a matter of ongoing disagreement between the U.S. and Canadian governments about which shifts supplier cost structures. In 2002 the U.S. Department of Commerce imposed a duty of 19.34 percent on such softwood lumber after deciding that the Canadian government unfairly subsidized the softwood industry. However, this allegation is disputed by both Canadians and some U.S. producers of softwoods, such as Weyerhaeuser. It has been under continuous review, and there is currently evidence that the U.S. tariff may be repealed, particularly because of lumber needs in the aftermath of Hurricane Katrina (http://www.safnet.org/archive/502_canada.cfm, and from http://foresttalk.com/index.php/2005/09/13/will_katrina_lower_softwood_tariffs [accessed Jan. 31, 2006]).

close attention to regular preventive maintenance and plant updating. Investing in their physical plants will mean that the portion of funds available for personnel must be more carefully planned than in the past. While adequate wages that provide basic sustenance are a matter of social justice, manufacturers must strike a wise balance between investment in compensation and physical plant.

All of these strategies may simply seem like good business. But the Christian's drive for greater productivity can also be a heightened sense of global resource stewardship in relationship to human need. This drive in manufacturing is an essential part of creating shalom.

A second part of shalom involves the distribution of wealth and opportunity over which the manufacturer has some control. Care in compensation decisions is one aspect of a much bigger covenant that must be made with employees. But it is here that manufacturers can make some of their greater contributions to social justice, by managing the pace and process of employee development. Manufacturing industries have a history of exchanging compensation for the completion of boring production jobs that provide little learning and little company ownership for those who do them. They reflect an era in which labor specialization and departmentalization complemented growth in mass national economies; there was a presumption that money was the principal motivator for people at work. It was assumed that labor brawn created economic power. At the same time, it was often the abuse of laborers that contributed to the development of employee unions; and the price of that abuse was the substantially higher compensation that manufacturers gradually paid. This cannot be a model for the future.

Instead, social justice for employees, which contributes to their universal flourishing, requires a different paradigm for those at work in the manufacturing firm. The exchange of effort for results should be based on different assumptions about people at work, assumptions that respect and honor them as God's image-bearers with abilities and ideas. Work must engage people's minds and beings as well as their bodies. At a minimum, social justice requires that the manufacturing firm provide education and training in transferable knowledge and skills. Even in the best of companies, given the ebb and flow of global demand, there will need to be some flexibility in their human labor capacity. However, an investment in the education and training of employees provides them with resources that cannot be taken away, even as particular tasks or company identities change. Transferable knowledge and skills are investments in employee futures that provide greater promise in an era of economic turbulence.

For many whose families and schooling have provided only a minimal floor of human development, the need to address such knowledge and skill deficiencies is substantial. Getting a degree, particularly the advanced higher education degree more readily needed in manufacturing, is closely correlated with having parents who went to college.[34] For many families who have traditionally associated themselves with manufacturing, the need for such advanced learning is not part of their inherited mindset, and the family finances to pursue it are limited. The needed mindset and the financial access must be cultivated not only by elementary and secondary schools but also by employers.

Beyond that, however, not all of the learning required is found in formal higher education. As Ruby Payne describes it in *A Framework for Understanding Poverty,* much of the required learning is in understanding how middle-class people have developed their personal capacities through different assumptions and habits.[35] Cascade Engineering, a manufacturer of engineered plastic systems and components, provides an example of a company that has taken Payne's analysis seriously. In their employee development programs, typically intended for ethnic minorities who have recently left welfare rolls, they provide ongoing employee training programs about personal accountability in the workplace, how to balance paid work and household demands, employer expectations, and appropriate styles of workplace communication. As their participants gain a greater understanding of the social codes and norms needed for self-sufficiency and workplace acceptance, they receive increased wages and opportunities for advancement. This more informal social learning has given a future to hundreds of their employees, even those who may not be stationed at this same company a decade later.[36]

34. "As Economy Shifts, A New Generation Fights to Keep Up," *Wall Street Journal,* June 22, 2005, A1.

35. Ruby K. Payne, *A Framework for Understanding Poverty* (Highlands, TX: aha! Process, 2001).

36. From "Triple Bottom Line Report," Grand Rapids, MI: Cascade Engineering, 2005, and from a classroom lecture by Mr. Ron Jimmerson, Human Resources Manager-Community Diversity, Cascade Engineering on May 3, 2005. It should also be noted that such social investment in employees is not a completely new phenomenon. From the 1920s through the 1950s, Henry Ford identified promising youth who had lost at least one parent and provided them with technical skills, a high school education, and social understanding

A different covenant with the people of the firm may also require that the firm's structure for decision-making be revisited to include production personnel with other decision-makers in the company. Involvement in decision-making builds a broader understanding of business enterprise: it necessarily involves the processing of financial and operational information beyond disconnected data points to their connected implications. And knowledge of economic implications shapes frameworks for the business judgments needed in any economic context. For example, when potentially vulnerable employees, through open decision-making, have learned more about a firm's systems for finances, budgets, inventory controls, and production planning, they have developed transferable knowledge that could benefit another employer. Opening up the decision-making processes of a firm is one of the greatest gifts that a manufacturer can give to employees. It is a commitment to their continued learning and development.[37]

---

at the Henry Ford School. Almost 3,000 students, all males, were organized into three cohorts. Each cohort rotated between two weeks of manufacturing equipment repair in the school's workshop and experiential coursework in science and engineering. Chemistry students, for example, were given bars of steel and told to determine the composition of their bars, using library and lab resources. In English classes students corresponded with worldwide inquirers about the nature of the Henry Ford School. Invited experts lectured students on the sayings of Ben Franklin. Students could be expelled for smoking, chewing tobacco, or swearing. Students who did well in Ford's school received small but consistent raises in their workshop wages; and if a young student put $2.00 per report card in the bank, Henry Ford would match it. These teenagers could also work at Henry Ford's farm a couple weeks each year so that their families could, without charge, harvest vegetables grown at the farm. Some of the best students combined this education with night school in the local public school system to prepare for college. A few then enrolled in professional programs in fields such as law so that they could become part of the executive team at Ford Motor Company. Sadly, during the 1960s the school declined because of a clash about the preferred route to technical licenses between union apprenticeship systems and the alternate Ford School system for accumulating such credits. These comments are based on personal conversation (1/2/06) with Carl Anderson, retired attorney for Ford Motor Company, a student at Henry Ford's School in the late 1930s and early 1940s. Cascade Engineering's approach might be seen as a contemporary attempt in a different legal and social environment to accomplish some of the same social ends.

37. The Lincoln Electric Company, an arc-welding firm based in Cleveland, is one good example of a firm that has such open information sharing. This is part of the legacy of James Lincoln, who developed some of these ideas from his Christian principles during the 1940s. For further information about Lincoln Electric, see *Lincoln Electric: Venturing Abroad*, Harvard Business School case #9-398-095, last revised on April 22, 1998.

For some firms, those kinds of investments in employee decision-making should lead them to consider different forms of firm ownership, forms that blunt the sharp divide between the preferences of owner and manager that is felt in publicly traded companies. Other forms of firm ownership, either private or employee-based, may have more potential for encouraging the convergence of owner and manager interests. Private ownership allows more latitude in balancing stakeholder interests over the long term, away from the pressures of short-term stock performance. When appropriately structured, employee ownership can also provide workers with a different vantage point from which to understand the goals and needs of the manufacturing firm. The vantage points of the employees, as partial owners of the enterprise, an option now readily feasible under U.S. law, are then stretched to consider the needs of all stakeholders in the firm. Employee ownership is not a panacea. But in many situations it can help employees understand the business in a broader way because they now hold multiple stakeholder roles themselves.

There will continue to be times when a given employer cannot sustain all the employees who have been hired. While this is tragic, it is a reality of the new global economy. If, however, instead of long-term jobs, employers promise opportunities to build knowledge, skill, and productive habits, they are creating more justice rather than less. Employers can then provide strong support in the out-placement process. Out-placement advisors can help released younger employees assess their personal finances and consider the value of further knowledge and skills education. They can assist the fifty-year-olds in presenting their daily life stability as an asset to a new employer or in planning a new business start-up. Counselors can support those who are even older in considering a phased retirement into modest part-time employment along with volunteer work. Not all people can adapt to change at the same rate. The ability to learn new ideas, shift one's paradigms for living, and deal with the stress of transitions is not evenly spread among personalities or family histories. Some will struggle, feeling rejected and discouraged. But employer support can ease the strain of such transitions. Overall, by providing carefully crafted promises, ample communication, and transition support, employers may be able to limit the damage of the change even if they cannot eliminate the economic pain of it.

Finally, employers influence the future through the ethical standards that they foster. Their ability to build a global manufacturing economy must presume and must model compassion, diligence, honesty, fairness, and stewardship if they aspire to provide a healthy global foundation for the future. Individual manufacturing firms may become the foundational models of ethics that are taught and learned by the specific communities, customers, employees, suppliers, and shareholders with whom they intersect across the globe. In that regard, Christian leaders in manufacturing firms are positioned to publicly acknowledge that providing a more sustainable daily life for others in the world may well require sacrifices from those who have controlled resources and wealth in the past. When those leaders communicate that Christian neighborliness involves sacrifice for the greater good of the whole global family, it is a powerful reminder of the Christian moral frame for all economic decisions. What these businesses do, how they do it, and how leaders interpret such decisions affects the global civil society that we are building together.

Granted, the voice of an individual firm, while potentially powerful within a certain range, is still bounded in the global conversation about change. Manufacturers must create partnerships with others. It is more likely that employers can positively affect policies regarding imports and exports, the pacing of tariff reductions, environmental safeguards, and needed infrastructure through trade groups or employer associations such as the National Association of Manufacturers. Employers can raise employee skill and knowledge levels; but governments and other not-for-profit groups, though imperfect, are still important actors. Such groups sustain those with severe physical, emotional, or mental challenges who cannot become qualified for jobs in the new economy. They dignify fellow humans who cannot develop the more sophisticated skills, capacities, and knowledge required to participate in the global platform for paid employment. To achieve greater shalom, Christians involved in manufacturing must share responsibility for social justice with such organizations.

Other partners, however, do not replace what manufacturers themselves must contribute to social justice. The efforts by single firms to manage the process and pace of change make for difficult but needed work. They require substantial new learning on the part of manufacturing leaders about global geography, politics, economics, and new business tools. Frameworks for employer/employee relations and business ownership structures must be rethought. The challenge of measuring and balancing value for each stakeholder group is immense and requires wise judgment as well as a sharing in the pain of change. This is new work that challenges comfortable patterns and exposes decision-makers to new unknowns. However, it is the necessary work of manufacturers to create the economic space and control the pace that social justice requires.

Conclusion

For manufacturers who live within the market system on Monday morning, who strive to do what Christian faith requires, I've tried to provide another angle of vision on business responsibilities for our neighbors near and far.

The Christian manufacturer's vocation should not be segregated from the responsibility of each believer to develop the shalom that Scriptures envisions, that is simultaneously a "banquet of rich fare for all the people" and a mandate to "set the oppressed free and break every yoke" (Isa. 25:6a; 58:6b). Each decision-maker in this environment is responsible for such flourishing in relationship with God, with others, and with nature. For the manufacturer, that flourishing will inherently involve intertwined responsibility to produce economic value and attend to social justice in the process. For Christian reasons, both economic value and social justice must be woven into the fabric of everyday business decision-making by those who produce and market products and services. While those directly involved in manufacturing make insufficient progress alone, the manufacturers' responsibility for global social justice is inherent in their calling before the face of God.

Manufacturers must then understand that, for them, social justice is not achieved by stopping economic change. Instead, they may well make their best contributions by rising to the forefront of global restructuring. At the cutting edge, manufacturers are best positioned to control the pace and process of change for the sake of global society. Yet the pursuit of social justice is a temporal, partial, and dynamic process. It is always limited because of the effects of sin and the distortions in our ability to reason. As Reinhold Niebuhr once noted, every attempt at justice is coupled with a perversion of justice.[38] We will always struggle between visions for shalom and particular historical situations in which we find ourselves.[39] Balancing

---

38. Lebacqz, *Six Theories*, pp. 84-88.
39. Lebacqz, *Six Theories*, p. 94, reflecting on Gordon Harland's ideas about justice.

the needs of all our global neighborhoods is a daunting challenge; the global market system will always be an imperfect means for doing so. Ethicists and economic theorists rightly recommend that global policies address challenges that the market is not positioned to consider.

Even within their realm of responsibility, manufacturing leaders who care about justice will not always rightly determine what their priorities should be. Some of the best efforts will have unforeseen adverse effects, and other serendipitous business choices will have stunning benefits over the longer run. Before the Second Coming, the Christian producer will often sense that the manufacturing life is in both the best and worst of times.

But as we move from the book of Genesis' garden to the book of Revelation's promised city, we know that God works for good through those who love the Creator. Christian efforts at social justice in the manufacturing environment, be they partial and rough, will still matter for the shalom — the universal flourishing — that we should promote and the future that is already promised through Christ. People of faith have often been placed in turbulent and uncertain environments in sorting out their neighborly obligations. But some people made morally imaginative choices in the midst of great uncertainty, which helped others flourish for the sake of God's global kingdom. Perhaps that is now the Monday morning calling of the Christian manufacturer.

CHAPTER 10

A Christian Perspective on the Role
of Government in a Market Economy

Rebecca M. Blank

Two kinds of institutions dominate our public lives, market-based institutions and government institutions. Most people find it obvious what market-based institutions do: they produce products that are bought and sold to customers, using management and production processes involving a mix of workers, physical structures (machines, buildings, etc.), and natural resources. But it is more difficult to provide a quick answer to the question of what government institutions do because of the wide range of activities in which governments engage. Answers such as "the government passes laws" or "the government levies taxes" name specific and limited activities that provide only a very partial view of government. In fact, in a democratic government, its institutions do whatever its citizens demand of them; therefore, the more appropriate question is perhaps, What *should* government do? This question has been hotly debated, of course, with very different answers over time and among nations.

In the first part of this chapter, I am particularly interested in the question of how government and market institutions should interact. In what ways (if ever) should government intervene to alter or limit the functioning of market-based institutions or to redistribute market outcomes? Section I provides a brief overview of various roles government might be expected to fulfill with regard to market-based institutions. These arguments for various kinds of government action are based on assumptions about the nature of government, the needs of citizens, and nature of markets. While this first section uses the language of social science, particularly economics and political science, to discuss the role of government, it is fundamentally about questions of moral choice. In a democratic society, "government" is an entity elected and directed by citizen voice. The social choices that determine a government's scope and power vis-à-vis the private sector will affect the distribution of resources within society and can influence the impact of economic institutions and economic changes on individual citizens.

The second part of this chapter directly engages the "moral choice" aspects of this discussion: it asks how a person in the Reformed faith tradition might interpret these different perspectives on the role of government. Section II focuses on this question: Should Reformed Christians have a different perspective from other citizens on the role of government? I argue that the call to engagement in the world, deeply rooted in Reformed theology, implies that one aspect of Christian vocation is a call to be an active citizen within democratic institutions. Indeed, the scope and reach of government provides a way for Christians to help create institutions that "serve one's neighbor" in a way that can extend and reinforce individual acts of outreach.

I should offer a few caveats about how I limit the scope of this paper. I am ignoring arguments about the role of government within nonmarket or nondemocratic nations. Hence, I set aside arguments about the particular citizen responsibilities that might occur within, say, dictatorial governments, and I focus on the issues most relevant in a current First World (and particularly U.S.) context. Second, I largely ignore federalism issues, which would lead to an extensive discussion about the appropriate role for local versus state versus federal governments. Here I talk about government activities without specifying which level of government should best fill which role.

I. The Role of Government in a Market Society

Markets are everywhere around us Americans. From the New York Stock Exchange to the farmers' market that sells local produce, markets organize our economic life. Markets determine the choice of what we purchase and the price we pay for it. They affect when we buy a new car and how much we pay for healthcare. If we are employed, most of us work for a market-based institution that provides a particular product or service to consumers, and our earnings are set by the labor market for workers with our sets of skills and experience.

I am an economist, and I believe in the value of markets. They are a useful way to organize economic life. When they work effectively, markets are efficient: they stimulate productivity; they help allocate resources with minimal administrative costs; competition creates an incentive to keep prices lower; and competition encourages new inventions and better ways of doing business, and helps fuel economic growth.[1] However, markets do not always work effectively, and there are limits to what they can accomplish. While available jobs, well-made products, and low prices are important to personal well-being, they are typically not all that is needed for humans to feel that they have a good life. Government institutions are often designed to do things that the market cannot do: they are considered civic institutions because they are typically concerned with issues relating not just to our individual economic life, but to the life of the entire community, including those not actively involved in market-based institutions.

Here I lay out three broad views of the role of government with respect to markets. The first claims that government's role is to help markets operate effectively, with government providing the infrastructure for effective market operations, along with corrections in the case of market failure. The second describes government as doing the things that the market cannot do but that society demands, redistributing resources from groups with greater economic earning ability to groups that might have lower earnings but are considered deserving of assistance. The third approach sees government as playing an oppositional role to markets, limiting the spread of markets to key areas of civic life and thereby directly confronting and constraining the market. As I will discuss below, these are not necessarily either/or choices: an effective government can do all of these things simultaneously.

A. Government's Role Is to Assist and Correct the Market

This argument comes straight out of economic theory, and it describes the role of government as helping markets to operate most effectively. Govern-

---

1. For the classic statement about the advantages of markets, see Milton Friedman, *Capitalism and Freedom* (Chicago: University of Chicago Press, 1962). However, even those less broadly supportive of markets recognize these advantages: see, for example, Amartya Sen, *Development as Freedom* (New York: Anchor Books, 1999), ch. 5.

ment institutions are created to help establish and enforce the "rules of the game" for the economy. Courts and legislatures determine the ways in which economic resources are obtained and transferred (i.e., setting up the rules under which property is bought and sold, inheritance laws, rules about the creation of a partnership or corporation, etc.), and to enforce these rules fairly, so that all economic participants can expect a predictable and standard set of procedures. Any economy needs a set of rules to create the infrastructure within which markets operate.[2] Just as the rules of the road reduce chaos and make transportation and travel easier, so the legal infrastructure that government imposes creates a set of economic rules (approved by popularly elected legislatures) that reduces chaos in the functioning of markets and helps them run smoothly. The rules provide predictability: for example, if I order and pay for something, I can expect to receive it as promised; if I sign an employment contract, I can expect to receive the promised wages at the end of a week's work. I have recourse to a legal system that punishes market participants who do not deliver on their contracts.

But markets need more than rules. There are times when markets fail, when the economic circumstances necessary for market solutions to be effective and efficient do not occur. In these cases, market outcomes may not result in efficient production or appropriately allocated resources or lower prices. Standard economic theory clearly describes the circumstances of market failure and indicates the appropriate ways government can step in to improve the functioning of the market. Four situations where government involvement can improve market outcomes are most frequently mentioned.[3]

1. *Lack of complete information.* Effective markets require that both buyers and sellers have similar information about the product that is being bought or sold. But that is not always the case. Sometimes buyers cannot obtain information about a product. For example, typically I cannot observe whether the milk is fresh, or whether a used car's odometer is correct, or whether the company in which I'm investing my pension funds is fol-

2. This argument goes back to Adam Smith.

3. The following section lays out a standard set of arguments for government regulation that are found in virtually any introductory economics text. For instance, for a much-used introductory economics text, see William J. Baumol and Alan S. Blinder, *Economics: Principles and Policy* (Mason, OH: Thomson, South-Western, 2004), esp. the chapter entitled "The Government and the Economy."

lowing appropriate financial accounting procedures. In these cases, there is a role for the government: it requires the disclosure of important information. Milk cartons have dates on them; used car salesmen have to accurately disclose mileage and other information; and companies are required to undergo regular independent audits, and the results must be publicly disclosed in annual corporate reports.

To correct situations where the buyer and the seller have different levels of knowledge and information (so-called asymmetric information) about a product, the government forces companies to make certain information public. This reduces the asymmetry of information that occurs in some market circumstances, and it "levels the playing field" for buyers and sellers. Of course, these disclosure regulations are not perfect, and companies sometimes avoid them or misrepresent information. But they are then legally liable for the harm that this might cause.

2. *Presence of monopoly power.* Buyers and sellers do not always meet on an even playing field. Companies can sometimes take advantage of particular situations that allow them to gain enough market power to limit competition and thereby raise their sales and prices. This can occur for many reasons. For instance, a market that is very expensive to enter (i.e., requires large up-front investments in equipment or in technology research) may give initial entrants enough leverage for them to keep out future competitors. Some products are considered "natural monopolies" because of the nature of their market, which favors a single large provider. Insider information, where knowledge is available to those in a market but hard to acquire by those outside the market, can also limit competition.

The U.S. government has extensive rules about what constitutes "undue market power," and a variety of tools are available to break up or limit the acquisition of market power by one or by a few firms. So-called antitrust regulation is explicitly designed to increase market competition and make markets function more effectively.

3. *Presence of externalities.* An "externality" is economics jargon for a situation in which an exchange between a buyer and seller affects someone not directly involved in the transaction. For instance, a classic negative externality occurs when a factory puts a lot of dirty smoke into the air while producing a product. The buyer, who lives elsewhere, doesn't care about this pollution, but the factory's neighbors all face costs from living near the smokestack. Effective government regulation will force the company to "internalize" the cost of pollution to the neighborhood. There are

a variety of ways to do this effectively, typically leading the company to reduce the pollution that is spewing out of its factory smokestack. While these regulations often result in higher-priced goods due to antipollution equipment that the factory needs to install, these higher prices are appropriate. The product was priced too low in the past: the costs of pollution created during production were not being taken into account.

4. *Presence of public goods.* Public goods are goods that, if produced or used by one individual, benefit the entire community. They are "nonexcludable" in the sense that my consumption doesn't limit their value to other potential consumers, and it may actually create value to others. Examples include things like defense (if I pay for neighborhood security, you receive the benefits if you live nearby), education (if I am a more educated citizen, you benefit from my improved income and citizen participation), or roads (I don't "use up" the road by driving on it). Public goods are typically best provided by government. Police forces or military defense forces provide security to all people; roads are open to all people; parks are available to the whole community. Because everyone benefits, we all pay taxes to support these government institutions. If they were privatized, some of us could refuse to pay and "free-ride" on those who continued to pay to support them.

In all four of these situations, the role of the government is to correct the market problem. Indeed, if the government regulation is done well, markets function more effectively because of government intervention, and there is a clear economic reason for government to take on these activities. These arguments are part of standard market-based economic theory. They are widely discussed in introductory economics classes as situations that may require government intervention. In fact, the cutting edge of much current economic research focuses on describing the nature of different types of market failure and the circumstances under which government can or cannot respond effectively to this problem.[4]

However, there is substantial disagreement among economists about the extent to which market failure occurs.[5] And there is disagreement about how effectively government can correct these problems. In particu-

---

4. For example, see Stiglitz's Nobel Prize lecture: Joseph Stiglitz, "Information and Change in the Paradigm in Economics," *American Economics Review* 92, no. 3 (2002): 460-501.

5. For an extended debate about what markets can and cannot accomplish, see Rebecca M. Blank and William McGurn, *Is the Market Moral? A Dialogue on Religion, Economics, and Justice* (Washington, DC: The Brookings Institution, 2004).

lar, some of the following arguments are made against extensive government involvement to correct market failure.

- Unnecessary or misapplied government regulations can make things worse rather than better. Government regulatory agencies sometimes lack the information or the expertise to effectively correct market failures. Regulations that are too extensive or that are not effectively targeted can waste economic resources and lead to costs that increase prices without reducing the problem the regulation was supposed to address.
- There are arguments about how extensively government has to be involved in these issues and whether the market can "self-regulate" to avoid these problems. For instance, companies may choose to share information with their customers under standard agreed-upon industry rules rather than face government regulation. Or there may be ways to reorganize the market to provide something more effectively than the government can. For instance, many people argue for the privatization of the post office, once viewed as an important public good. Perhaps, in a rural economy with limited transportation, the post office was a necessary public good. In a modern economy, with a much greater range of communication and transportation technologies, the delivery of letters and packages might be better provided by a host of competing private companies. The rise of companies such as UPS and Federal Express reflects these technological changes.
- Government regulation requires resources to monitor and enforce. It is costly to set up and fund regulatory organizations, and it is often difficult for them to function effectively. Even if government regulation of market failure might seem attractive theoretically, some level of market failure may be preferable to government regulation. If market failure occurs infrequently, and its effects are small, the "cure" (government regulation) may be worse than the "disease."

In short, while almost all economists agree that market failure is possible and that appropriate government involvement can correct it, honest and smart economists argue about how frequently market failure occurs and where the lines should be drawn between useful and wasteful government activity. Joe Stiglitz, the 2001 Nobel laureate in economics, has argued that market failures are pervasive. Milton Friedman, the 1976 Nobel laureate in economics, is well known for arguing that market failure is extremely rare and the need for government regulation is very limited.

B. Government's Role Is to Redistribute Market Outcomes Where Necessary to Respond to Specific Citizen Needs that the Market Does Not Address

If the previous argument was based on economic theory, this argument typically emerges from the field of political economy. The claim is that markets provide only partially for economic needs. Those who can rely on the market for support are people who have resources to bring to it, people who can invest capital or who have the skills and talents to hold a job that pays adequate earnings. Not all people at all points in their lives have such resources. In many cases, a society will want to provide support to those who are excluded from the market, or those whose market skills might be too limited to provide an adequate income but who are an important part of the civic community.

As a result, the government taxes a share of resources from those who hold them and redistributes to support those whom society considers deserving. For instance, our government taxes earnings and provides support to some groups of nonworkers (retirees, disabled persons, and the unemployed); the government taxes wealthier people and supports poorer families (through housing subsidies or food stamps); and the government transfers tax money from childless families to families with children (supporting public education or child-based tax deductions).

Why would we choose to redistribute resources rather than simply letting market outcomes determine everyone's level of income? There are a variety of valid social and citizen concerns that the market cannot address and to which these redistributive government programs respond.[6] Let me describe some of the most important of them here.

1. Redistribution enhances long-term economic well-being by investing in persons so they can become fuller market participants in the future.

---

6. A well-known and extended discussion of the role of government redistribution can be found in John Rawls, *A Theory of Justice* (Cambridge, MA: Harvard University Press, 1971).

Government support for low-income families with children or for training programs for low-skilled adults may be viewed as a public investment in groups that cannot afford to invest in themselves. Thus we support Head Start for poor children, or Pell Grants for low-income college students, and public healthcare for those without access to health insurance. All of these programs are designed to increase the education, skills, or health of particular groups over the long run. If they are effective, these investments should result in a more productive set of adults who can support themselves better in the market. The most optimistic adherents of this point of view will often argue for redistribution as a form of public investment, claiming that these investments more than pay for themselves, that they provide a larger overall economy because redistribution programs make our citizens better educated and healthier.[7]

2. Redistribution enhances long-term political stability; and an effective market economic system requires political and economic stability. Civic unrest or frequent government changeovers can limit the ability of markets to function, because they limit the predictability about which rules will be enforced or whether there will be a long-term and stable demand for products. One argument for redistribution from market participants to those with limited market resources (the unemployed, the disabled, the poor) is that such redistribution makes these groups more satisfied with the current political and economic system and reduces civic unrest. Redistribution may prevent social protests, riots, or political discontent with current leaders.

In its more pessimistic version, this argument suggests that current political leaders and successful market participants are willing to share a small part of their gains to "buy off" those who are discontented with the system.[8] In a more optimistic version, empathetic political and business leaders recognize that markets do not provide resources to those who do not have the skills to participate in them, so they respond to citizen demands and to their own consciences and give a share of the country's economic wealth to the aged, the young, and the disabled.

7. See Rebecca M. Blank, "Can Equity and Efficiency Complement Each Other?" *Labour Economics* 9, no. 4 (2002): 451-68, where I provide examples of programs where evaluations suggest that the benefits from the programs exceed their costs.

8. For example, this view about welfare is expressed in Frances Fox Piven and Richard A. Cloward, *Regulating the Poor: The Functions of Public Welfare* (New York: Vintage Books, 1971).

3. Redistribution ensures everybody against unpredictable future economic risk. Redistribution programs can be viewed as a form of future insurance for those currently in the market. And these programs also provide minimal levels of resources to those who are outside the market or whose earnings are low. This protects all of us against future conditions in the world in which we might find ourselves disabled, poor and elderly, or unemployed. Thus citizens demand redistribution programs as a form of future insurance for themselves and their families.[9] As long as food stamps are broadly available to low-income families, I know that my children and I will never actually starve.

4. Redistribution responds to religious and ethical arguments for providing support to those who are economically marginalized. In addition to the political economy arguments for redistributive programs, there are also religious arguments for such programs. Most religions recognize the value of human life and the importance of respect and dignity for fellow human beings.[10] Hence, redistributive programs respond to the demand that human beings are not treated as market commodities, valuable when they can produce and discarded when they cannot. Children, the disabled, elderly people, or less-skilled and lower-wage individuals may have much to contribute to our life together even if they have very little ability to generate economic earnings. Ideally, such individuals might be supported by their families; but not all families have the resources to support all of their members, and not all individuals have families who can or will support them. Consequently, these programs recognize the value of human life by providing resources and (when appropriate) public investments into the skills, life, and health of society's more disadvantaged members.

These four arguments for redistributional programs by government may be viewed in three ways. On the one hand, such programs can be viewed as complementing the role of the market. The government acts as a partner to the market, providing things the market cannot. In this view, the redistributive programs provided by government are an extension of its role in providing public goods and assuring that investments with positive externalities (such as public schools) are made within the society. Gov-

---

9. This is a key argument for redistributional programs in Rawls, *A Theory of Justice.*

10. Douglas A. Hicks, *Inequality and Christian Ethics* (Cambridge, UK: Cambridge University Press, 2000), provides an extensive discussion of these issues, comparing the views of H. Richard Niebuhr and Gustavo Gutiérrez.

ernment's redistribution programs add to the effective functioning of the market and may (in argument 2 above) even be necessary for long-term stable political and economic environments.

On the other hand, these redistributive programs can be viewed as a separate sphere for the government. The market produces resources and makes certain distributions of its wealth and resources, while the government taxes and redistributes a share of that wealth for other purposes. The role of the government is separate from that of the market. In a democratic society, if there is a demand for redistribution, the government can and should do it; but these actions operate separately from the market activities of a society.

A third view argues that these redistributive activities are actually harmful to the market, and they should be limited or abolished. Those who make this argument typically point to several concerns:

- It is difficult to decide which transfers are good and which are bad. Once government transfers become possible (i.e., once there is a tax and transfer system with an effective and strong central government), this largess can be captured by any group with a well-organized political lobby. Thus we redistribute not only to poor children and elderly adults, but also to beekeepers, peanut farmers, those who buy hybrid cars, and those with capital gains income. Given how hard it is to limit transfers or to pick and choose appropriate transfers, society is simply better off making as few transfers as possible and not allowing this sort of pork-barrel politics to take place.
- Transfers create disincentives and hence have efficiency costs. Public transfers to the elderly lead to earlier retirement and reduce economic productivity. Public transfers to those who are not working produce an incentive to leave the labor market and receive public assistance, again reducing economic productivity. Major concerns about the disincentive effects of cash welfare on single mothers' involvement with the labor force led to a major welfare reform in 1996 that reduced the availability of cash support and emphasized moving single mothers into work.[11]

11. See Arthur M. Okun, *Equality and Efficiency: The Big Tradeoff* (Washington, DC: Brookings Institution, 1975), for the classic statement about how redistributive programs inevitably produce inefficient outcomes, discussing the "leaky bucket" of welfare programs.

• There are alternative and less costly ways of providing for redistribution. One option is to do so through the market. For instance, if people want old-age assistance, they should save or invest in pensions rather than relying on the government. Those who cannot afford such insurance must live without it. A second option is to do it through private transfers. Families should be expected to support their children and their elderly parents, and governmental support should only be for orphans or childless elderly. Or if some group of people — say, Christians — want to provide assistance to the poor, they can organize and support nonprofit institutions to provide such assistance. (Of course, this runs into the free-rider problems with regard to public goods that I mentioned above. If a religious group provides the support to house and feed the poor, nonmembers will benefit from this even if they don't contribute to it, since they will not have to confront hungry or homeless people.)

In short, there are ongoing arguments about the value and the extent of redistribution that government should provide. Very few people argue that the government should provide *no* redistribution of resources, but honest and well-meaning people can come to different answers about the range and generosity that redistributive government programs should offer.

C. Government's Role is to Confront and Limit Market Involvement in Certain Spheres of Activity

This position argues that there are certain areas of family and civic life that should not be subject to the market calculus of demand and supply or where certain commodities are so valued that their access should not be limited by the income of those who need them. Because the market is a powerful force in most nations, one needs a powerful government to confront the market and to limit its reach in certain areas of activity. There is a tendency to view a growing set of behavioral choices through the lens of market reasoning. Hence we talk about marriage markets: young men and women evaluate each other's long-term economic and partnership potential in making their marriage choices. Similarly, people unhappy in their marriage are advised to make a cost-benefit calculus: Are you better off with him or without him?

In what areas of life might such market calculations seem offensive, inaccurate, and perhaps even destructive or immoral? There are a variety of situations in which we enact laws to protect a particular sphere of behavior from cost/benefit market calculations.[12] Let me name a few.

1. We protect a public sphere of civil justice. Large parts of the legal and criminal justice system are placed outside the market. For instance, jury votes should not be bought or sold; judges, prosecutors, and police officers should not be bribed; each adult citizen has one vote and cannot buy more nor sell the one he or she has. In all of these cases, we would find the application of market principles of buying and selling offensive, and we judge that market behavior is illegal in this sphere.

2. We protect a private sphere of family behavior. For example, we give protection to certain activities within marriage. Up until a certain age, parents are legally expected to support and nurture their children: they are not allowed to kick their children out by arguing that the benefits they receive from their annoying children are not worth the cost of supporting them. Similarly, marriage is viewed as more than just an economic contract; it is not comparable to the contract between your office and the company that maintains your copy machine. We have traditionally limited the circumstances under which divorces may be obtained and (particularly when children are involved) force divorcing couples to deal with a host of noneconomic as well as economic issues.

3. We protect human beings from commodification. In most cases, for instance, we do not allow individuals to sell their bodies or themselves. Prostitution is illegal in most places; people cannot sell themselves into voluntary slavery; the sale of body organs is usually prohibited. Prohibitions against child labor protect young children from becoming just a market commodity.[13]

4. In some situations we establish laws that enforce certain behaviors in the market regardless of their economic costs or benefits and regardless of whether people "prefer" to follow them or not. For instance, we require employers to ignore race or gender in hiring; we demand that restaurants serve anybody who has money to pay, regardless of ethnicity or religious

---

12. For an excellent discussion of these issues, see Elizabeth Anderson, *Values and Ethics in Economics* (Cambridge, MA: Harvard University Press, 1993).

13. For an extensive discussion of the problems created by the "commodification" of human beings, see Margaret Jane Radin, *Contested Commodities* (Cambridge, MA: Harvard University Press, 1996).

background; we require that workplaces provide "reasonable accommodation" for those with disabilities; and we mandate that employers may not demote or fire persons who take time off to serve in the National Guard or to respond to a jury summons.

The range of appropriate situations in which government should constrain market behavior is much disputed. Clearly, agreement about what constitutes governmentally protected spheres of behavior varies over time and among countries. The regulation of child labor, the presence of equal-opportunity laws, and the legality of buying or selling one's civic obligations has changed in this country as the sense of acceptable social norms regarding this behavior has changed. (In the Civil War, for example, richer young men could pay poorer young men to fulfill their draft obligations.) Some of the most intense political issues in the United States today can be viewed as arguments about whether or not the market should be constrained. For instance, the debate over abortion is a debate about whether access to abortions should be governed by the market, where abortions are available to anyone with the income to buy one and provided by anyone with the skill to perform one, or whether their access should be taken outside of price/market calculations and placed into a separate nonmarket sphere of decision-making.

The role of the government in protecting certain spheres of behavior from the market is often less discussed than its role in regulating industry or providing redistributive programs. Perhaps we take some of these laws on the part of government entirely for granted and never think that the market could be involved in some of these spheres. For instance, virtually everyone in a democratic government system will agree that some areas of civic behavior should not be marketized, such as individual voting or judicial decision-making. However, exactly where the lines get drawn, distinguishing those areas protected by government and those areas subject to market forces, is not obvious. An extended public decision-making process has to determine which spheres are worthy of this special governmental protection.

But there are those who argue strongly that markets should be allowed to function in as many places as possible and that government constraints on markets should be extremely rare. These arguments come most urgently from those who claim a libertarian perspective, and they tend to make at least three arguments:

- A primary goal for a democratic system of government should be to allow people to pursue their own self-interest, defined in any way they want to define it. The government should never second-guess individual choices. People who want to sell their organs or to sell their body for sex should be allowed to do so without government intervention. In general, therefore, individual self-interest is a higher priority than some vaguely defined social interest. Government should never play the paternalistic role by deciding for individuals what is best for them. Only a few exceptions to this should be allowed, such as when individual self-interest might lead to injury or death for someone who would not choose this outcome voluntarily. (Of course, those who wish to die should be allowed to.)[14]
- It is problematic to start allowing government to regulate behavior. Like markets, governments are powerful and may seek to expand their power over time. Hence, what may start as well-intentioned limitations on personal choices can lead to extensive and unjustified limits on freedom of expression and behavior imposed by a powerful government on the citizenry. It is always better to have too little government than too much government. This argues for giving government limited jurisdiction over as few spheres of behavior as possible.
- If there are social norms that individuals would like to see imposed on behavior, these individuals can form voluntary associations that promote the value of such behavior and pledge to follow these behaviors among themselves. Indeed, if their arguments are powerful and persuade others, then others will behave this way as well. If they cannot *persuade* others that behaviors should be constrained, they should not be allowed to *impose* such beliefs via government legislation. If they can persuade others, then government legislation is unnecessary.

While the previous two roles of government could be viewed as complementing the operation of markets, the role of government in this third area is to confront and limit the operation of markets. Government's job is to ensure that markets exist only in those areas where they are deemed appropriate, protecting other spheres of behavior from commodification and market forces.

14. For a classic presentation of these arguments, see Friedrich von Hayek, *The Constitution of Liberty* (Chicago: University of Chicago Press, 1960).

D. How Do These Three Roles for Government Compare with Each Other?

These three roles for government — correcting market failure, redistributing market outcomes, and limiting markets to protect certain spheres of behavior — are not either/or choices. Most modern governments do all of these to one extent or another.

How does this kind of government activity affect the market and our economic institutions? Because government imposes constraints on market institutions in all of these roles, this is often interpreted as implying that government is inherently in conflict with the market. In the U.S. business press and in public discussions of the government, one frequently encounters the view that government action always makes market outcomes worse. Therefore, a healthy economy needs a very limited government.

I disagree with this view. These different roles of government may complement the market rather than affect it negatively. By providing effective regulation, government can improve on market outcomes in its first role of correcting market failures. In both its first role and its second role (redistributing market outcomes), the government may provide goods that are highly valuable for market operation but that the market itself has difficulty providing. This may include such things as a broadly educated workforce, healthier citizens, infrastructure to support market operations, and protection and support for new innovations through patent laws or basic research support.

Even in its third role, the government may benefit the market by placing some highly important social interactions outside the market. One effect is to refocus social conflict over issues relating to marriage, civil rights, or child labor from the private sector to the public sector. Indeed, one might argue that the public sector is better equipped to make decisions about social issues where opinion is divided, and that market institutions function more effectively when they can operate under well-defined rules and do not have to establish their own standards for appropriate behavior with regard to hotly contested commodities or behavior.

All of these arguments presume an effectively functioning set of government institutions. If government institutions are corrupt, none of these benefits may accrue from government regulation, redistribution, or limitation. The same is true if government institutions are simply incompetent and are not able to design, monitor, or enforce effective laws or regula-

239

tions. But one could say the same things about markets. Market institutions no longer provide the economic benefits ascribed to markets once they become corrupt, or if companies are no longer able to monitor or enforce appropriate and productive employee behavior. This is not to dismiss problems of corruption or incompetence. Such problems occur too frequently and seriously limit the service that market institutions or government institutions provide to their clients and to citizens.

Both kinds of institutions must put controls in place to monitor and reduce such behavior, and it may be harder for government to do this than for the private sector (partly because "performance" is often less easily measured in government institutions).[15] But bribery scandals involving our local congressman should no more lead us to give up on the value of representative democratic governmental institutions than should the gross economic mismanagement and illegal behavior of a company like Enron lead us to give up on the value of an effectively functioning market economy. As citizens, we need to demand good government and put in place the institutions that help make government function more effectively, such as a professional and equitably paid civil service and limitations on the extent to which elected officials can receive gifts from organizations whose behavior they can affect through legislation.

II. A Religious View of Government and Markets?

The discussion in the first section of this chapter uses the language of social science to discuss the role of government and the role of markets. None of the arguments that I have made require any particular religious motivation; however, as I have observed above, many of these arguments are closely tied to ethical arguments about appropriate community responsibilities and behavior. In this second section I want to ask whether theological beliefs should have any influence over how someone from a Reformed Christian background would view these arguments. Do Christians have a particular "viewpoint" on the role of government relative to the market?

15. For an excellent discussion of the management issues in the public sector, see James Q. Wilson, *Bureaucracy: What Government Agencies Do and Why They Do It* (New York: Basic Books, 1989).

The Reformed tradition typically resists making fundamentalist arguments about biblical truth and its application to modern society. Religious truth is revealed in many ways; the Bible provides guidance, but humans are expected to use both their minds and heart when confronted with ethical and behavioral questions. While the Bible provides a number of direct mandates for individual behavior (honor your father and mother; do not murder, covet, or commit adultery, etc.), it does not contain many specific mandates relating to government action in our modern world. However, a number of religious standards emerge from a biblically grounded faith about the nature of the human community that have implications for civic institutions. One can make theological arguments from these that lead to broad goals for policy.

For instance, there is a strong biblical concern that all persons within God's community have access to the things they need for life. The Bible ascribes value and dignity to all human beings. This suggests that we should also ascribe value and dignity to human beings who are part of our civic community and provide them with the basic resources of life, if at all possible.[16] Of course, exactly how we do this is open to debate, and well-meaning people can disagree about whether the best policy to fight hunger involves providing food stamps, cash assistance, or subsidizing food prices. Similarly, the Bible clearly declares a concern for God's creation and proclaims its goodness. This suggests that, as citizens and as consumers, we should be concerned with preserving the goodness of God's creation in the world around us. But it is a matter of open debate whether this is best done by signing the Kyoto accords on global warming, by preserving wilderness areas, or by developing the technology for hybrid cars.

Let me suggest five broad theological messages that are commonly accepted within the Reformed Christian tradition, messages that have been widely discussed in theological writings over the years. These religious messages have implications for how people of faith should prefer to organize public life, including our economic and governmental institutions.[17]

1. Christians should be concerned about others. It is not just self-

16. A number of statements about the economy from a Christian point of view have been written over the past two decades, both within Catholic and various Protestant traditions. While these statements disagree on a variety of points, virtually all of them explicitly agree with this statement.

17. See my first essay in Blank and McGurn, *Is the Market Moral?* for a more extensive discussion of the implications of these religious beliefs for economic life.

interest that should dominate our motives in all times and places; we should genuinely care about the well-being of others even when their interests may be different than our own. (This is in direct conflict with the assumption of self-interest that is typically made within standard economic theory.)

2. The "others" about whom Christians are concerned should be very broadly defined. Jesus' teachings and actions demonstrate clearly that answering the question "who is my neighbor?" is not easy. Our neighbors are not just those who look like us, talk like us, or even who share our same national, cultural, or religious commitments. Samaritans are just as human and just as worthy of Jesus' concern — and by implication, of our concern — as are those who belong to our own community.

3. Values and choices matter. Our Christian faith provides behavioral guidelines about what constitutes "good behavior." Hence, some desires are less worthy than others, and some actions are preferred over others. Not all personal wants should be satisfied, and not all behavioral choices are approved. Our religious faith is, by and large, not consistent with the libertarian approach that allows each individual to define what is good for himself or herself — without any reference to community concerns.

4. We should be concerned about more than material goods. We should care about our spiritual well-being. In fact, material goods, while not bad in themselves, can tempt us to focus on the accumulation of riches in this world and make us lose sight of the more important things that provide spiritual abundance and salvation. We should not use material abundance as a measure of human worth. Material wealth can be used well or ill; it is well used if it is used in service to God.

5. We should be specifically concerned about the poor. We should not shut out those on the margins of our community, but we should invite them in. The widows and orphans among us (to use the language of the Old Testament) must be treated fairly by our community. Indeed, Jesus specifically tells us that we will be judged by how we deal with those who are the least among us.

This is hardly an exhaustive set of religious/ethical beliefs within the Christian tradition, and those of us from different religious traditions can argue long and hard about the nuances of what these beliefs actually mean for our religious communities and our own behavior. My primary point is that there is a core set of beliefs about appropriate behavior by human beings in community with each other that most of us Christians will agree with to some degree. Our Reformed tradition emphasizes that these beliefs should affect our lives; they should affect not just our Sunday morning behavior, but our attitudes and behavior throughout the week. These beliefs about Christians' behavior and values should thus have some effect on how we think about our modern economic and political community and the institutions that govern our social behaviors.[18]

It is utterly appropriate for our Christian faith to inform our views about how our governmental institutions should be organized and what they should do. This does not imply that such institutions should be explicitly Christian in any sense. But it would be strange indeed if the Christian beliefs we hold, as citizens in a democratic society, did not have some direct effects on the values that we espouse when acting as voters and citizens. The following are four particular concerns about the role and nature of economic and government institutions that might be expected to emerge from the beliefs and values listed above.

- We should be concerned about the potential injustices that a market economy can create. We care about the real material well-being of our neighbors, as well as their spiritual well-being. We should care when market failure results in higher prices or a less effective use of the human skills of employees. No humanly created institutions are fully satisfactory, and our economic life — as well as our spiritual life and our family life — must always be subject to God's judgment.
- We should value the redistributive ability of government. Governmental institutions give us the ability to address inequities or injustices. They provide a way to serve the "widows and orphans" in our community. This is particularly important in a larger and more complex society, in which individual outreach may not be satisfactory and where we need to create public organizations or programs to deal with the needs of those who are not able to be economically self-sufficient through the market. Note that I am not arguing for a particular kind of redistributive program. We can disagree about whether inequities are best addressed by cash support for low-income families, for example, or by work programs for the adults in

18. For an extended theological discussion of this issue, see M. Douglas Meeks, *God the Economist: The Doctrine of God's Political Economy* (Minneapolis: Augsburg Fortress, 1989).

those families.[19] The primary point is that government provides a mechanism through which we can collectively reach out to those neighbors who are suffering economically.

- We should believe in the necessity of supporting certain value choices within society. This means supporting governmental institutions that facilitate decision-making to deal with difficult and divisive social questions. Such institutions can provide an avenue through which faithful persons can present the arguments to support their values and beliefs, even to others in the community who may not share their religious affiliation.
- We should value the need to insulate some parts of our lives from the market. Our beliefs suggest that large areas of our well-being are not linked to the market, but rather to how we treat each other. Protecting human dignity and human rights is more important than protecting economic institutions.

In short, there is justification from our Christian values that would provide general support for all three roles of government discussed in the previous section. We should care about correcting market failures, about redistributing market outcomes when some in our society do not have enough, and about limiting the market in some places. Our government institutions are one way (though hardly the only way!) through which we can express and act on these commitments. Government institutions provide a mechanism through which we can act as a community and reach out more broadly than we could through our own personal lives.

If we truly believe that we have commitments to neighbors far and near, government institutions can provide an avenue through which we, as people of faith, can meet these obligations. The taxes that we pay to support the food stamp program, for example, allow the government to run a nationwide initiative that determines need and provides greater access to food, especially among low-income families with children. We can also view the taxes that we pay to support international relief aid to Africa, for

19. For instance, there is a debate on how Christian viewpoints might inform antipoverty policy in Mary Jo Bane and Lawrence M. Mead, *Lifting Up the Poor: A Dialogue on Religion, Poverty, and Welfare Reform* (Washington, DC: The Brookings Institution, 2003).

example, as an outgrowth of our Christian commitments to serve those in need wherever we find them.

I am not arguing that we should seek to make government programs an arm of the church, or that such programs should explicitly reflect Christian theology. Indeed, in a democratic process within a large heterogeneous country, the details of any government program will be formed through a collaborative decision-making process in which Christian voices are joined with persons who have different faith commitments and many different agendas and perspectives. But from the perspective of Christians as voters and as citizens, one reason to support at least some U.S. governmental programs (foreign aid spending by the United States for the least-developed countries in the world, food and housing assistance programs, disability assistance, etc.) is that these programs fulfill our Christian commitments as well as our civic commitments. These programs — assuming they are effectively run — are good not just from my point of view as a social scientist but also from my point of view as a Christian.

In short, my support for particular government actions is very much based on my faith commitments. I do not apologize for this, nor do I shrink from it. As a person of faith, I do have a different perspective on government and what I expect from government institutions.

III. Conclusion

We live in a market economy, but as people of faith we are called on to be aware of the promises as well as the limitations of markets. Our New Testament faith indicates that we should be as concerned for our neighbors as for ourselves: Jesus made it very clear that our neighbors are more than just those who live next door and look like us and talk like us. Our "neighbors" also include those of different cultures, languages, and races.

This message has particular resonance in a global economy. Increasingly, our economic lives are connected with the lives of rural agricultural workers, urban factory employees, and computer programmers from around the world. Our economic actions — what we buy and what we sell — affect people not just in our local community or our national community, but they ripple across the world. Of course, this is particularly true of Americans whose buying power has so much impact on the global economy. In this world, we must take our faith-based responsibilities to our global neighbors very seriously, because those neighbors who live far away have become even more closely connected to our lives. Our economic actions have an impact on people in many countries, and our subsequent responsibilities have increased so that we need to pay attention to those impacts and to reach out to those who may be disadvantaged by a global economic system that greatly benefits citizens of the First World.

We often have little ability to respond to these individuals at the personal level or even (in many cases) through church-based organizations. However, the activities of our government institutions provide a way to help fund assistance and services to poor and disadvantaged people both in this nation and around the world. In that sense, government actions can be viewed as a complement to church-based outreach programs. In many cases, especially in a more global world, the government programs may be more effective than church-based efforts because of their scope and their ability to reach across nations and across communities to provide assistance.

Let me make one last cautionary and balancing statement. This chapter has tended to focus on what governments can and should do. This is purposeful. In our modern society, the typical argument is always promarket and antigovernment, so I find myself arguing the progovernment side because I think the antigovernment claims are often not well thought out. But there is clearly also government failure and some areas where public decision-making is hard or public-sector action is more limited and difficult.

Faithful people should always resist the secular temptation to deify the market, but neither should they deify the public sector as a more "moral" sector of society. I do not believe that market outcomes are inherently "right," but neither do I believe that the public sector naturally produces better outcomes. Like the human beings that participate in them, both private and public institutions have the potential for good and for evil. Which of these directions they follow depends a great deal on the choices that are made by the people who establish, shape, and participate in these systems.

Given that statement, the government provides an imperfect but important institution that regulates and limits the market, and we can hope that it creates a better balance between the market and society. When the market is functioning effectively, it can increase human potential and should be supported. But the market can also encourage greed, create pain, and limit economic participation. In this case, we should be critical of the market and seek to build nonmarket institutions that can offset and regulate the market to correct these problems.

Sometimes "faithful criticism" is best expressed through civic participation, shaping the political leaders we select and the policies that we support. This is work that may be part of our vocation as Christians in a democratic society. The values that we hold as religious people, and the characteristics of the religious spirit — discernment, mercy, and kindness — are not just relevant to our private lives among our family and friends. They are also an important touchstone in our public lives as well, and we should refer to and call on those values as we make choices both as market participants and as citizens.

Well-functioning government institutions are critically important to our lives. I believe this, not just as an economist who thinks markets regularly fail to behave quite as effectively as economic theory suggests they should, nor just as a political scientist who thinks there is a need for redistribution, but as a religious person who takes my responsibilities to my neighbors seriously. We are fortunate to live in a democratic system where our public institutions can help us express these values. If our government is failing us, it is because we are failing as citizens to shape a government that expresses these values.

CHAPTER 11

Critical Economic Engagement: On the Perennial and Novel Dimensions

Douglas A. Hicks and Mark Valeri

For two millennia Christians have faced the perennial dilemma of how to embody and express the values of the reign of God in everyday practices within a society shaped, at least in part, by human fallenness — not to mention human diversity and the complexity of human motivations.[1] From the New Testament letters of St. Paul to the present, Christians have variously interpreted and applied Jesus' declaration to his disciples, that he "sent them into the world" but "they do not belong to this world" (John 17:16-18; cf. Rom. 12:2; 1 Cor. 5:10). How should Christians engage the society, including the economy, in which they find themselves?

Theologians have offered many responses to this question. Augustine distinguished between the perfect moral order of the city of God and the order of the city of man in which we currently live, in which strict social discipline is needed to constrain sinful human actions. Thomas Aquinas offered a more hopeful account of the social order, presenting a moral account for organizing human economic and political life based on natural law. The Protestant Reformers Martin Luther and John Calvin emphasized the need to model the Christian gospel in everyday life (including economic activities). Despite their differences on such matters as the uses of the law and the precise meaning of vocation, Luther and Calvin acknowledged the tensions between the freedom of the Christian life and the need for social discipline.[2] And as we will discuss in more detail below, Protestants in America have long struggled thoughtfully over how best to apply

---

1. See Jeff Van Duzer's essay, ch. 6 of this volume.
2. See Eric Gregory's essay, ch. 2 of this volume.

Christian ideals to the complex and changing economic institutions of the modern era.

The question of how we should live economically has always included attention to the organization of social, political, and economic structures of exchange that meet human needs as well as possible. The modern era has been marked by an increasing role for the complex institutions that shape the context and conditions for everyday human activities, including the bureaucratization analyzed most definitively by Max Weber. However, one of the most basic of human needs is freedom, including the freedom from institutional coercion, and from the mid-eighteenth century onward, political, social, and economic systems have had greater and greater potential to make undue demands on human beings. As Theda Skocpol and other sociologists have documented, the rise of the welfare state in the latter part of the nineteenth and into the twentieth century provided both powerful mechanisms to alleviate human misery such as poverty but also the potential to create dehumanizing rules and regulations and alienating social conditions.[3]

In theological terms, Christians hold, as a fundamental commandment, the prohibition against making idols of any person or system. The threat of a totalizing system to human freedom in general and Christian life in particular has been an enduring one, but arguably more so now than ever before. The theological ethicist H. Richard Niebuhr provides a useful framework for identifying the danger of falling into social, political, or economic idolatry. In Niebuhr's language, economic, political, or social systems should at most require our *penultimate* loyalty; they must never hold our ultimate allegiance, which is due only to God. Because our fundamental value-orientation should be directed toward God, all systems, ideologies, and persons that might otherwise become value centers — or idols — are "relativized" in light of the absolute commitment to God.[4]

We submit that the moral challenge for Christians in every time and

---

3. Theda Skocpol, *Protecting Soldiers and Mothers: The Political Origins of Social Policy in the United States* (Cambridge, MA: Belknap Press, 1992); Skocpol, *Social Policy in the United States: Future Possibilities in Historical Perspective* (Princeton, NJ: Princeton University Press, 1995). See also Rebecca Blank's essay, ch. 10 of this volume.

4. H. R. Niebuhr, *The Responsible Self: An Essay in Christian Moral Philosophy* (San Francisco: Harper and Row, 1963), pp. 137-41; H. R. Niebuhr, *Radical Monotheism and Western Culture* (New York: Harper and Row, 1970), p. 37; H. R. Niebuhr, *Christ and Culture* (New York: Harper and Row, 1951), p. 28.

place has been to live together in economic life in ways that humanize their neighbors without making idols of any economic ideology. It is wrong-headed (and sinful) for Christian individuals or Christian communities to attach themselves too completely or uncritically to any social, economic, or political system of ideas or practices. Rather, at individual and corporate levels, Christians are called to humanize any system while naming its shortcomings and seeking to correct them.

Critical Economic Engagement: Four American Moments

In fact, the most creative moments of interaction between Christian communities and the economic order in America have involved just such a dynamic: criticism by thoughtful persons of faith of the excesses and dehumanizing effects of the market even as they have participated in it. Of course, many Christians, in various times and places, have "baptized" the economic theory du jour without critical reflection. Yet others have expressed ambivalence and worked actively to resist what they perceived to be the moral threats of modernizing commerce. It is far beyond the scope of this essay to provide a thorough narrative of Christians and the economy throughout history, even a narrative within the American context alone; but a brief (and admittedly selective) review of four crucial episodes in this history, focusing on Protestantism in America, illustrates the complex engagement between Christians and the development of the modern market system. In each period, Christians sought to live faithfully while applying moral ideas to ever-shifting economic practices.

First, during the mid-seventeenth century, Anglo-American Puritans expressed deep reservations about the effects of the expansion and growing specialization of commerce. During the first half of that century, midsize and middle-distance merchants and the great merchants of overseas trading companies turned to new modes of exchange that expanded and strengthened business networks: formalized correspondence between suppliers and merchants; the use of professional factors, or agents; a nearly total dependence on paper credit (book accounts and bills of exchange, i.e., signed promissory notes akin to personal checks); the extension of credit by contract with guaranteed profits to the creditor; determination of prices by market demands and current fashion; and the use of civil law courts to enforce contracts and coerce repayment of debts. These techniques, while facilitating long-distance exchange and economic forecasting, appeared to their critics to depersonalize commerce: to "unmoor" it (a properly maritime metaphor) from local, neighborly obligations. In sum, the growth of market mechanisms challenged the current customary assumptions about commerce, which were moral axioms derived from a blend of medieval, humanist, and Protestant teaching.[5]

We have become so accustomed to reading the story of Protestantism and the market through popularized versions of Max Weber (that Protestants were perforce enthusiasts for capitalism) that we may miss what Weber himself admitted: early Protestants, especially the Reformed churches of western Europe, England, and colonial America, resisted the depersonalization of exchange — often vehemently. To be sure, many Puritans were merchants, and no religious spokesman worth his salt denied the essential importance of trade, the value of profits (for employment, charity, and civic projects), and the courage of overseas merchants. Nonetheless, street preachers in London, learned divines in Cambridge, pastors of rural parishes outside London, and the religious founders of New England all voiced a nearly incessant critique of new techniques that threatened to sunder local moral solidarities.

They condemned new credit practices as usury cloaked in various guises. These critics used such metaphors as "cannibals," "cormorants," and "murderers" to describe a rising class of lawyers, loan-brokers, and inhumane creditors. Puritans fretted about price fluctuations as temptations to oppress the neighbor. They issued dire warnings against those who presumed to follow putatively rational procedures — the determination of prices solely to enhance profits, litigation over unpaid debts, business with unknown customers at the expense of local neighbors — as a betrayal of Christian charity. They damned the merchant who took his accounts more seriously than he did the biblical mandates. Most tellingly, they used their local congregations as instruments of discipline against wayward merchants. In isolated parishes in England, and in the settled churches of New England, pastors and lay leaders formed disciplinary committees that excommunicated traders who oppressed their neighbors through egregious prices, who sued indigent debtors, and who invested their profits in new

---

5. Bernard Bailyn, *The New England Merchants in the Seventeenth-Century* (Cambridge MA: Harvard University Press, 1955); Stephen Innes, *Creating the Commonwealth: The Economic Culture of Puritan New England* (New York: Norton, 1995).

ventures rather than relieve the poor in their communities. The Puritans recognized the significance of economic production and exchange, including trade across the Atlantic, for enhancing human well-being, but they refused to give up the communal moral practices that could harness commerce for Christian living.[6]

Second, during the mid-eighteenth century, American Protestants faced different moral challenges from a market system that had developed far beyond the overseas trading networks of the preceding century. To make short work of a long story, Anglo-American commerce became entangled in imperial politics: the century-long conflict among England, France, Spain, and the Netherlands. To abet its dynastic program and fund imperial warfare, the British monarchy and Parliament increasingly co-opted commercial interests. They promoted a regularized system of national debt through the Bank of London; they worked in concert with new trading companies to contest colonial ventures, especially French ones; they promoted the African slave trade; they issued lucrative monopolies to manufacturing and mercantile firms; and they attempted to control trade with its colonies through navigation laws and ever-mounting tariffs and regulations.

In America as well as in England, the result was a remarkable stratification of wealth among merchants: the growth of hugely wealthy trading houses accompanied the failure of many smaller firms, as well as an inability to address the increasing problem of poverty. Indeed, several economic thinkers of this period, most famously Adam Smith (but also his intellectual predecessors in London and Edinburgh), broke with the imperial-mercantile ideology precisely because they could foresee only a vicious trend toward monopoly, dynasty, slavery, and widespread starvation. Of course, they proposed what has become known as a "free-market" or "laissez-faire" economic system: individuals seeking profits and commodities according to their internal desires and rational acumen without state intervention, except for the restrictions against anticommercial tactics such as monopolization and the basic rules for justice in economic exchanges and relationships. These important caveats, often overlooked in popularized renditions of Adam Smith, were a hedge against a totalizing economic ideology, even when the chief concern of the day was political imperialism.[7]

---

6. Mark Valeri, "Religious Discipline and the Market: Puritans and the Issue of Usury," *William and Mary Quarterly*, 3rd. ser., 54 (1997): 747-68.

7. See Rebecca Todd Peters's essay, ch. 5 of this volume.

For the most part, American Protestants during the second half of the eighteenth century embraced the critique of the mercantilist system, gradually accepting many of the assumptions of a free market. Leading up to the movement for independence from Britain, they obviously had interests as colonials to resist parliamentary prerogatives and the imperial program. Yet their moral arguments over a long period of time — long before the movement for independence and during the early national period — stressed the humane, even benevolent, agendas implied in unrestricted trade. Adam Smith, for instance, had emphasized the capacity of the market to lift many persons out of the dehumanizing condition of human poverty. Evangelicals such as Thomas Prince (a devotee of Jonathan Edwards), severe Calvinists such as Samuel Hopkins (who denounced the slave trade as a vile analogue to imperial political oppression), liberal Bostonian clergy such as Jonathan Mayhew, and Philadelphia-region Presbyterian leaders such as John Witherspoon condemned imperial economics as oppressive, impoverishing, and inhumane. To their lights, a free market offered the possibility of economic exchange and prosperity without political favoritism, slavery, dynastic ambition, and artificial restrictions against social mobility. They did not imagine that the market would end poverty, but they did envision that wide commercial channels would speed the diffusion of wealth and prevent devastating, widespread poverty.[8]

This is not to say that Protestant leaders embraced every aspect of the market in the eighteenth century. Indeed, unaccustomed to an undiluted market ideology, they alerted their congregations and political leaders to the dangers of a purely self-serving mode of exchange. Edwards and other evangelicals denounced high fashion, the emergent consumer culture, unbridled material ambition, and the inattention to private poor relief. Mayhew and other liberals winced at the rise of financial speculators and the fall of overly ambitious debtors. Moral thinkers such as Witherspoon challenged the assumption made by the more extreme market advocates, who, drawing from the cynical philosophy of Enlightenment provocateurs such as Bernard Mandeville, were urging people to pursue their private passions and self-interests without restraint from customary moral teaching.

8. Alan Heimert, *Religion and the American Mind: From the Great Awakening to the Revolution* (Cambridge MA: Harvard University Press, 1966); Mark Valeri, "Jonathan Edwards, the Edwardsians, and the Sacred Cause of Free Trade," in *Jonathan Edwards at Home and Abroad: Historical Memories, Cultural Movements, Global Horizons,* ed. David W. Kling and Douglas A. Sweeney (Columbia, SC: University of South Carolina Press, 2003).

Mandeville argued that the reasonable pursuit of self-interest would in fact tend toward the common good in the end. But Protestant moralists suspected that such a formulation masked a perverse resistance to Christian virtue and would bring calamity. That is, these early American Protestants valued the benefits of trans-Atlantic trade and promoted the dismantling of imperial restrictions on international commerce without accepting the whole apparatus of a free-market system. They hoped that the kinds of exchange defended by the likes of Adam Smith would redress the more oppressive effects of the old imperial system, from its implied political tyranny to its economic favoritism.

Third, throughout the second half of the nineteenth century and into the early decades of the twentieth century, many American Protestants identified a new set of social problems as the market developed into an industrial capitalist system. Among those problems, the status of labor and the laboring classes appeared quite acute. Evangelical social reformers, along with proponents of the Social Gospel such as Washington Gladden and Walter Rauschenbusch, equally admitted that the growth of economic inequality, the powerlessness of uneducated workers and a decline in wages, and the miseries of a truly indigent urban class bespoke widespread moral failure. Inspired by Christian socialists in England such as F. D. Maurice and Charles Kingsley, the leaders of the Social Gospel movement advocated the common ownership of large companies and government protection for labor unions. Critics of commercialization in nearly all of its forms, they argued that the unregulated industrial system dehumanized laborers and degraded the meaning of economic production.[9]

Evangelical and moderate social reformers of the same period suggested less radical remedies: temperance, the political enfranchisement of women, temporary assistance through inner-city missions (the YMCA grew out of such efforts), and enhanced public education. The various proposals and efforts for social reform, legitimated through hundreds of tracts and sermons, all indicated sensitivity across the theological spectrum to the failures of the regnant economic ideology and the demands for critique and response.

Although the depth of critique of the economic system varied a great deal, from calls for reform to calls for revolution, Christian critics of this

---

9. Ronald C. White, Jr., and C. Howard Hopkins, *The Social Gospel: Religion and Reform in Changing America* (Philadelphia: Temple University Press, 1976).

Gilded Age shared a sense of the humanity of consumers and workers alike. They were willing to challenge the wave of industrialization and sought significant transformation in light of its deficiencies. Indeed, there were some overly optimistic Social Gospelers and social reformers who placed too much hope either in human perfectibility or in the technological wonders of the age that together promised, in Rauschenbusch's memorable phrase, "to Christianize the social order."[10] Yet these radicals and reformers found resources in their Christian faith enabling them to take a critical stand against industrialization in their common struggle to uphold human dignity.

Fourth, in the age of the American welfare state, roughly from the 1930s to the end of the twentieth century, many Christians combated the modern consumer economy that threatened to exacerbate social inequalities. Building on the spirit of the Social Gospel, Protestants joined forces with Catholics to support minimum-wage legislation and the social safety net that was pieced together during the New Deal era. Steering between the more utopian proposals of the Social Gospel for a Christianized economy, on one hand, and the more personalistic or charity-based social outreach, on the other, Protestants like Reinhold Niebuhr joined Catholics like John A. Ryan to offer hard-headed, policy-based approaches to socioeconomic amelioration in the United States. Niebuhr's writings on economic life, derived from his experiences as a pastor to employees of the Ford Motor Company in Detroit,[11] and his public essays in periodicals such as *Christian Century* and *Atlantic Monthly*,[12] emphasized the joint tasks of maintaining a critical distance from the contemporary economic system and designing countervailing political institutions to keep its power in check. Niebuhr's influential analyses had not merely come full circle from earlier eras, when political imperialism was more feared than economic ideology; but Niebuhr also identified the mid-twentieth century by the twin threats of economic power and political power.

From the perspective of the church as an institutional voice, the mid-

---

10. Walter Rauschenbusch, *Christianizing the Social Order* (New York: Macmillan, 1912).

11. See Reinhold Niebuhr's reflections on this period and his pastorate in his *Leaves from the Notebook of a Tamed Cynic* (New York: Richard R. Smith, 1930).

12. Many of these essays are collected in Reinhold Niebuhr, *Love and Justice: Selections from the Shorter Writings of Reinhold Niebuhr*, ed. D. B. Robertson (Philadelphia: Westminster Press, 1957).

dle and late twentieth century saw the decline (for better and for worse) of a unified or influential voice of Christendom. Ecumenical Protestants, working through the National Council of Churches, lacked Niebuhr's realism at times but certainly embraced his critical distance from economic powers and a concern for the impacts of the economy on the lives of poor people in America. In the age of contextual theologies (from the 1960s onward), the fragmentation of Protestant as well as Catholic theological-ethical voices brought with it space for perspectives that addressed the economic conditions of women, African-Americans, and other disempowered groups in society. As Eric Gregory notes in his chapter, a proliferation of moral issues (e.g., war and peace, nuclear questions, civil rights, environmentalism, and bioethics and sexual ethics) in the latter decades of the twentieth century attenuated the direct focus of Christian ethics and theology on the economy that had been present, for example, during the Social Gospel period.

Yet, for many thoughtful scholars, pastors, and businesspeople, issues of economic justice stood centrally within Christian life, and they were closely related to those other moral questions as well.[13] And the end of the twentieth century was marked by various critiques of the culture of consumerism that increasingly accompanied market-based economics as it was practiced in America.[14]

Taken together, these four periods reveal a remarkable pattern: provoked by the problems of a particular set of market institutions, Protestant Americans gradually developed a social critique without attaching themselves wholeheartedly to, or removing themselves from, any one economic ideology. To reiterate a rather commonsense observation, none of these religious communities or movements opposed economic production, exchange, and prosperity wholesale. Most did not reject the idea that trade/commerce/business (whatever term we use) should yield some economic returns to the producer, laborer, merchant, or entrepreneur. At the same time, they did manage, within broadly divergent and changing contexts, to

13. See Janet Parker's essay, ch. 7 of this volume, as one example of this kind of economic and environmental analysis.

14. M. Douglas Meeks, *God the Economist: The Doctrine of God and Political Economy* (Minneapolis: Fortress, 1989); Michael Budde and Robert Brimlow, *Christianity Incorporated: How Big Business Is Buying the Church* (Grand Rapids, MI: Brazos Press, 2002); Vincent Miller, *Consuming Religion: Christian Faith and Practice in a Consumer Culture* (New York: Continuum, 2003).

develop critical tools for working toward justice and the improvement of social conditions.

These four episodes in the story of American Christians and the growing market system suggest the general framework that has informed our conversation in the chapters of this book. Too often, public debate about Christian moral teaching and the economy lapses into facile and simplistic dichotomies: religion against commerce, ministers against merchants, virtue against profits. More accurately, we should speak of identifying specific moral dilemmas and forging humanizing responses within systems of exchange to which we owe no lasting allegiance. For the Puritans, the early market broke apart local communities; their response included corporate discipline. For eighteenth-century evangelicals and liberals, the imperial system threatened liberty and fairness with oppression and dynastic agendas; they embraced a (largely) free market. For religious social reformers and Social Gospelers in the industrial age, capitalism degraded laborers and produced frightening disparities of wealth and poverty; these transformers advocated a series of far-reaching remedies. And for twentieth-century Christians, the modern economy exacerbated social inequalities and threatened to overpower our political and social institutions; these more contemporary people of faith helped piece together a social safety net and questioned the excesses of American consumerism.

Our Economic Dilemma:
Globalization and a Christian Response

Social commentators and economic analysts today perceive a new turn in the development of the market: a new episode, so to speak, with its own peculiar challenges. Perhaps most significantly, this contemporary era of globalization intensifies the impersonal nature of economic relationships. Although we were distant from many of our economic partners in earlier eras, the notion of the economic neighbor as nearby grows more antiquated. It is more and more difficult to imagine who our economic neighbor is. Indeed, in our so-called virtual economy, or network economy, an increasing proportion of economic exchanges take place with little or no personal interaction. The deregulation of futures trading, the turn to derivatives and hedge funds, and the use of mathematical-game theorems to run computer programs that trade billions of dollars a day without any moral reflection — all of this has produced an eerie sense of detachment in many quarters. According to one recent commentator, each day the economy "becomes increasingly spectral, until it is virtually nothing but the play of floating signifiers" that "are unmoored [again, the maritime analogy] from what once was called the 'real' economy."[15]

Meanwhile, the degree of human deprivation across the planet is staggering. As Douglas Hicks noted in Chapter 3, over a billion people survive on less than one U.S. dollar per day, and almost a billion people (many, but not all, of whom are those in absolute poverty) suffer from severe malnutrition. The relationship between economic deprivation — as well as economic inequality — and globalization is hotly contested. Some tout globalization as the solution to all economic ills, while others vilify globalization as a force of oppression of the poor and alienation for all of us. As people of faith have demonstrated in earlier periods, we are called to engage the global market critically and selectively, rejecting as too simplistic either a wholesale embrace of it or wholesale rejection of it.

But what does critical engagement with the global economy look like? The contemporary dilemma involves, at bottom, an economy of unprecedented scale that renders individual consumers and workers powerless. Or, to say it better perhaps, it leads us to believe that we are powerless. It is difficult to think of helping our economic neighbors when we do not know who they are. Informed by the resources of their past, Christians must continue to think carefully and creatively about these new "signs of the times." The authors of the chapters in this book have pointed to directions of analysis and practice. Rather than offer a definitive list of components in a Christian approach to the global market — beware any such totalizing ideology! — we will, in the remainder of this chapter, offer some points of leverage for Christian reflection and action in light of the economic challenges of our moment.

As a prerequisite, a Christian response to the global market must have a place to stand where it will be possible to assume a critical distance from any would-be totalizing ideology or system. This requires acknowledging, as Jeff Van Duzer emphasizes, that there is a tension between "kingdom values" and "market values" and practices. Too often, the temptation of our day (and, arguably, of any age) is to accept the so-called free

15. Mark C. Taylor, *Confidence Games: Money and Markets in a World without Redemption* (Chicago: University of Chicago Press, 2004), p. 180.

market and the accompanying culture of consumerism as unchangeable facts of life. Reacting to an airline's tightening of security in light of a recent terrorist threat, one parent who was traveling with her teenaged children was quoted in a news story: "The security officials aren't allowing anyone to take our video games, iPods or computers onto the airplane. What are my children going to do for eight hours?" For most readers of this book, the ubiquity of electronics is far more palpable than the reality, say, of surviving on less than one U.S. dollar per day. Yet this latter economic condition is the reality for roughly one in six humans on the planet. Thus the ability not only to imagine alternatives, but also to understand the various realities of the global economy, requires being at a critical remove from our everyday practices.

It also means questioning those taken-for-granted elements of a so-called free-market ideology that are often invoked to trump all other moral arguments. "Business is business," for example, is a mantra that implies that some ethical practices necessarily need to be overlooked or overruled in the hard-edged world of commercial competition. A variation of this mantra was invoked to convince Denny McFadden, in William Goettler's prologue to this book, to play his part in the outsourcing of a New York-based plant, and then of a Mexican one. Kent Van Til shows that human needs are not adequately accounted for in an economic theory that cannot distinguish between mere wants and genuine basic needs. Environmental ethicists, including Janet Parker, note that standard economic theory treats the environment as merely a series of inputs to the economy or as an inconvenient "externality" to be taken into account. As the best exemplars of earlier periods did, Christians in our time must be willing to call into question the taken-as-gospel elements of economic practice and theory.

It is important to repeat that this does not require a wholesale rejection of the market mechanism. On the contrary, the market system has the tremendous capacity, in the language of economics, to allocate scarce resources to alternative ends. If individuals and communities can determine the most important ends — both individual goals and collective goals — and can agree on acceptable means to reach those ends, then social coordination by the market (as opposed, for example, to centralized decision-making by the state or the church) can have tremendously positive outcomes. The challenge, as the Catholic moral theologian and economist Daniel Finn puts it, is to decide on the moral fences that a society is going to place around the market.[16] Stated positively, the various institutions of society, including the state, the market, the nonprofit sector, and religious institutions, all should work together in social coordination.

The danger, at this moment, seems not to be the threat of a hegemonic takeover of society by the nonprofit sector or religious institutions. Although some social commentators (including those of a libertarian stripe) would take issue with our claim, it is also not the state that is the greatest threat to be a totalizing force vis-à-vis personal well-being in any of the modern industrialized countries. It is the global market, accompanied by a culture of consumerism, that has predominant position in shaping our lives, and thus it deserves our careful moral scrutiny. The challenge of the global market involves not only distance and (in)visibility, but also a change in common moral sentiments. The ideology of consumerism has constrained our imaginations in ways we have never before experienced. We are captivated by stories of products, even as competing Christian narratives (the Good Samaritan, manna in the wilderness, the loaves and fishes, prophetic calls for Sabbath and Jubilee) become less and less familiar.

One central concept in this volume for understanding Christian faith in the global market has been imagining our economic neighbor. Thomas Walker's chapter illustrates the value of thoughtful engagement with biblical texts in this regard: the power of the Bible to enlarge our moral sentiments and perspectives. Following Walker's biblical analysis, Eric Gregory demonstrates how Christians should apply neighbor-love along the lines of equal regard in ways that challenge contemporary practices contributing to increasing inequality. Douglas Hicks tells of how the ONE Campaign, with its virtues and pitfalls, is attempting to mobilize a largely faith-based effort to aid impoverished neighbors, particularly in Africa. It is at this point, though, that the question of self-interest comes into view in our framework, which Kent Van Til analyzes thoughtfully in this volume. Not even the relatively modest effort needed to eliminate extreme poverty has been mustered thus far. As the economist Amartya Sen has demonstrated, self-interest narrowly considered need not be the exclusive (or even predominant) motivator in a market system.[17] Indeed, the challenge here is

16. Daniel Finn, *The Moral Ecology of Markets* (Cambridge, UK: Cambridge University Press, 2006).

17. Amartya Sen, "Rational Fools: A Critique of the Behavioural Foundations of Economic Theory," *Philosophy and Public Affairs* 6 (1977): 317-44.

not so much the market mechanism of allocating scarce resources; rather, it is the "tastes and preferences" that consumers bring to the market in the first place. This book's reflections on and analyses of neighbors, justice, vocation, and the like can, we believe, serve as resources for a more robust critique of consumerism and those cultural, political, and even religious practices that condone and perpetuate it.

The chapters in Section III focus on labor, especially the concept of vocation as a key to our response to the global market. It is true that vocation can be, and has been, interpreted in ways that encourage oppressed people to accept their "fate" as ordained by God. In contrast, however, Reformed theologians in particular have emphasized the moral equality of vocations, at least within a good and just society.[18] Vocation is a life-encompassing invitation to full personhood extended by God to all people. Vocation illuminates the active, responsive agency of each person and the positive contribution to human societies that each person can make. The practice of vocation necessarily takes place in the social-relational context of creation. In H. Richard Niebuhr's language, all of life should be lived as a grateful response to God, and consequently in responsibility toward other human actors and all of creation. While vocation illuminates the responsive agency of *each* person, it must also be noted that all such actions are made within a community of agents. Humans pursue their vocations not only to fulfill their own personhood, but to help others realize their dignity as well.[19]

18. Nicholas Wolterstorff expresses a view of such equality in this way: "Some [vocations] may be more crucial than others for the welfare of society, but all are equal. . . . What the Calvinists especially had their eye on with this radical leveling of occupations was of course the monasteries. . . . A friend of mine told me how annoyed he was, upon visiting the St. Bavo Kerk in Haarlem, to see how the Calvinists had put representations of good solid Dutch burghers in the windows where the medievals would have had saints — until he realized that these *were* the Calvinist saints" (*Until Justice and Peace Embrace* [Grand Rapids, MI: Eerdmans, 1983], p. 17). See also Michael Walzer, *The Revolution of the Saints: A Study in the Origins of Radical Politics* (Cambridge, MA: Harvard University Press, 1965).

19. In his commentary on the story of Martha, Mary, and Jesus, Calvin writes: "We know that people were created for the express purpose of being employed in labor of various kinds, and that no sacrifice is more pleasing to God, than when everyone applies diligently to one's own calling, and endeavors to live in such a manner as to contribute to the general advantage" (quoted in Ronald H. Stone, "The Reformed Economic Ethics of John Calvin," in *Reformed Faith and Economics* [Lanham, MD: Univ. Press of America, 1989], p. 37). This notion of vocation was taken up and expanded by the English and American Puritans, most notably in William Perkins's "Treatise on Vocations," in *The Workes of that famous and worthy minister* [William Perkins], Vol. I (London, 1608); see also John Cotton, *The Way of Life* (London, 1641).

Thus it becomes part of one's vocation to strive to enable others to fulfill their vocation. This has implications for socioeconomic and political policies alongside occupational choices, as Rebecca Blank also emphasizes. All aspects of one's life play a part in realizing human dignity. Of course, this includes, but is not limited to, one's occupation or career. In Calvin's words, one's work must be contributing to (or at a minimum, not hindering) "the general advantage."[20] Occupation or labor in this framework is much wider than the economic definition of the formal labor market, which excludes "domestic" work and volunteer service (which continue to fall disproportionately on women). This account of vocation requires that a life of faithful response "is to be rendered *per vocationem* and not merely *in vocatione*" (through positions and not merely in positions).[21] That is, one's very commitment to remaining in a particular position requires reflection on whether it is enabling one to live a life that contributes to social justice. The English Puritan William Perkins put it this way: "A vocation or calling, is a certaine kind of life, ordained or imposed on man by God, for the common good." One implication of this view is that persons can be called either to refuse jobs or to quit them when they determine that they are not able to fulfill their call to work for social justice through them. While theologians have not always pursued these justice dimensions, it is an important aspect of "vocation" that connects personal contribution to wider structural arrangements and public policy.[22]

To be sure, it is important to acknowledge that for many people without socioeconomic status or sufficient educational attainment, the range of "choice" of occupation or position is severely limited. It is arguably a privilege to be able to refuse or leave a job because it is seen not to promote either one's own well-being or social justice. We certainly do not intend to condemn persons who must hold such jobs, but rather to promote actions and policies that overcome inhumane working conditions and unjust economic activities that obstruct human dignity. The chapter by Robert Austin and Lee Devin on the changing and context-dependent

20. This is Calvin's term, quoted in n. 19 above.
21. Wolterstorff, *Until Justice and Peace Embrace*, p. 17.
22. Perkins, "Treatise on Vocations," p. 727. Following Ernst Troeltsch, Wolterstorff argues that a Lutheran understanding of vocation does not emphasize this constant reflection on whether one's occupation is serving the cause of justice (*Until Justice and Peace Embrace*, p. 16).

nature of work underscores the challenges (and the privilege) of contributing to the common good through meaningful work.

Pursuing our vocation and contributing to the common good requires moral imagination and contextual analysis. We must see who our neighbor is and understand how interpersonal relationships as well as wider social, political, and economic systems shape our own reality and that of others near and far. It also means using the technological means (perhaps made possible by the global market) at our disposal. Richard Niebuhr puts it aptly: "The Christ who commended a good Samaritan for pouring oil and wine into wounds would scarcely likewise honor a man who, trained in contemporary methods of giving first aid, regarded the Biblical example as his absolute guide."[23]

Responsible socioeconomic contribution and participation require just public policies as well as deliberative reflections about the interests and well-being of others by all persons as a dimension of their vocation. Shirley Roels highlights this point about contribution well in her chapter on the manufacturing sector. Roels emphasizes the value of productivity for justice and recounts contemporary struggles to make a contribution within a downsizing sector. The background of her acute analysis is the conviction that, as societies are transformed toward greater justice, more people will be able to realize their own vocations.

The noble and often-perplexing work of living faithfully within our current globalizing and already globalized economy presents us with the challenge of bringing together a number of elements: economic acumen and moral-theological analysis; reflection on individual economic decisions and society-wide (indeed, global) economic systems; and understanding both historical and contemporary realities. It is important to add one explicitly theological dyad: divine and human agency. Each of the chapters in this book has focused on thinking and acting in the economic sphere in ways that are faithful to God. The emphasis has been on human agency: how we can respond morally to the challenges before us. But it is fitting to acknowledge expressly that Christian faith also entails the understanding that God is acting in the present order, including the economy, in ways both known and unknown to us. As Richard Niebuhr puts it, God is acting through us and despite us.[24] We should not use the theological conviction

---

23. H. Richard Niebuhr, *Christ and Culture*, p. 234.

24. H. Richard Niebuhr, "A Christian Interpretation of War," in *Theology, History, and*

that God is acting in creation, indeed is sovereign over all of creation, as an excuse for human inaction, or for irresponsible or narrowly self-interested action. But it is a reminder that we should embrace the moral task without believing that we are going to fix the world on our own.

As we have noted above, some overzealous Social Gospelers, especially as their work was popularized, came near to declaring that the kingdom of God could be created on earth within the human-oriented institutions that promised innovation, productivity, and enhanced quality of life for all persons. In contrast to such unbridled optimism and excessive faith in human agency, a reminder that God is acting through us and despite us serves to maintain the perennial tension between kingdom values and economic values. We should strive, in our contemporary economic reality, to live faithful lives, but always acknowledging that the tension is not ours fully to resolve. Richard Niebuhr upholds the dialectical model of Christ transforming culture, in which we engage our society as best we can, maintaining our ultimate loyalty to God alone, and thus relativizing the trust we place in any economic ideology or system of practices.[25] Wolterstorff puts it slightly differently, calling contemporary people to practice a "world-transformative Christianity" that speaks up for justice and peace in our own time and place.[26]

Like Christians in earlier epochs, we see a daunting challenge before us: the pace of change is dizzying; the apparent rate of degradation of our environment is horrifying; and the subhuman standard of living of a billion human beings is almost incomprehensible. But, like those before us, the contributors to and the readers of this volume have the opportunity to critically engage a powerful economic system that holds the potential to influence, for good or for ill, the well-being of humans and all of creation. The theological, moral, and economic resources at our disposal, including the ideas we offer here, seem meager in light of global economic forces. But we are surely not the first persons to have that sense. Our first act of moral imagination might be to believe that we can muster the moral agency to shape our relationships with our global neighbors.

Culture: Major Unpublished Writings of H. Richard Niebuhr, ed. William Stacy Johnson (New Haven, CT: Yale University Press, 1996), pp. 159-73.

25. H. R. Niebuhr, *Christ and Culture,* pp. 190-229.

26. Wolterstorff, *Until Justice and Peace Embrace.*

Index of Names and Subjects

abortion, 21n.
Adams, Robert M., 29n.
affluence, 17, 20, 22, 25-30, 41-42, 47, 51, 59
agape, xx, 25, 161
AGAPE (organization), 154, 157, 161
agapism, 25, 38-39
agency, divine, 263-64
agency, human, 85-88, 261, 263-64
AIDS. *See* HIV/AIDS
Alticor Corporation, 215
Altieri, Miguel A., 158n.
American Protestantism, 250-57
Annan, Kofi, 135
Anderson, Carl, 219n.
Anderson, Chris, 189n.
Anderson, Elizabeth, 236n.
anthropology:
   biblical, 65-69
   mainstream economic, 65, 73-76, 77
   Smith's understanding of, 92, 103, 104, 108
Applied Energy Systems (AES), 215-16
Aquinas, Thomas, xx, 30n., 33, 36-39, 168, 248
Arendt, Hannah, 168n.

Assayas, Michka, 54
Augustine, xx, 23, 33-37, 40, 248
Austin, Robert D., xxiii-xxiv, 91n., 167n., 177n., 188n., 190n., 191n., 193n., 263

Bagwell, Catherine, 43n.
Bailey, Kenneth E., 11n.
Bailyn, Bernard, 251n.
Bakke, Dennis, 211n., 215-16
Bane, Mary Jo, 20n., 244n.
Barkin, David, 149n.
Barmen Declaration, 155
Barro, Robert J., 53
Barrow, Julia, 172n.
Barth, Karl, 23n., 38, 39n.
basic needs, 78, 82-84, 259
Basing, Patricia, 172n.
Bathsheba, story of. *See* David-Nathan, story of
Battles, Ford Lewis, 73n.
Baumol, William J., 227n.
Beatitudes, 47
Becker, Gary, xxi-xxiii, 65, 81-85, 88
Beckley, Harlan, 88
Bender, Frederic L., 170n.
Berkes, Fikret, 149n.

The editors would like to thank Lisa Rivero for her work on the indexes.

Berkman, John, 21n.
Berry, Wendell, 157n.
Bhide, Amar, 121
Bible. *See* Beatitudes; Commandments; Creation narratives; David-Nathan story; Flood narrative; Golgotha; Good Samaritan, parable of; Lazarus, story of; love commandments; Naboth's vineyard, story of; "Who is my neighbor?" (Luke 10:25-37)
biblical anthropology, 66-69
biblical imagination, xxi, xxiii-xxiv, 5, 134
biodiversity, 133, 135-40, 146, 148-52, 158-60, 162
Bishop, Morris, 172n.
Blair, Claude, 172n.
Blair, Tony, 46
Blank, Rebecca, xxiv-xxv, 129n., 200, 207, 229, 232, 241, 249, 262
Blinder, Alan S., 227n.
Blomberg, Craig, 70
Boccia, Lionello G., 172n.
Bono, xxi, 43, 44-62, 196
Bradley, Stephen P., 188n.
Brett, Mark, 140n., 141n.
Brimlow, Robert, 256n.
Bromiley, G. W., 23n., 66n., 69n.
Brown, Raymond, 12n.
Brubaker, Pamela K., 145n.
Brueggemann, Walter, 3-5, 6n., 15
Brunner, Emil, 170n.
Budde, Michael, 256n.
Bush, George W., 20, 46, 47, 55, 204
business ethics, 20

Calvin, John, 73, 169, 177, 248, 261n., 262
Calvinism, 253, 261n.
Campbell, R. H., 94n.
Campolo, Tony, 47
Caparaso, James, 74-75
capitalism:
    Christian apologists for, 112-13, 118-19
    globalization of, 137, 143-45, 155-56

McNamara and, 102, 105-6
neoliberal, 133, 143-45, 155-56
Protestantism and, 18, 251, 254
religious social reform and, 20, 257
Schumpeter on, 202
Smith and, 92, 97-98, 108
Third World, 78-81
Carr-Ruffino, Norma, 125n.
Carter, Stephen L., 115n.
Cascade Engineering, 218-19
Castillo, Maria, 149, 150n.
Catholicism. *See* Roman Catholic Church
Caufield, Catherine, 99n.
celebrity activism, 44-53, 58-62
Central American Free Trade Agreement (CAFTA-DR), 204
charity, 17, 26, 28, 35-37, 40, 45, 57, 60, 83, 251
Chatterjee, Deen K., 42n.
Cherry, John, 172n.
Chery Automobile, 204-5
Christian ethics, 18, 21, 24n., 25, 28-30, 32, 111-12, 128, 132
Christian Platonism, 33
Christian witness, xxi, 4-5, 19, 59, 134, 198
civil rights movement, 18
Claggett, Marshall, 172n.
Clemons, Eric K., 188n.
Clinton, Bill, 53
Cloward, Richard A., 232n.
Cobb, 92n., 93n.
collective intellectual-property-rights regime, 160n.
Collins, Jim, 113
commandments, 68
common good, 24, 36, 129, 161, 208-9, 212, 254, 262-63
commutative justice, xix, 208
compassion, 9-16, 29, 31, 33-35, 40n., 42, 56, 93-101, 104-8, 156, 161
compassion fatigue, 34
compassionate conservatism, 20

consumability, 4
consumerism, 14, 20, 59, 144, 256, 257, 259-61
Convention on Biological Diversity, 162
Cotton, John, 261n.
Cox, Taylor, 125n.
Craddock, Fred, 10n.
Creation narratives, 4, 66-67, 140-42, 163
creative destruction, 110, 202-3, 213
Cuban, Mark, 115
Culpepper, R. Alan, 9n.
customization, 188n., 189
Cyberton, xi, xiii-xvii

Daft, Richard L., 215n.
Daly, Herman, 92n., 93n.
Daniels, Denise, 192n.
DATA (Debt, AIDS, Trade, Africa), 46
David-Nathan story, 6-9, 12, 15, 70
Davidson, Clifford, 172n.
Davis, John, 74n.
de Soto, Hernando, xxi-xxii, 65, 77-81, 85, 88
Dearborn, Tim, 192n.
deism, 93, 96-97
del Mastro, M. L., 168n.
DeMarco, Tom, 191
Deming, W. Edwards, xv, 189
demographics, 125-26
destitution, global, 48-51
Devin, Lee, xxiii-xxiv, 167n., 177, 193, 263
DeWitt, Calvin, 142
Diabre, Zephirin, 137n.
dissonance theory, 114
distance, 14-15, 17-18, 22-24, 26-31, 38-41, 61, 260. *See also* proximity
distributive justice, xix, 18, 208
diversity:
    cultural, 86, 125-26, 133, 146, 149, 151-53, 159
    economic, 133, 156-63
    See also biodiversity

dominion, 66-68, 141
Dragun, Andrew, 151-52
Drucker, Peter, 189
Duchrow, Ulrich, 161-63
Dumas, Maurice, 172n.
Dyson, Robert, 34n.

ecofeminists, 139, 163
economic democracy, 146, 162-63
ecosystems, 134-37, 159
Edwards, Jonathan, 253
ejidos, 149, 160-61
embryo adoption, 21n.
Emergent Church movement, 4
Emerson, Ralph Waldo, 36
Enriquez, Juan, 194
equality, 25, 28, 30n., 35, 54-59, 86-88, 110, 261
Ewing, A. C., 24
exploration costs, 176-77, 183, 185-87
externalities, 118, 127-28, 144, 228-29, 233, 259

Fahy, Evertt, 172n.
FAO. *See* United Nations, Food and Agricultural Organization
Faust, Betty, 147n.
feminist ethicists, 29
Ficino, Marsilio, 169n.
Field, Erica, 81n.
Finn, Daniel, 260
Finnis, John, 30n., 37n.
Fiske, Susan, 114n.
Flescher, Andrew, 21n.
Ford, Henry, 179-83, 188, 218n., 219n.
Ford Motor Company, 99, 205, 255
Frank, Robert H., 29
Franz, Randal S., 192n.
Frechette, Louise, 136
freedom, 28, 36, 55, 87-88, 111, 134, 146, 163, 200, 209, 248-49
Friedman, Milton, 226n., 231
Friedman, Thomas, 124, 205
Frink, Al, 197

functionings, 85-87

Gates, Bill, 44, 53
Gates, Melinda, 44, 53
Gates Foundation, 196
Geldof, Bob, 46
General Agreement on Tariffs and
    Trade (GATT), 203
Gladden, Washington, 254
Gleick, Peter, 137
Global Biodiversity Strategy, 149n.
globalization:
    alternatives to, 134
    of business, 126, 130
    Christian response to, 257-64
    education and, 194
    interdependence and, 23
    of manufacturing, 197-207
    moral and religious concerns about,
        20, 92, 133, 137, 143-47, 154-55
    mystification of production and, 104
    "neighbor" and, 38, 40
    neoliberalism and, 143-47, 154
    poverty and, 80
    self-interest and, 61
globalized elites, 80
Goettler, William, xviii, 91n., 259
Golgotha, 13-14
Gonzalez, Nelson, 20n.
Good Samaritan, parable of, xx-xxi, 8-
    15, 16, 18, 21, 24-25, 28, 31-34, 39-44,
    56-62, 65, 72, 242, 260, 263
Google, 189-90n.
government regulation, 128-30, 227-31,
    239
Gray, Andrew, 153
Great Economy, 157
Green, Garrett, 22n.
Green, Joel B., 72
Green, R. P. H., 33n.
Gregory, Eric, xviii-xix, 43, 54, 248n.,
    256, 260
Gregory the Great, Pope, 168
Griffiths, Richard Owen, 31n.

Gu, Ben, 188n.
Guerrero, Eugenio, 150
Guruswamy, Lakshman D., 136n.
Gushee, David P., 68n.
Gutiérrez, Gustavo, 50, 233n.
Guttierez, Carlos, 197

Habel, Norman C., 140n., 141n.
Hadsell, Heidi, 20n.
Hale, David, 124
Hallett, Garth L., 24n., 30n., 37n.
Hammond, Jan, 167n.
Hammond, Pete, 122n., 123n.
Hands, Wade, 74
happiness, 75, 95-97
Hardy, Lee, 168n., 169n.
Harrison, Beverly, 139
Hassall, W. O., 172n.
Hatcher, John, 172n.
Hausman, Daniel M., 20n.
Heap, Shaun Hargreaves, 74n.
Heimert, Alan, 253n.
Helms, Jesse, 53, 55
hendiadys, 66
Hennessey, Eileen, 172n.
Henry Ford School, 219n.
Hessel, Dieter T., 142n.
Hewson, Paul, 45. *See also* Bono
Heyne, Paul, 74n., 75
Hicks, Douglas, xxi, xxv, 20n., 43n., 50,
    86n., 87n., 88, 233n., 258, 260
Hiebert, Ted, 141
Higton, Mike, 33n.
Hill, Edmund, 37n.
Hill, Frank Ernest, 181n.
Hiltzik, Michael A., 190n.
Hinkelammert, Franz, 161-63
HIV/AIDS, 46, 49, 53, 55-56, 59, 107, 137
Hobbes, Thomas, 83n.
Hoffman, W. Michael, 131n.
Holt, Lucinda Duncalfe, 190
Holwerda, David, 69n.
homo economicus, 90, 156-57, 162, 163
Hope, xii, 170, 193-94, 196, 209, 248

Hopkins, C. Howard, 254n.
Hopkins, Samuel, 253
human capability, xxii
hunger, 48-49, 78, 137, 145, 241
Hunn, Eugene, 158-59
Hurricane Katrina, 17, 19, 135, 216

image of God, 4, 28, 54, 66-68, 72-73,
111, 119, 141, 163, 169
indigenous peoples and cultures, 134,
146-54, 160-63
individualism, 97, 103
industrial making, 179-84
Industrial Revolution, 169-70, 186
industrial revolution, new, 205-6
inequality, 18, 27, 90, 110, 137, 161, 254,
258-60
Innes, Stephen, 251n.
International Monetary Fund (IMF),
143, 162
Israel, Robert, 198n.
iteration costs, 176-77, 186

Jamieson, Dale, 28n.
Jimmerson, Ron, 218n.
John XXIII, Pope, 111
John Paul II, Pope, xix, 46
Johnson, William Stacy, 264n.
Johnston, Carol, 106n.
Jubilee, 47, 71, 260
Jubilee 2000 campaign, 45-46
justice, 7, 25, 28, 36-37, 107, 109, 134, 139,
144, 220, 262-64
civil, 236
distributive, 18
ecological, 134
economic, 44, 90-91, 96, 100, 106, 111,
154, 214, 243, 252, 256-57
faith-based understanding of, 47-48,
56
in Isaiah, 72
in Israel, 69
productive, xxiv, 208

social, 54, 57-60, 106, 198-99, 207-17,
221-23, 262-63

Kalafatic, Carol, 153n.
Kanigel, Robert, 181n.
Kant, Immanuel, 25, 53n.
Karns, Gary L., 192n.
Kaufmann, Walter, 34n.
Keller, Charles M., 176n.
Keller, Janet Dixon, 176n.
Kelly, Betsy, 43n.
King, Martin Luther, Jr., xxiv-xxv, 31,
32n., 54-55
kingdom values, xxii-xxiii, 5, 109, 117,
122, 126-28, 131, 258, 264
Kingsley, Charles, 254
Kling, David W., 253n.
Knupp, Jackie, 53n.
Kreuger, Alan B., 81
Krueger, David, 207-8
Kruse, Kevin, 22n.

La Rocca, Donald J., 172n.
Larkey, Patrick D., 190n.
Lawrence, C. H., 168n.
Lazarus, story of, 57
Le Goff, Jacques, 172n.
Lebacqz, Karen, 207n., 208n., 222n.
Leo XIII, Pope: *Rerum Novarum,* xix
Leopold, Aldo, 141
Levine, David, 74-75
Levitt, Theodore, 201n.
liberation theology, 18
Licklider, J. C. R., 185-86
Lincoln Electric Company, 219n.
Lindblom, Charles, xix, 110n., 128n., 144,
200
Live 8 concerts, 46, 59
Live Aid, 44, 45
love commandments, 8, 11-12, 33, 111, 161
Lula Da Silva, Luiz Inácio, 46
Luther, Martin, 169, 248

Macfie, A. L., 94n.

MacKay, A. T., 23n.
"Made in America," xviii, 203
Maffi, Luisa, 147n., 152n., 153n.
mainstream economics, 65, 85, 87-88
    anthropology and need in, 73-76
    the poor in, 76-77
Make Poverty History Campaign, 43, 46
management, 99, 126, 182n., 189-93, 224,
    240
management, scientific, 169, 185
Mandeville, Bernard, 253-54
Marcel, Raymond, 169n.
Marcic, Dorothy, 215n.
marginalization, 19, 70, 72, 84, 88, 99n.,
    100, 145, 233
market fundamentalism, 144n., 159
market economy:
    relationship of government to, 225-40
    religious view of, 240-45
marketing, 59, 130-31, 188n.
Markopoulis, Panos, 188n.
Marsh, Richard, 56n.
Marshall, Alfred, 50
Marshall, I. Howard, 9n., 10n.
Marshall, Katherine, 56n.
Marx, Karl, 170n.
mass customization, 188n.
Massey, Douglas, 22n.
Maurice, F. D., 254
Mayhew, Jonathan, 253
McConville, J. G., 70n.
McCulley, Lucretia, 43n.
McFadden, Denny, xi-xviii, 259
McFarland, Ian A., 21n.
McGurn, William, 129n., 200n., 229n.,
    241n.
McHugh, Alexandra, 191-92
McLaren, Brian, 4-5, 5n.
McLennan, Scotty, 113n.
McNamara, Robert, xxii, 91, 99-106
McNeely, Jeffrey A., 135n., 136n., 137
McNeill, John T., 73n.
McPherson, Michael S., 20n.
Mead, Lawrence M., 20n., 244n.

Meeks, M. Douglas, 243n., 256n.
Meisel, Anthony C., 168n.
Milbank, John, 39-41
Millar, J. Gary, 71n.
Millennium Ecosystem Assessment
    (MEA), 135-36
Miller, Edward, 172n.
Miller, Fred D., Jr., 83
Miller, Vincent J., 3, 20n., 256
milpa, 148
Mintzberg, Henry, 191-92
Mirsky, Jeannette, 180n.
Mitchell, William J., 188
Moe-Lobeda, Cynthia, 143n., 156n.
Moessner, David P., 7n.
monopolies, 194, 228, 252
moral imagination, xix-xxi, xxiii-xxiv,
    44-45, 52, 56-62, 263, 264
moral justification, 50, 52
moral sentiments, 52, 92n., 93-104, 106,
    260
Mosher, David L., 34n.
motivation, 48-52
Mott, Stephen, 68, 70
Myers, Bryant, 72

Naboth's vineyard, story of, 71n.
Nash, Laura, 113
National Council of Churches, 138, 256
National Prayer Breakfast, 47-48, 57n.
national tithe, 47
nationalism, 38-39, 54
natural disasters, 17, 19, 135, 216
natural law, 93, 95-98, 248
Naughton, Michael, 192n.
Nazarea, Virginia D., 148n., 158n.
"near one," 9-15
"neighbor," 9, 14, 16, 36, 163, 245
neighbor-love, xxi, xxiv, 22, 36, 39, 44,
    56, 65, 260
neoliberalism, 133, 143-46, 149, 154-56
Neuhaus, Richard John, 20n.
Nevins, Allan, 180n., 181n., 183n.
Nickel, Helmut, 172n.

Niebuhr, H. Richard, 233, 249, 261, 263, 264n.
Niebuhr, Reinhold, 18, 208n., 222, 255-56
Nietschmann, B. Q., 153n.
Nietzsche, Friedrich, 34n.
Nijar, G. S., 160n.
Nolan, Richard L., 193n.
nongovernmental organizations (NGOs), 19, 50
Norman, A. V. B., 172n.
North American Free Trade Agreement (NAFTA), xiii, 143, 147-51, 160, 203-4
Novak, Michael, 112
Nussbaum, Martha, 20, 20n., 35, 52, 85

O'Donovan, Joan Lockwood, 30n., 40n.
O'Donovan, Oliver, 30n., 40-41
Ogletree, Thomas, 28n.
Olasky, Marvin, 20n.
O'Neill, Paul, 46
ONE Campaign, xxi, 44-49, 58-61, 260
Oppenheimer, Mark, 20n.
ordo amoris, 23
Outka, Gene, 22n., 25n., 38
Ovitt, George, Jr., 172n.
OXFAM, 26, 42

Pareto optimality, 76-77, 84-85, 87
Parker, Janet, xxiii, 91, 139n., 256n., 259
Paul, Ellen Frankel, 83n.
Paul, Jeffrey, 83n.
Payne, Ruby, 218
Peralta, Athena, 157
Perkins, William, 261n., 262
Peters, Rebecca Todd, xxii, xxiv, 20n., 50, 92, 109, 252
Peterson, Eugene, 3
Pfaffenbichler, Matthias, 172n.
Pfeil, Margaret, 32n.
Piore, Michael J., 180n.
Piven, Frances Fox, 232n.
place-based cultures, 149
Plato, 168

Platonism, Christian, 33
pluralism, 19
Pogge, Thomas W., 17n.
political economy, 18, 75n., 98, 104, 106, 231, 233
Posey, Darrel Addison, 153n., 158n., 160n.
postindustrial making, 185-87, 189
Pounds, Norman John Greville, 172n.
poverty, 19-22, 249, 252
  absolute, 41, 49, 58, 258
  affluence and, 25, 29
  Becker and, 83-85
  Biblical view of, 81
  Bono on, 50-51, 55, 60
  capital accumulation as solution to, 106
  Christian response to, 21, 50-51, 88
  deaths from, 17n., 137
  definitions of, 77, 88
  de Soto and, 77-81
  diseases related to, 137
  economic growth as solution to, 145
  economic language and, 77
  environment and, 138, 142
  "evangelical," 29
  extreme, 17, 26, 28-30, 48-52, 59-62, 260
  free market and, 253, 257
  information about, 41, 53
  injustices of, 100
  justice and, 71
  King on, 31
  Latin American, 137
  mainstream economics and, 76-77
  marginalization and, 72
  McNamara and, 99-106
  neighbor-love and, 56, 61
  romanticization of, 96
  Sen and, 86-88
  Singer and, 18, 20, 25-30, 199
  Smith and, 96, 253
  statistics on, 17n., 49, 53, 137

See also Make Poverty History Campaign, ONE Campaign
Powell, Mark Allan, 46n.
pragmatism, 113, 170
Preece, Gordon, 20n.
preindustrial making, 171-78, 187, 189
Prince, Thomas, 253
Pringle, William, 169n.
private property, 144, 159-60
processus confessionis, 154
prodigal son parable, 10-11
productivity, 4, 78, 97, 115, 119, 197, 207, 214, 217, 226, 234, 263
professional specialization, rise of, 19
proximity, 13, 18, 25, 26, 29-31, 36, 39-41. *See also* distance
Puritans, 250-52, 257, 261n., 262
Pyhrr, Stuart W., 172n.

Quinn, Steven, 46n.
Quixtar, 215

Radin, Margaret Jane, 237n.
Raphael, D. D., 94n.
Rasmussen, Larry, 139n., 141n., 142, 147n., 157n.
Rational Choice Theory, 74-75
rational man, 104n.
rationality, 74, 98, 103-4, 107, 208n.
Rauschenbusch, Walter, 254-55
Raven, Peter H., 135n., 137
Rawls, John, 19, 231n., 233n.
Ray, Stephen, 32n.
Reagan, Ronald, 143
reconfiguration costs, 176-77, 183, 185-87
redistribution, 199-200, 231-35, 239, 247
Reeder, John P., Jr., 21n.
reemergence of Christian ethics and economics, 18-19
Reformed Christian tradition, 225, 240-41
Reich, Robert, 115n.
Ricardo, David, 143
Riley, Father, xi, xii

Rima, Ingrid Hahne, 76
Robb, Carol, 104n., 139n.
Robbins, John W., 31n.
Robertson, D. B., 255n.
Robertson, Pat, 47
Robinson, William, 144-45
Roels, Shirley, xxiv, 263
Roman Catholic Church, 18, 21n., 32, 207-8n., 241n., 255-56, 259
Roosevelt, Theodore, 168n.
Rosenberg, Alexander, 83
Ruether, Rosemary Radford, 142n.
Rule of Indigenous Environments, 152-53
Rumpza, Stephanie, 192n.
Ryan, John A., 18, 255

Sabel, Charles F., 180n.
Sachs, Jeffrey, 53, 58n., 137n.
Samaritan, parable of. *See* Good Samaritan, parable of
Sant, Roger, 215-16
Sayers, Dorothy, 117
Schlabach, Gerald, 32n.
Schumpeter, Joseph, 202-3
Schwartz, Barry, 188n.
Schweiker, William, 23n.
Scrimale, Jessica, 43n.
Scully, Matthew, 68n.
Seccombe, David, 69
segregation, residential, 22
self-interest, xxii, 51-52, 93-94, 97-104, 110-11, 238, 242, 253-54, 260, 264
Sen, Amartya, xxi-xxii, 20, 20n., 51, 65, 85-88, 226n., 260n.
sequential processes, 182-84
shalom, 116, 209-17, 221-23
Shapley, Deborah, 99n., 100n., 101, 103
Shaw, Nancy, 193n.
Sider, Ronald, 67-68, 70
Sinclair, Upton, 167-68n.
Singer, Peter, xx-xxi, 17-18, 20-30, 34, 36-42, 54, 56, 199-200
Skinner, A. S., 94n.

Skocpol, Theda, 249
Smith, Adam, xxii, xxiv, 50, 52, 75, 91,
    104-12, 143, 227, 252-54
    compared with Robert McNamara,
        102-3
    as moral philosopher, 92-93
    Theory of Moral Sentiments, 92-99,
        102
    understanding of anthropology, 92,
        103, 104, 108
    Wealth of Nations, 93-99, 102, 104
Smith, Michael W., 47
social cognition theory, 114
Social Gospel movement, 18, 254-57, 264
social sin, 32
Spitler, Rick, 188n.
stable preferences, 83-85
Stearns, Richard, 44n.
Steelcase Corporation, 201
Stevens, R. Paul, 122n.
Stevenson, Howard, 121
stewardship, 116, 141, 209n., 217, 221
Stiglitz, Joseph, 229n., 230-31
Stockman, Steve, 46n.
subsistence economies, 136, 158-59
Summers, Lawrence, 53
sustainable development movement,
    145n., 153
Sutherland, Ivan, 190
Svanoe, Todd, 122n.
Sweeney, Douglas A., 253n.

Taylor, Frederick, 179-85, 189-90
Taylor, Jerome, 172n.
Taylor, Mark C., 258n.
Taylor, Shelley, 114n.
Terkel, Studs, 167n.
Thatcher, Margaret, 31, 143, 156
Thiemann, Ronald, 31n.
Third World. *See* Two-Thirds World
Thomke, Stefan, 186
Thompson, Ginger, 150n.
Thomson, Judith J., 21n.
Thurow, Lester, 130n.

Tilgher, Adriano, 168n.
tithes, 47, 70
Toledo, Victor M., 147n., 148, 150, 151n.
Tomlinson, John, 23n.
Torah, 4, 8, 12
Torrance, T. F., 23n.
trade liberalization, 143-45, 151-52
traditional ecological knowledge (TEK),
    148-49, 151, 159
Traub, James, 44n.
Troeltsch, Ernst, 262n.
tsunamis, 17, 135
Two-Thirds World, 80, 87, 90, 99, 102,
    106
Tyrangiel, Josh, 53n.

UNAIDS, 49
Unger, Peter, 20, 26n.
UNICEF, 26, 42
United Nations, 49, 59, 145, 147n., 153
    Development Programme (UNDP),
        137n., 138n.
    Food and Agricultural Organization
        (FAO), 48-49
    Millennium Development Goals
        (MDGs), 62
    Millennium Ecosystem Assessment
        (MEA), 135
universalism, 16, 25, 39-41
Unocal, 214-15
Usher, Albert Payson, 172n.
utilitarianism, 25, 29-30

Valeri, Mark, xxv, 43n., 252n., 253n.
van der Vlist, Leo, 160n.
Van Duzer, Jeffrey, xxii-xxiii, 192, 248n.,
    258
Van Til, Kent, xxi-xxiii, 51, 68n., 259-60
vocation, 116, 169-71, 179, 192, 212-13,
    222, 225, 261-63
von Hayek, Friedrich, 238n.
von Rad, Gerhard, 66n., 67

Waldron, Jeremy, 40-41

Walker, Alice, 156
Walker, Thomas, xx-xxi, 43, 260
Wallace, Howard, 141n.
Wallis, Jim, 47
Warren, Rick, 47
Washington, James M., 31n.
Waters, David, 43n.
Waters, Tony, 28n.
Watkins, Jane, 172n.
Weber, Max, 18, 249, 251
welfare reform, 20, 104, 234
Wenham, Gordon J., 66n., 67n.
Wesley, John, 37n.
White, Lynn, Jr., 172n.
White, Maunsel, 181
White, Ronald C., Jr., 254n.
Whitney, Eli, 179-83
"Who is my neighbor?" (Luke 10:25-37),
    7-15, 16, 57
Williams, Bernard, 39n.

Williamson, Thad, 43n.
Wilson, James Q., 240n.
Witherspoon, John, 253
Wolters, Albert M., 118n.
Wolterstorff, Nicholas, 40, 200n., 208-
    10, 261n., 262n., 264n.
Wong, Kenman L., 192n.
World Alliance of Reformed Churches,
    xxiii, 134, 144, 154-55
World Bank, xxii, 17, 48, 55, 91, 99-103,
    143, 162, 215
World Council of Churches (WCC),
    xxiii, 134, 138-39, 145-46, 154-55, 161
World Trade Organization (WTO), 143,
    160n., 162, 203n., 204, 212, 215
Wurst, Shirley, 140n.

Zapatista Mayan rebellion, 147
Zink-Sawyer, Beverly, 43n.

Index of Scripture References

OLD TESTAMENT

Genesis

1:4-31	142
1:26-27	66
1:28	67, 209n.
1:31	163
2	67
2:1-3	141n.
2:15	209n., 210
3:17-19	117
9:2-3	68

Exodus

20:8	68n.
22:21-4	70

Leviticus

19	8, 9-10, 12
25:29-31	71n.
27:30-33	70

Deuteronomy

6	12
6:5	8

14:22-29	70
15:13-15	70

2 Samuel

11–12	6
12:5-6	70
12:7	7

1 Kings

21:1-19	71n.

Psalms

14:6-7	69
24:1	155
72	69
82:3f	69
146:5-6	70

Proverbs

19:17	70
29:7	70
29:14	69
29:18	156

Isaiah

3:15	69

14:32	69
58:6-7	71, 73

Jeremiah

22:16	70

NEW TESTAMENT

Luke

1:5	10
1:5-39	12
1:46-55	13
1:50-78	10
4:18	72
5:14	10
6:20	72
7:13	10
7:22	72
9:51	7
10:25-37	xx, 7-15, 16, 43, 56-57
14:13	72
15:20	10

16:19-31	57n.	23:49	13	**1 Corinthians**	
16:20	72			5:10	248
16:22	72	**John**		12	6
17:14	10	4:5	9		
18:10-17	13	17:16-18	248	**2 Corinthians**	
19:44	7			8:14	29
23:34	13	**Romans**			
23:34	14	5:3-4	xii, xiv	**Revelation**	
23:43	14	12:2	248	6	209, 223